C Y B E R
SECURITY
in industrial automation

K S MANOJ

INDIA · SINGAPORE · MALAYSIA

Notion Press

No.8, 3rd Cross Street
CIT Colony, Mylapore
Chennai, Tamil Nadu – 600004

First Published by Notion Press 2020
Copyright © K S Manoj 2020
All Rights Reserved.

ISBN 978-1-64919-976-8

**Dedicated
to
the lotus feet of Goddess Saraswathy and
my professors of Physics and Engineering**

CONTENTS

LIST OF FIGURES

LIST OF TABLES

PREFACE

MESSAGE FROM THE AUTHOR

The evolution of industrial automation is extremely fascinating. As it continuously innovates and appropriately amalgamates Information and Communications Technology (ICT), sophistication of cyber-attacks also increases. Today almost in every month, in every day, in every hour and in every minute, the security researchers encounter hundreds and thousands of cyber attacks on Industrial Control Systems with new worms and viruses. Hence understanding how to defend automated critical infrastructure systems such as energy, water, oil & gas, etc. becomes indispensible for OT system security experts. Hence this book is written with the intention to impart the essential information that an automation engineer need to understand the vulnerabilities of the distributed Supervisory Control and Data Acquisition (SCADA) and its mitigation strategies.

Present day automation of ICS mainly based on the SCADA technology and the security requirements of the SCADA is quite different from IT security as it involves mission critical operations. In SCADA systems or Industrial Control Systems, the fact that any logic execution within the system has a direct impact in the physical world warranting safety to be paramount. The field devices being on the first frontier to directly face human lives and ecological environment, the field devices in SCADA systems are deemed with no less importance than central servers. The ultimate target of ICS attackers is to sabotage the ICS causing catastrophically damaging it and not stealing or corrupting the data. The motivation for the cyber attacks are varied and indeed includes industrial espionage and ultimately causing damage to physical plant. These make addressing the cyber security of the ICS a timely and important issue. Ensuring the security and resilience of the ICS is necessarily multidisciplinary endeavour requiring expertise in Industrial Control Systems, ICS security, control theory, information security, secure communication, etc. All these facts form the motivation for this book. Sincere attempt has been made to elaborate important topics appropriately while others are cited briefly.

This book provides a comprehensive overview of the security fundamentals of Industrial Control Systems (ICSs) and Supervisory Control and Data Acquisition (SCADA) systems. Careful attention is given to providing the reader with clear and comprehensive background and pertinent to ICS security. This book also provides information regarding specific operating and security issues and methods which are suitable to monitor and protect the system and design strategies to reduce threats. It also offers chapters on ICS cyber threats, attacks, metrics, risk, intrusion detection and security testing for current system owners who wish to securely configure and operate their ICS.

There are very few books available in the market on the cyber-security of SCADA and ICS. Hence this book may be a good addition to industrial cyber security. It is written in such a manner that it is quite readable even by novices. Also written with an imagination that it can be used for teaching a course on the cyber-security of ICS and SCADA.

AUDIENCE FOR THIS BOOK

This book is intended for a specific range of readers who want to secure the environment of ICS and SCADA systems will indeed benefit from an understanding of ICS physical-cyber security concepts, challenges, mitigation strategies, ICS security standards, secure communication, attack vectors, risk assessment, etc. This includes professionals who are engaged with design and implementation of DCS, Power System Automation, ICS security auditing, Smart Grid, etc. and the Electrical, Electronics, Computer Science and Automation Engineering students. As an academic text book, it is most useful for the senior under graduate and post graduate students. For ICT professionals who are interested to work in the demanding industrial cyber security domain will find this book very useful. All the chapters of the book are very structured and modular to provide a considerable deal of flexibility for the design of courses in industrial cyber security. Security solution architects and technocrats who conduct research in ICS security may also be interested in addition to automation project managers, national security agencies, cyber security analysts and auditors, cyber security consultants, and cyber security policy makers.

SALIENT FEATURES

Written in an easy to understand style, this book provides a comprehensive overview of the physical-cyber security of Industrial Control Systems (ICSs). It benefits the computer science and automation engineers in obtaining essential and required understanding of the ICS cyber security from concepts to realization.

The Book

- ➤ Covers ICS networks, including zone based architecture and its deployment for product delivery and other Industrial services.
- ➤ Explores the industrial communication basics in detail.
- ➤ Discusses SCADA networking with required cryptography and secure M2M communication that define the modern ICS.
- ➤ Provides the reader with a fundamental understanding of both physical-cyber-securities in detail.
- ➤ Discusses a detailed description of the cyber-vulnerabilities and mitigation techniques.
- ➤ Presents many real-world documented examples of attacks against industrial control systems, and mitigation techniques.
- ➤ Provides information about industrial cyber security standards presently used.
- ➤ Explores defense-in-depth strategy of ICS from conceptualisation to materialisation.
- ➤ Is a suitable material for the students of automation engineering to learn the fundamentals of OT security.

ABOUT THE AUTHOR

K S Manoj is an electronics and communication engineer with design interest in physical-cyber security of Industrial Control Systems (ICS) who continues to explore the adoption of new security strategies in order to promote safer and more reliable automation infrastructures. He first specialized in design and development of SCADA systems.

However after realizing the importance of the cyber security of ICS, later focused towards the attack vectors of advanced threats in the interdependent critical cyber infrastructures and framing mitigation strategies. He holds a Masters in Technology (Communication Electronics) from Department of Electronics, CUSAT, India and another Masters in Solid State Electronics from University of Kerala, India. He worked for KELTRON, SCTIMST and KSEBLtd and having over 30 years of experience in Automation and Energy Engineering. He has authored two more titles viz. Industrial Automation with SCADA and Smart Grid-*Concepts to Design*. His research interests include Machine Learning and its application in Clinical Diagnostic Support Systems (CDSS). He may be contacted *ksmanoj321@gmail.com.*

STRUCTURE OF THIS BOOK

This book is arranged in twelve chapters to give a holistic awareness of industrial cyber security, mainly intended for computer science and automation engineers, Electrical, Electronics, ICT and Instrumentation engineering students who are interested to pursue a career in the most demanding industrial cyber security domain including the physical cyber security of the critical infrastructure of a Nation.

Chapter 1: CYBER SPACE AND THREATS: This chapter begins with explaining the cyber space and security definitions which an industrial security professional may familiar with. Then it proceeds in explaining the motivation for cyber attacks to ICS and various threat sources. The common cyber attacks to SCADA and ICS are briefly explained. Then it gives a brief account of dreadful malwares which attacks SCADA such as BlackEnergy, Stuxnet, Havex, Sandworm, Duqu and Flame. This chapter conclude with describing the End Node Security, Flash Drive Usage, BadUSB and Cyber Incidents using USB.

Chapter 2: OPERATIONAL TECHNOLOGY AND ICS: Chapter begins with explaining Operational Technology (OT) and its difference with Information Technology (IT). Then this chapter describes the Industrial Control Systems, its various types, functioning, control and network components. The chapter ends with attack strategies of ICS.

Chapter 3: ICS ARCHITECTURE AND DESIGN CONSIDERATIONS: This chapter begins with describing the communication architecture of basic SCADA. Then moves on to describing the common communication philosophies adopted in DCS. As the reliability and availability of DCS functions are the most important, they are briefly introduced, but cater the necessary understanding to industrial security professionals. It then explains the concepts of Fault Tolerant Systems, Fail Safe redundant systems, High Availability, etc.

Chapter 4: INDUSTRIAL NETWORKING BASICS: The advancement of ICT innovates the four major areas in industry viz. Data Acquisition Systems (DAS), computer and communication, cyber-security and the pertinent ICS applications. The present domain of the ICS does not require much knowledge of secure M2M communication. But engineers who wish to associate with the development and implementation of the advanced and distributed SCADA and ICS, a basic understanding of computer and communication, is most essential. Hence this chapter Industrial Networking Basics, which describes the basic terminologies and the most fundamentals of computer and communication needed for an industrial security engineer is included.

Chapter 5: INDUSTRIAL COMMUNICATION: This chapter has focused on various communication aspects of the industrial ICS with an emphasis on DCS and Smart Grid. It begins with discussing various types of transmission technology in very modest way so that it is very apt and most essential for automation engineers and security professionals who are engaged in the design and implementation of DCS and Smart Grid. The chapter then discusses the guided and unguided media used today for communication in such a manner that it is very useful for a practicing communication professional, which includes the various cabling issues as well. Various but most relevant communication technologies, which find space not only in industrial SCADA but also in other smart automation technologies today are discussed comprehensively. Finally the chapter focused on the security issues of the wireless communication technology.

Chapter 6: ICS AND SCADA PROTOCOLS: In DCS, whatever data is gathered in the field including those from remote sites, has to be send to the control room for processing and decision making. Being an industrial process, which is to be controlled in real-time mostly from a remote control room, the data and the control information have to be exchanged in a most secure manner. In computer science, this is achieved by encrypting the data and using proper protocols. Hence an essential and appropriate knowledge of various relevant protocols adopted and developed for ICS are required for an automation engineer to get a proper control over the automation process. This chapter begin with the evolution of communication protocols and then move on to explain the various communication protocols used today such as DNP3, Modbus, Profibus, IEC 60870, IEC 61850, and ICCP TASE 2(IEC 60870-6). Other relevant ICS protocols such as IEEE C37.118.1 Synchrophasor Measurement Standard, IEC 61968 standard, IEC 61970 standard, IEC 62325 standard, IEC 61508, IEC 62351, IEC 62056 and IEC 62056-21 are also fleetingly presented. Finally the important points to select the right protocols are also described.

Chapter 7: ESSENTIAL CRYPTOGRAPHY: This chapter begins with explaining cryptography components and their relationships, definition, need for cryptography, etc. Then move on to explain symmetric cryptography and types of symmetric systems. Various encryption methods such as Data Encryption Standard (DES), 3DES (Triple DES), Blowfish, Twofish, International Data Encryption Algorithm (IDEA), RC4, RC5, RC6, Advanced Encryption Standard (AES), Secure and Fast Encryption Routine (SAFER) and Serpent are explained. Asymmetric or Public Key Infrastructure (PKI), Certificate Authorities, Certificates, Registration Authority, Certificate Generation and Destruction are briefly explained. This chapter concludes with a description of hashing algorithms and uses.

Chapter 8: ICS CYBER SECURITY: FOREMOST CHALLENGE: This chapter gives a description about how the OT (SCADA) security is different from IT security and its importance. The requirement of open communication system and standardization are discussed with emphasis on security. The VPN and MPLS technology with their advantage and disadvantages, selection criterion are also discussed. The critical infrastructure protection requirements are also introduced in this chapter. Security concerns of the substation automation and control center are briefly deliberated.

Chapter 9: DEFENSE IN DEPTH ARCHITECTURE: This chapter begins with explaining the Purdue Reference Model which is generally accepted as the basic security architecture model in industry. Then explains Physical and Environmental Security, Attacks and Mitigation Strategies. Then it explains Network Security, Computer Security, Device security and Application Security. Briefly describes the software development security cycles and attacking the air gapped systems tactics.

Chapter 10: RISK ASSESSMENT: Risk and vulnerability assessment are very important issues in an automated ICS and SCADA systems. This chapter begins describing with risk calculation, risk assessment steps such as asset identification, system characterization, threat modelling and mitigation strategies. The chapter concludes with a brief description of Security Assessment Tools.

Chapter 11: ICS SECURITY STANDARDS: This chapter briefly explains the various security standards presently existing in the industrial sector and their selection requirements. IEC 62443, NIST 800, NERC CIP and ISO 27001 standards are briefly explained.

Chapter 12: DOCUMENTED ICS CYBER ATTACKS In recent years ICS is one of the main target of cyber-attackers and a number of cyber incidents have occurred to the ICS. This chapter describes some of the cyber-incidents as well as different sources of attacks to make the ICS engineers aware of the severity of the attacks. It also briefly describes the different types of threats that ICS may encounter from the perspective of the utility and implementation agencies. It then explains the lethal malware threats like Stuxnet which is a nightmare for Power System SCADA and ICS as it mainly exploits the Zero Day Vulnerabilities of the Windows OS.

ACKNOWLEDGEMENTS

First and foremost, let me contemplate over the kindness of the Almighty for giving me the thought, inspiration and ambience to write this complex technical book. I also remember my parents and uncles with due respect and affection and sincerely thank all my friends, colleagues especially Er.Vipin C Chacko and Er.Arun Raghavan and classmates who helped me with many technical debates and especially for reading and commenting on presentation of this book. At this moment of completion, I do recognize the contribution of my wife Dr. Shreelekshmi and my sons Harishankar and Harikrishnan. I express my gratitude for the spiritual and ethical support of Swami Rithmbarananda of Sivagiri Mutt and Sri. M.S. Bhuvananji of Ganesholsava Trust. I also remember all my cousins especially Sri. K.S. Jayamohan, Sri. R. Ranjith, Sri. Saji Natarajan, Sri.V.S. Ram Mohan, Sri.V.S. Madan Mohan and Smt.Bindu Chitharanjan, for their genuine love and support which have also been very crucial in non-academic aspects. Special thanks to my brother-in-law Maj.G.Chitharanjan for his encouraging words.

Dealing with cyber threats in an automated world is extremely complex and challenging as it requires expertise and co-ordination of multiple domains. Cyber security is not a readymade product rather it is a continuous process which needs real time updating to have a robust physical-cyber security system. Many parts of this book is written through contribution and cooperation from my colleagues and friends with the hope that it would be beneficial to many IT and OT technocrats who are engaged in the effort of building secure ICS and SCADA systems.

In addition to my early morning habit of scribbling with a cup of tea, most of my writing time for this book has been squeezed into spare moments in evenings and weekends which I have been spending for sightseeing or hilarity with friends. My thanks go, therefore, to my classmate and friend Smt. Ananda Parvathy T.G, for resuscitating and engaging me in my passion for writing with a good mindset of creativity. I also remember my dear professors with great respect especially Prof. S. Sooryadas, Dr. M.S.Valiyathan, Dr. G.S. Bhuvaneshwer,

Dr. M. Harishankar, Dr. K.G. Nair, Dr. C.S. Sridhar, Dr. P. Mohanan, Dr. Tessamma Thomas, Dr. R. Gopikakumari, Prof. P. Saraswathy and Dr. P. Sethumadhavan for their blessings. Finally I dedicate this work to the lotus feet of Goddess Sarada Devi of Sivagiri Mutt and to all my professors of Physics and Engineering.

In spite of all my efforts, there may be quite a few errors remaining in the book, and there would have been many more. Without the help of the expert reviewers, they may not be corrected and any suggestions for improvement of this book are always welcome. The author will be definitely privileged, if the readers get the intended sense which is the sole aim of this effort. Finally my sincere thanks to Notion team especially to Smt. Divya, Smt. Vandana, Smt. Lakshmi Parvathy and their colleague Sri. Hamza Natamkar for their support and co-operation on this project.

K S MANOJ

CHAPTER ONE
CYBER SPACE AND THREATS

1.1 INTRODUCTION

Today, the increasing cyber attacks are seriously drawing attention because of the enormous capability of the information age to challenge and redefine our security assumptions and the dependence on connected devices is developing more quickly than their ability to secure those devices. The microprocessors and the smart devices are the instruments of the present age and cyberspace is the oxygen of the internet. The interconnected, globalised, and technologically advancing world depends so much on cyberspace to fulfil our needs and requirements. From the emails to social networking to the high priority banking services, government systems, communications, transport, oil and gas and may be most important, our military organizations, the sophisticated weapons and the power sector, all increasingly place reliance on the World Wide Web (WWW) and everything connected to it. In fact, presently cyberspace is indispensible in our daily life. This chapter gives a brief description about the cyber space, cyber security definitions, different types of attacks on SCADA and Industrial Control Systems (ICS) which an automation security professional must be aware of.

1.2 CYBER SPACE

Cyberspace refers to the virtual computer world, and more specifically, is an electronic medium used to form a global computer network to facilitate online communication. It is a large computer network made up of many worldwide computer networks that employ TCP/IP protocol to aid in communication and data exchange activities. In fact, it is a digital medium with an interactive world but not a copy of the physical world. It is dynamic, undefined, and growing exponentially. It is as vast as human imagination and has no fixed shape.

1.3 SECURITY DEFINITIONS

Automation engineers often use the cyber security terms vulnerability, threat, risk, etc. However very few use those terms in the right sense by comprehending the correct meaning and their relationships between them. Some of the important cyber security terms of importance are briefly explained below.

Vulnerability: It is a weakness in a SCADA system for a countermeasure and could be exploited by a threat. It can be a software, hardware, procedure, or human weakness that can be exploited.

Threat: It is any potential to destructively impact a SCADA system that is associated with the exploitation of vulnerability. The threat is that someone, or something, will identify a specific vulnerability and use it against the company or individual. The entity that takes advantage of a vulnerability is referred to as a *threat agent.* A threat agent could be an intruder accessing the network through a port on the firewall, a process accessing data in a way that violates the security policy, or an employee making an accidental mistake that could expose confidential information.

Risk: It is the probability that a specific threat exploiting a vulnerability and the consequent impact or harm to the SCADA system. If a firewall has several ports open, there is a higher probability that an intruder will access the network in an unauthorized method.

Exposure: It is an instance of being exposed to losses. Vulnerability exposes an organization to possible damages. If password management is lax and password rules are not enforced, the company is exposed to the possibility of having users' passwords captured and used in an unauthorized manner. If a company does not have its wiring inspected and does not put proactive fire prevention steps into place, it exposes itself to potentially devastating fires.

Control or countermeasure: It is put into place to mitigate or reduce the potential risk. A countermeasure may be a software configuration, a hardware device, or a procedure that eliminates vulnerability or that reduces the likelihood a threat agent will be able to exploit vulnerability. Examples of countermeasures include strong password management, firewalls, a security guard, access control mechanisms, encryption, and security-awareness training.

Safeguard: A countermeasure or security control designed to reduce the risk associated with a specific threat.

Impact: The effect or consequence of a threat realized against a SCADA system.

Cyber War: The unauthorized invasion by a government into the systems or networks of another, aiming to disrupt those systems, to damage them partially, or to destroy them entirely. A specific target is to slow down if not curtail the military systems of the target state, there is no point having excellent missiles and weapons if the delivery systems can be paralyzed. As the military establishments become more and more dependent on sophisticated technologies, the risk of equally sophisticated attacks on them grows. The Stuxnet attack on Iran nuclear facility and Blackenergy attack on Ukraine power sector are typical examples to Nation sponsored cyber attacks.

Cyber Espionage: Governments can invade the systems of their rivals to steal sensitive information that would be useful for their own purposes. These attacks are usually hard to discover. As it has been reported, approximately for five years hackers had access to 70 government and private agencies around the world as they secreted away gigabytes of confidential information. By the time it has been spotted, 49 networks had been infected in the U.S alone along with several others in other countries.

Cyber Crime: It is the kind of threat which is the most familiar. This also has military and political implications. Cyber Crime also includes pornography, Internet stalking, and personality imitation.

Cyber Terrorism: This includes websites spreading extremist propaganda, recruiting terrorists, planning attacks, and otherwise promoting terrorists' political and social objectives. It also involves the use of hackers by terrorists to debilitate states and governments, much like in Cyber War, with the only difference that this involves a non-State actor. Cyberspace offers a great advantage for the shrouded business of terrorists, making their work murkier than ever to those outside.

If users are not aware of the processes and procedures, there are chances that an employee will make an unintentional mistake that may destroy data. If an Intrusion Detection System (IDS) is absent on a network, the attack probability is very high. Risk ties the vulnerability, threat, and likelihood of exploitation to the resulting business impact.

1.4   MOTIVATION FOR ATTACKS

Hackers attacking ICS have different motives, including financial gain, political reasons and military objectives. Attacks can be state-sponsored or from competitors, insiders with a malicious goal, and even hacktivists. They are also people with curiosity, convictions, apathy, anger, greed, hope, and honor. Just like people, hackers or groups of hackers may fall on a spectrum of good and evil. Where they fall may be dependent on the day or mood of that individual, or even the convictions of the larger collective.

1.5   THREAT SOURCES TO ICS

Both threat and vulnerability are evaluated based on the consequences and the amount of loss or damage occurred from a successful attack. Distributed Control System (DCS) is a typical Cyber Physical Systems (CPS), which tightly integrates a physical power transmission system with the cyber process of network computing and communication at all scales and levels. Obviously it is susceptible to cyber threats and vulnerabilities and can be exploited by different attack groups. They are mainly classified as described below.

- *Threat from crackers:* Crackers break into computers for profit by exploiting vulnerabilities. Internet provide information regarding the availability of hacker tools along with information industrial control systems,

- *Threat from insiders:* They disrupt their corporate networks. It can be by accident or by a disgruntled employee for revenge.

- *Ransomware threats:* They break into computers with a strong financial motive for cyber-crime to exploit vulnerabilities,

- *Threat from terrorists:* who attack systems for cause or ideology, and

- *Threat from enemy nations:* Nations which attack computers and servers of the enemy nations.

1.6 ICS VULNERABILITIES

With the integration of ICT, transition to a smarter ICS is very much optimistic and promising. However it introduces cyber vulnerabilities to the ICS. The major points which lead DCS vulnerable to cyber attacks are briefly described below.

- *Bi-directional Communication:* Though bi-directional communication provides great benefits to the utility and the end user with the capability to communicate and share information, it makes the system vulnerable to cyber-attacks.

- *Customer Data Privacy:* The information shared over the DCS is intrinsically sensitive, requires high level privacy and personal security.

- *Device Security: Device Security* of various manufactures roll out devices with different security features with different security levels built in, making it a challenge to standardize security practices. A cyber-attacker may compromise some of the communication devices such as modems, routers, etc. and infiltrate the system using it as a backdoor to launch attacks. A cyber-attacker may compromise some of the communication devices such as modems, routers, etc. and infiltrate the system using it as a backdoor to launch attacks. Malwares developed by an attacker can infect the AMI, RTU, PLC or control center servers or utility's corporate servers. Malwares can replace or alter the device functions or a system including sending false commands.

- *Spreading Malwares:* Malwares developed by an attacker can infect the AMI, RTU, PLC or control center servers or utility's corporate servers. Malwares can replace or alter the device functions or a system including sending false commands.

- *Distributed Connectivity: In DCS especially which are not confined to a specific geographic area like* Smart Grid, the network continue to expand and become more difficult to secure.

- *Access Controls:* As the number of customers, suppliers and contractors increases, it becomes difficult to gain access to the network resulting in identity theft.

- *Employee Training and Awareness:* Without proper training and awareness, there are chances of increasing the insider threats and lapses.

- *Guidelines and Policies:* This may pose the potential for gaps in visibility, defense and recovery. These threats are real that many Nations have declared its digital infrastructure as strategic asset and made cyber-security a national agenda with highest priority. They are setting up security policies to force utilities responsible for protecting the critical electrical infrastructure. Many Nations entrusted their secret agencies to monitor hackers. Hence utilities have to take spontaneous and significant steps to secure their networks. The techniques which attackers use to gain control of an ICS or cause different levels of damage are mostly similar to those in case of IT. But they also possess certain explicit techniques and some of the techniques used are briefly described below.

1.7 ALARMING ICS THREATS

The present day ICS threats are much advanced technically and the implemented ICS and DCS are secured just because of *security through obscurity*. A brief description of the technically advanced lethal threats and vulnerabilities are described in the following sections.

➢ Zero Day Vulnerabilities (ZDVs)

The term zero day implies that the developer does not get enough time to develop and deploy a patch to overcome the flaw. Before that, an attacker exploits the flaw and/or creates and deploy malwares to attack the SCADA system. There are many zero-day flaws that may affect a SCADA system. Stack overflow is one of them. This attack can occur on the field devices as well as the servers. The stack buffer in the memory can be corrupted by a malicious player, leading to injection of dangerous executable code into the running program and thus usurping the control of the industrial process. The vulnerability reported in China is a well-known example. Zero Day Attacks can also occur in the form of DoS attacks that overload computer resources. Stuxnet is a lethal computer worm which uses four zero-day Windows vulnerabilities. It was primarily written to target Iranian nuclear centrifuges. Its final goal is to disrupt ICSs by modifying programs implemented on PLCs to make them work in a manner that the attacker intended and to hide those changes from system operators. It is believed that Stuxnet is introduced to a computer network through an infected removable drive. To hide itself while spreading across the network and realizing the final target, the virus installs a Windows rootkit by exploiting four zero-day vulnerabilities. The success of this virus in penetrating the PLC environment shows that traditional security measures are not sufficient for the complete protection of safety-critical infrastructures.

➢ Non-prioritization of Tasks

This is a serious flaw in real-time operating systems of many Industrial Control Systems (ICS). In certain embedded operating systems, there may not have the feature of prioritization of tasks. Memory sharing between the equally privileged tasks lead to serious security issues. The features such as the accessibility to create Object Entry Point (OEP) in the kernel domain can lead to loopholes in security. Non-kernel tasks maybe protected from overflows using guard pages. But the guard pages may be small and cannot provide stringent protection.

➤ Database Injection

Detrimental query statements can be injected to exploit the vulnerabilities in a ICS especially when the client inputs are not properly filtered. This is widely reported for SQL-based databases. Here the attacker sends a command to SQL server through the web server and attempt to reveal critical authentication information.

➤ Communication Protocol Issues

Today with the developments in encryption and authentication, IT security is capable of encountering the sophisticated cyber-attacks and threats. But they are not adopted in an adequate manner in ICS and DCS especially when the process is controlled with the client server architecture.

Earlier SCADA security was not a major concern and hence communication protocols did not give sufficient importance to authentication. This does not mean that authentication and encryption methods cannot be used with these systems. It should be noted that encryption is effective only in an authenticated communication between entities. To have a secure TCP/IP communication, internet Protocol Security (IPSec) framework has to be employed. It will help to create a secure channel of communication for ICS. IPSec uses two protocols for authentication and encryption viz. Encapsulating Security Payload (ESP) and Authentication Header (AH). Advanced Persistent Threat (APT) attacks which monitor network activity and steal data for a future attack, can be effectively dealt with protocols like Syslog that keeps security logs which provide a means for detecting stealthy attempts to gather information prior to building sophisticated attacks by malicious players.

➤ Stealthy Integrity Attack

Stealth attacks are targeted to disrupt the service integrity, and make the networks to accept false data value. Security experts reports that powerful adversaries equipped with in-depth knowledge, disclosure resources, and disruption capabilities who are capable to perform stealthy attacks which partially or totally bypass traditional anomaly detectors. The detectability of an attack strategy depends on the capabilities of adversaries to coordinate attack vectors on control signals and sensor measurements.

➢ Replay Attack

These are the network attacks in which an attacker spies the communication between the sender and receiver and takes the authenticated information e.g. stealing the key and then contact the receiver with that key. In replay attack the attacker gives the proof of his identity and authenticity. The negative effect of a replay attack on a feedback control system has been found that this attack strategy is carried out in two steps which are mentioned below.

- The hacker records sensor measurements for a certain window of time before performing the attack.

- The hacker replaces actual sensor measurements with previously recorded signals while modifying control signals to drive system states out of their normal values.

A replay attack is capable of bypassing the classical detectors.

➢ False Data Injection Attack

DCS may operate in very hostile environments. AMI components lacking tamper-resistance hardware increases the possibility to be compromised. The attacker may inject false measurement reports to disrupt the DCS operation through the compromised meters and sensors. The objective of the attacker is to fool the state estimator by carefully injecting a certain amount of false data into sensor measurements. Those attacks are denoted as false data injection attacks. It can upset the grid system and lead to a false state estimation resulting to the disruption of the energy distribution. Security experts are of the opinion that the false data injection attack is a discrete-time state-space model driven by Gaussian noises. A Kalman filter is generally used to perform state estimation, and a failure detector is employed to detect abnormal situations.

➤ Zero-Dynamics Attack

In ICS Zero-Dynamics Attack (ZDA) is one of the hardest attacks to defend, especially in closed-loop feedback system which possesses an unstable zero, such as an unbounded actuator or sensor. These attacks cannot be observed by the monitoring data. The ZDA can be easily implemented in the cyber space or injected into the communication links by an attacker who has a proper understanding of Data Acquisition System (DAS). As modern control systems are implemented on digital computers using sample and hold mechanisms, where the controllers can be dealt with in a Sampled Data (SD) framework, can generate vulnerability to stealthy attacks due to the unstable sampling zeros in the SD system.

➤ Covert Attack

This attack is a targeted attack, but it is constructed and deployed using public tools. These are custom-made and minimally equipped. The strategy of covert attack consists of coordinating control signals and sensor measurements into a concerted malicious attack. This attack is executed in two steps as described below.

- The state attack vector can be chosen freely based on malicious targets and available resources.

- The sensor attack vector is designed in such a way that it can compensate for the effects of the state attack vector on the sensor measurements. The covert attack strategy can be considered as the worst case attack because it has the capaability to bypass traditional anomaly detectors. However, the covert attack needs to compromise numerous sensors to assure its stealth. Therefore, ICS defenders can remove a covert attack by protecting some critical sensors or deploying secure sensors.

➤ Surge Attack, Bias Attack and Geometric Attack

The three types of stealthy attacks, viz. the surge attack, the bias attack, and the geometric attack are also important and is to be addressed by a cyber-security expert. The surge attack seeks to maximize the damage as soon as possible, while the bias attack tries to modify the system by small perturbations over a long period. The geometric attack integrates the surge attack and the bias attack by shifting the system behavior gradually at the beginning and maximizing the damage at the end.

1.8 DREADFUL ICS MALWARES

As ICS and DCS improve the efficiency and performance of the power grid, they also increase the grid vulnerability to potential cyber attacks. Black Energy, Stuxnet, Havex, Duqu, and Sandworm are all recent examples of malwares targeting ICS. The AMI components especially the Smart Meters and increase in External Access Points (EAP) added with the integration of Renewable Energy Sources (RES) introduced new additional areas through which a potential cyber-attack may be launched on the grid. The present malware intrusions have resulted in a significant disruption of grid operations like what it had occurred to Ukraine by the dreadful malware BlackEnergy. The following sections are dedicated to describe some of the SCADA malwares.

➢ BlackEnergy

BlackEnergy is a Trojan horse malware program which infects the SCADA systems. Though it has been detected in 2007, the vehemence of destruction is realized only in 2015 with the Ukraine power sector attack. Till the Ukraine power sector attack, it has been believed that BlackEnergy was designed only for nuisance spam attacks and not targeted ICS or critical energy infrastructure. Today, BlackEnergy is a special concern for Critical Infrastructure companies especially to ICS because the software being used is in an Advanced Persistent Threat (APT) form, apparently to gather information. BlackEnergy specifically targets HMI software which is typically running 24/7, with the provision of remote access. It is rarely updated, thus making it a favorite target for opportunistic hackers. While no attempts to damage, modify, or otherwise disrupt the victim systems' control processes immediately after infection of BlackEnergy, indicates that the APT variant of BlackEnergy is a special concern as it is a modular malware capable moving through network files.

➢ Ukraine Incident

The December 23rd 2015, a cyber-attack has been carried out by the BlackEnergy malware which resulted in disrupting the ICS network almost completely in a brilliant sabotage operation which is briefly described below.

The hackers penetrated the ICS networks through the hijacked VPNs and sent commands to disable the UPS systems they had already reconfigured. Then they issued commands to open breakers. But before they did, they launched a Denial-of-Service (DoS) attack against customer call centers to prevent customers from calling in to report the outage. DoS attacks sent a flood of data to the web servers and as a result, the phone systems of the control center were flooded with thousands of bogus calls, in order to prevent genuine callers from getting through. This clearly demonstrates a high level of complexity, cleverness and organization of the attackers. Expert cybercriminals and even Nation sponsored attackers often fail to anticipate in all likelihoods. However, regarding BlackEnergy attack, it has been observed that the attackers put very concentrated effort to make sure that they are covering all aspects without any lapse so that nothing could go wrong. The move certainly required considerable time to the attackers to complete their operation. But by the time the operators realized this adverse situation that their machine has been hijacked, a number of substations had already been taken down and the situation had been totally slipped out of their control. In fact the operators become silent witness of this attack.

By gaining the remote control and opening the breakers, the attackers switched off a series of substations from the grid. They carried out these most clever operations in fact paralyzed the grid. They overwrote the firmware of the substation serial-to-Ethernet converters, replacing genuine firmware with their malicious firmware and rendering the converters thereafter inoperable and unrecoverable, unable to receive commands. As a result, these gateways are blown and cannot be recovered until they got new devices and integrate them.

Once the attackers have completed all of these, they used a malware called KillDisk to wipe out files from operator stations to make them inoperable. KillDisk wiped or overwrote the data in essential system files, causing computers to crash. Because it also overwrote the master boot record, the infected computers could not reboot. All these happened during the beginning of night peak, and the power utilities posted a note to their web sites acknowledging that power was out in certain regions and reassuring that they are working vehemently to identify the cause of the crisis. But within half an hour, the KillDisk completed its dirty action and left power operators without any doubt what caused the blackout. The utilities then posted another note to customers intimating the cause of the outage was hackers.

In effect, up to 95% of daily electricity consumption in Ukraine was not supplied. Though the cyber-attacks on the energy distribution companies has been attributed to the Russian APT group, the BlackEnergy cyber-attack on Ukrainian power sector not only wrecked the Nation economically, but also worsened the energy customers confidence in the Ukrainian power companies and government. Most of all this power sector cyber attack gave a message to the entire world concerning the consequences of cyber attack on critical infrastructures of a Nation especially the power sector.

> ➢ **Stuxnet**

Stuxnet, the Nation sponsored world's first lethal digital weapon, was unlike any other virus or worm that came before. Rather than simply hijacking targeted computers or stealing information from them, it escaped the digital realm to wreak physical destruction of equipments which are controlled by the computers. Initially it designed specifically to infect the Siemens SIMATIC WinCC and S7 PLC products, either installed as part of a PCS 7 system, or operating on their own. It starts operation by taking advantage of vulnerabilities in the Windows operating systems and Siemens products. Once it detects a suitable victim, it modifies control logic in of PLCs or RTUs. Undoubtedly the objective is to sabotage a specific industrial process using the vendors' variable-frequency drive controllers, along with a supervising safety system for the overall process. Though there has been much speculation on Stuxnet's intended target, recent information suggests it was Iran's nuclear program and more specifically, its uranium enrichment process. Stuxnet is capable of infecting both unsupported/legacy and current versions of Windows including Windows 2000, Windows XP, Windows Server 2003, Windows Vista, Windows Server 2008 and Windows 7. It also infects the Siemens STEP 7 which is one of the world's best known and most widely used engineering software in ICS in such a way that it automatically executes when the STEP 7 project is loaded by an uninfected Siemens system. Some of the important characteristics of the worm are,

1. It propagates cleverly between targets, typically via USB flash drives and other removable media,

2. Once migrated the target, It propagates quickly within the target via multiple network pathways,

3. It very cunningly searches for numerous vendors' anti-virus technologies installed on machines and modifies its behavior to avoid the detection,

4. It contacts a command and control server on the internet for instructions and updates,

5. It establishes a peer-to-peer network to propagate instructions and updates within a target, even to equipments without direct internet connectivity,

6. It modifies PLC or RTU program logic, causing physical processes to malfunction,

7. It hides the modified PLC or RTU programs from control engineers and system administrators who are trying to understand the reason for the malfunctioning of the system,

8. It is signed with certificates stolen from major hardware manufacturers, so that no warnings are raised when the worm is installed, and

9. If a particular machine is not the intended target, the worm removes itself from the machine.

➢ **Iranian Experience**

In 2012 it has been confirmed that the Iranian nuclear facilities were attacked and infiltrated by the first *cyber-weapon* or the *digital missile* of the world known as the Stuxnet. It is believed that this attack was initiated by a random worker's USB drive. One of the affected nuclear facilities was the Natanz nuclear facility. The first signs that an issue existed in the nuclear facility's computer system was in 2010. Inspectors from the International Atomic Energy Agency (IAEA) visited the Natanz facility and observed that a strange number of uranium enriching centrifuges were breaking. The cause of these failures was unknown at that time. Later Iranian technicians contacted computer security specialists in Belarus for examining their server and network systems which control the facilities. This security firm eventually discovered multiple malicious files on the Iranian computer systems. It has subsequently revealed that these malicious files were the Stuxnet worm. Although Iran has not released specific details regarding the effects of the attack, it is currently estimated that the Stuxnet worm destroyed 984 uranium enriching centrifuges. By current estimations this constituted a 30% decrease in enrichment efficiency. It is reported that in 2017, once again Iranian critical infrastructures and networks have been vehemently attacked by a new variant of Stuxnet which is more sophisticated than its former variant leaving extreme concerns to the security of the industrial automation world.

➢ Spreading of Stuxnet

As already explained Stuxnet is one of the most complex, lethal and well engineered 500kilobyte computer worms the world has ever seen. It took advantage of at least four Zero Day Vulnerabilities (ZDVs) with remarkable sophistication. The worm propagates using three totally diverse mechanisms as described below.

- Via infected removable drives such as USB flash drives and external portable hard disks,
- Via Local Area Network communications such as shared network drives and print spooler services, and
- Via infected Siemens project files including both WinCC and STEP 7 files.

Within these three, it uses the following vulnerability exploitation techniques for spreading to new computers in a system.

The worm initially exploits a Zero Day Vulnerability in Windows Shell handling of LNK files which is a vulnerability present in all versions of Windows since at least Windows NT 4.0. Then uses several techniques to copy itself to all accessible network and spread from there to all possible locations. It also copies itself to printer servers using a zero-day vulnerability, The Conficker RPC vulnerability is also used to propagate through computers which are not properly patched up. If any Siemens WinCCSQLServer database servers are present, then the worm installs itself on those servers via database calls and puts copies of itself into Siemens STEP 7 project files to auto-execute whenever the filesare loaded. Certain versions of the worm used a variant of the old *autorun.inf* trick to propagate via USB drives.

In addition to the propagation techniques described above, the worm uses two ZDVs to escalate privilege on targeted machines. This provided the worm with system access privileges so that it could copy itself into system processes on compromised machines. When first installed on a computer with any software, Stuxnet attempts to locate Siemens STEP 7 programming stations and infect these. If it succeeds, it replaces the Dynamic Link Library (DLL). Mostly Stuxnet spreads through the infected removable devices especially the USB. However it is a misconception that it spreads through only removable devices and an effective disabling of the storage device access can prevent the spreading of Stuxnet.

> **Havex**

The modified version of Havex malware mainly targets the energy sector. Originally, Havex was distributed via spam email or spear-phishing attacks. The new version of Havex appears to have been designed as a Trojan horse specifically to infiltrate and modify legitimate software from ICS and SCADA suppliers, adding an instruction to run, code containing the Havex malware. In the instance discovered, Havex malware was used as a Remote Access Tool (RAT) to extract data from Industrial Control System (ICS) related software used for remote access. The cyber-attack leaves the company's system in what appears to be a normal operating condition, but a backdoor has been opened by the attacker to access and control the utilities ICS or

SCADA operations. The Havex malware possibly enter the control systems of targeted utilities using one or multiple levels of attack as described below.

1. Top level management are targeted with malicious PDF attachments.

2. Websites are likely to be visited by people working in the energy sector. Such websites can be infected and visitors are redirected to another compromised legitimate website hosting an exploit kit. Using this exploit kit, the RAT may be installed.

3. Through software downloads from ICS related vendors which they include the RAT malware.

Havex is also called as *Backdoor. Oldrea* or the *Energetic Bear RAT* as it contains the malware known as *Kragany.* Havex is a product of the Dragonfly group, which appears to be a state-sponsored undertaking focused on espionage with sabotage as a definite secondary capability. The malware allows attackers to upload and download files from the infected computer and run executable files. It was also reported to be capable of collecting passwords, taking screenshots and cataloguing documents.

➢ Sandworm

Sandworm is a type of Trojan horse, focused on exploiting vulnerability in the Windows operating system. USB storage devices with automatically run files, carrying the malware is used for the attack. The primary mode of Sandworm attack is spear phishing. Using well written emails with topics of interest has been sent to the target. The malware contains an attachment that exploits the vulnerability to deliver variants of the BlackEnergy Trojan.

Various reports released regarding the Sandworm team and investigations of the malware samples and domains, realized that Sandworm team is targeting SCADA centric victims especially who are using GE Intelligent Platform's CIMPLICITY HMI solution suite. The HMI can be viewed as an operator console that is used to monitor and control devices in an industrial environment. Sandworm can potentially have greater impacts on an enterprise, as the malware could be transferred to other corporate business systems.

It is important to note that CIMPLICITY is mainly used as an attack vector by Sandworm. However, there is no sign that this malware ismanipulating any actual SCADA systems or data. Since HMIs are located in both the corporate and control networks, this attack could be used to target either network segment, or used to cross from the corporate to the control network.

➢ **Duqu and Flame**

Duqu and Flame are computer malwares that were discovered on 1st September 2011 and 28th May 2012, respectively. Duqu is almost identical to Stuxnet but with a different tenacity. Flame is also known as Flamer or Sky-wiper. The goal of Duqu is to collect information that could be useful in launching an ICS attack later. Flame like Stuxnet and Duqu, uses rootkit functionality to evade information security methods. Unlike Stuxnet, which was designed to sabotage ICSs, the target of Flame is to gather technical diagrams such as AutoCAD drawings, PDFs, and text files. Though Duqu and Flame were not designed to target ICSs directly, their penetration and acquiring information about the systems, is an indication of a targeted stealthy attacks in the future.

1.9   FLASH DRIVE USAGE AND END NODE SECURITY (ENS)

USB attacks are becoming more sophisticated, affecting all classes of USB device instead of just storage. As USBs have become a common method for easily sharing information locally between devices, they have become a common source of information system cyber-compromise. As per NERC CIP guidelines, use of USB or USB type ports are strongly discouraged because a USB port is not immune to protection from *unauthorized access*.

It would be helpless against connecting modems, network cables that bridge networks or insertion of an infected USB pen drive. Cyber protection for USB ports can be enforced, however, it is often cost prohibitive and is not one hundred percent effective. There is no essential requirement for using a USB instead of other standard and more secure interfaces such as Ethernet and serial ports. Some of the common methods to protect the USB ports are,

- disabling (via software) the physical ports,
- prominent physical port usage discouragement such as, a port cover plate or tamper tape, and
- physical port obstruction using removable locks.

These measures are examples of defense-in-depth methods, but the CIP guidelines acknowledge that these control approaches can be easily circumvented. It is also not uncommon for an employee or authorized contractor to inadvertently compromise a device simply by plugging in an infected smart phone to charge the battery. USB flash drives pose two major challenges to critical infrastructure cyber-security viz.

- ease of data theft owing to their small size and transportability, and
- system compromise through infections from computer viruses, malware and spyware.

It is a well-accepted fact that a USB supported portable peripheral device can trigger a massive cyber-attack, even when the computer system targeted is isolated and protected from the outside with firewalls and other types of security devices.

➢ BadUSB

Any computer which can be reached by a USB port is potentially vulnerable. This is particularly true for ICSs where malicious code can be injected into critical devices just by plugging a USB device for a few seconds into them. BadUSB is an USB which includes firmware in addition to disk space. It is inherently a microcontroller with writable storage memory registers. This firmware however can be embedded with executable codes which cannot be verified by third party security software applications since the firmware is not an open source. This flaw in USBs opens the door to modification of USB firmware, which can easily be done from inside the operating system, and hide the malware in a way that it becomes almost impossible to detect. The BadUSB software can transforms the firmware of the USB device so that it appears as a keyboard to the operating system. The flaw is even more potent because complete formatting or deleting the content of a USB device won't eliminate the malicious code, since it is embedded in the firmware. Patches made for BadUSB have been largely ineffective and a fix is years away. In fact till date, there has been no practical defensive solution against BadUSB attacks and it exposes the fundamental vulnerabilities of unconstrained privileges in USB devices. This being the situation, ICS and DCS design and implementation must be in such a manner that it completely eliminates the need for a USB port which is advised and recommended in the interest of reliable and safe operations. Security engineers consider BadUSB attacks are highly dangerous to ICS since most antivirus and malware scanners usually have no way to access the firmware on the USB devices and cannot protect the computer.

➢ Cyber Incidents using USB

- Two US based power plants were infected with malware after using USB drives in their ICS. At one of the plants this resulted in downtime and delayed the plant's restart by three weeks. This caused considerable financial loss.

- Another cyber incident of malware wreaking havoc includes the recent widespread infections at Saudi Aramco and Ras-Gas, where malware were planted by USB drives. At Saudi Aramco approximately 40,000 computer hard drives were completely wiped off. As none of the infected power plants had updated anti-malware softwares, the infected computers were totally incapable of detecting the malware on the inserted USB drives.

Usually, almost every vendors or implementation agencies offer or sign the contract stating that the control system shall be protected by an automatically updated antivirus system. The agreement is reasonable, but it may be very difficult to comply with. The ICS industry is very much aware of this problem. Different solutions have been tried, including the use of glue guns to disable USB ports and physical USB locks.

Summary

This chapter begins with explaining the cyber space and security definitions which an industrial security professional may familiar with. Then it proceeds in explaining the motivation for cyber attacks to ICS and various threat sources. The common cyber attacks to SCADA and ICS are briefly explained. Then this chapter gives a brief account of dreadful malwares such as BlackEnergy, Stuxnet, Havex, Sandworm, Duqu and Flame. This chapter conclude with describing the End Node Security, Flash Drive Usage, BadUSB and Cyber incidents using USB.

CHAPTER TWO
OPERATIONAL TECHNOLOGY AND ICS

2.1 INTRODUCTION

The ICS control a physical process which is a real time system having unique network configurations and protocols. The data can become stale in a fraction of seconds, if not kept secured, resulting in loss of process efficiency, damage or shut down. As a result, ICS reliability is crucial and continues to operate even during a cyber attack. Process inefficiencies and shutdowns are often very expensive, with millions of dollars or much more for large process. In critical infrastructure, loss of the ICS can have significant, detrimental impact in the health and functionality of society. Earlier, ICS were physically isolated or air gapped from the outside world. Now systems are linked into the corporate WAN and internet to allow process monitoring and maintenance. Control engineers, operators are usually not skilled in cyber security. Conversely, the IT professionals are not skilled in process control. They have sometimes conflicting goals and management in the corporate structure. This chapter briefly explains the Operational Technology (OT), its difference from the IT and the changing culture of ICS.

2.2 OPERATIONAL TECHNOLOGY (OT)

Operational technology (OT) is the use of hardware and software to monitor and control physical processes, devices, and infrastructure. Present operational technology demands that decision-makers to understand OT in its traditional sense and as an area of exciting innovation. At very fundamental level, OT refers to a technology which monitors and controls specific devices especially the field devices and processes within industrial workflows.

When compared with IT, OT is unique with its hardware and software and is usually designed to do specific things such as control physical parameters like heat, pressure, humidity, flow, etc. and monitor mechanical performance, issue emergency shut offs, etc on proper decisions. Typically, this is done through Industrial Control Systems (ICS) based on Supervisory Control and Data Acquisition (SCADA) technology.

2.3   INFORMATION TECHNOLOGY (IT) VS OPERATIONAL TECHNOLOGY (OT)

In the simplest sense, IT deals with information, while OT deals with machines and process. The former manages the flow of digital information such as Customer Relationship Management, Enterprise Resource Planning, Email, etc, while the latter manages the operation of physical processes and the machinery used to carry them out. Some examples of OT are SCADA, PLCs, HMIs, etc.

From power plants and oil rigs to manufacturing and inventory management, OT is an essential part. Today some of the IT systems invented to manage are now being applied to operational technology to manage the flow of water, lubricating oil, controlling physical parameters, packing food grains, etc. In fact, OT and IT now work hand-in-hand to monitor and regulate essential industrial processes. Although these processes will differ from one industry to industry, ICS has a central role to play in the success of many modern enterprises and manufacturers. Table 2.1 gives a comparison between IT and OT.

Table 2.1 Functional Comparison of IT and OT

Function	Information Technologies (IT)	Operational Technologies (OT)
Objective	IT focuses on the storage, recovery, transmission, process and security of data.	OT is more oriented to the control of processes or their change through the monitoring and control of devices.
Application Domain	Business-oriented.	Process-oriented.
Access	Connected with the external world.	Highly secured with very restricted access mostly through role based access.
Frequency of Change	Constantly changing with new employees	Slow changing environment
Main priority	Confidentiality, Integrity and Availability.	Uptime is very critical Availability, Integrity and Confidentiality.
Updates	Constant due to software updates. Service interruptions are tolerable.	Updates must be tested carefully in advance before installing and usually involve restarting.
Life cycle	Shorter life cycles of 3-5 years.	Longer life cycles of 15-20 years.
Latency	Minutes to Days.	Miliseconds to Seconds.
Security	The objective is to protect confidential information. Requires cyber security.	The objective is to protect the environment, people and infrastructures. Requires Physical-Cyber security.
Operating System	Using standard Operating Systems.	Using specific purpose equipment with Custom-developed software and Operating Systems.

2.4 INDUSTRIAL CONTROL SYSTEMS (ICS)

An industrial control system is a combination of a variety of systems like computers, electrical and mechanical devices. It can be considered as the combination of several control systems such as Supervisory Control and Data Acquisition (SCADA) systems, Distributed Control Systems (DCS) and Programmable Logic Controllers. They are used to provide automated or partially automated control of the equipment in manufacturing and chemical plants, electric utilities, distribution and transportation systems, and many other industries. It can also be described as the automatic regulation of unit operations and their associated equipment as well as the integration and coordination of the unit operations into the larger production system. ICS is used in manufacturing operations and it can also be applied to material handling. Present ICS are mostly based on SCADA technology and has been evolved through four stages which are mainly described below.

2.5   SUPERVISORY CONTROL AND DATA ACQUISITION (SCADA)

Supervisory Control and Data Acquisition (SCADA) is a system that operates with coded signals over communication channels so as to provide control of remote equipment (using typically at least one communication channel per remote station). In SCADA, the control system is combined with the data acquisition system by fetching the coded signals over communication channels to acquire information about the status of the remote equipment's for displaying or for recording or controlling equipment functions. SCADA systems historically distinguish themselves from other ICS systems by being large-scale processes that can include multiple sites, spread out over large areas. These processes can be industrial, infrastructure, and facility-based processes.

Industrial processes include those of manufacturing, production, power generation, fabrication, and refining. The process can be run in continuous, batch, repetitive, or discrete modes. Infrastructure processes may be public or private, and include water treatment and distribution, wastewater collection and treatment, oil and gas pipelines, electrical power transmission and distribution, wind farms, civil defense siren systems, and large communication systems. Facility processes occur both in public facilities and private ones, including buildings, airports, ships, and space stations. They monitor and control heating, ventilation, and air conditioning systems (HVAC), access, and energy consumption.

Evolution of SCADA

SCADA systems have been evolved through the following four generations.

- *Monolithic SCADA:* These SCADA systems were in use before the revolution of computer networking. They were stand-alone systems having no connectivity to other systems and developed as local SCADA. These mostly used guided communication with proprietary protocols. Further these systems did not envisage the fail safe and fault tolerant design aspects seriously. Hence these SCADA systems faced reliability issues considerably. The hardware used was mainly minicomputers capable of large computing capabilities.

- *Distributed SCADA:* This generation came into existence when the computer networking technology has been developed and incorporated into the SCADA systems. Here the data gathered and the data processing across the multiple stations are connected through computer networking. The latency has been reduced considerably to an extent that system as a whole functioned in near real time. These SCADA systems were economical when compared with first generation, as each station has been assigned with particular tasks. However the protocols used was still proprietary and was not interoperable. But the proprietary protocols had an advantage that beyond the developers, the extent of security or the security flaws are unknown. In other way these SCADA systems were secured through *security through obscurity.*

- *SCADA with standard protocols:* The advancement of communication technology and with the introduction of interoperable SCADA protocols, SCADA broke the geographical barriers and spread across more than one LAN network called Process Control Network. The master station may have several servers running parallel to handle various tasks, such as historian, SCADA, NMS, Development, etc. This makes the system very economical and real-time. However the physical-security is a major concern and must be addressed while designing and implementing.

- *Internet of Things:* By appropriately integrating the advancement of cloud computing, SCADA has taken a new shape and adopted the name Internet of Things. The advantages of amalgamating the various technologies are:

1. Capable of being flexible and affordable with the ability to go private,

2. Capable of ingest massive amount of machine data,

3. Capable of connecting different machines and systems such as SCADA, DCS, and historians,

4. Capable of connecting various machines having net connectivity and process data across all these sources together,

5. Capable of real time complex and real time processing of data from multiple sources,

6. Capable of Big data processing and apply supervised and unsupervised machine learning algorithms to predict outcomes,

Another advantage of incorporating the cloud computing technology is that it significantly reduces the infrastructure costs and increases the ease of maintenance. Further the SCADA operations become near real time and the use of open protocols with TLS security improves the security boundary considerably.

Certain ICT professionals envisage IoT as an appropriate amalgamation of Machine to Machine (M2M) communication, Wireless Sensor Networks (WSN), Radio Frequency Identification (RFID), and SCADA as shown in Figure 1.1.

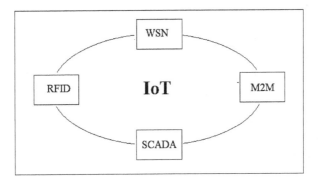

Figure 2.1 Fourth generation SCADA or IoT

In fact, the fourth generation SCADA or IoT transforms the human centric internet into objects or things centric. It is expected that about 70 billion things may be hooked into internet in the near future while people hooked into the internet may be only 7 billion. However at present, IoT is not a tangible reality but it is a prospective vision of a number of technologies. But once materialized, it can drastically change the way of functioning of our society. Realizing the potential and the opportunity of business, IoT has become a buzzword in many countries. Further it is anticipated that the whole world will be soon under the influence of IoT wave.

2.6 TYPES OF INDUSTRIAL CONTROL SYSTEMS

ICSs are classified based on their uses and the separation between the controller and the supervisory components and they are,

- *Process control system:* This system does the automation function in a manufacturing unit, process control systems are mostly seen in factories,

- *Safety instrumented system:* These systems are used in the automation process it will check the process and it prevents unsafe operation processes. They have sensors which will send signals to the controller which can prevent any fault operation,

- *Distributed Control System:* DCS can handle multiple automation processes in a factory, it can control all the automation or it can monitor or supervise the factory process,

- *Building Automation System:* Building Automation System (BAS) controls and monitor the whole building process such as air-conditioning, ventilation, energy management, and fire protection. So one can control the whole building from a control room with the help of BAS.

- *Energy Management System:* An energy management system can control and monitor the transmission and generation of electricity. It can be considered as a type of SCADA which can control the power generation and transmission and

- *Supervisory Control and Data Acquisition:* SCADA is a type of industrial control system which can observe the automation process across geographical areas which will be miles away. SCADA system can control and monitor remote field controllers, and the result will be given to operators by a human-machine interface. SCADA system can control one or more distributed or process control systems at distant locations.

2.7 CONTROL COMPONENTS OF ICS

Control server: This provides the control software for DCS or PLC which is designed to communicate with lower-level control devices.

SCADA server or master control unit: SCADA server acts as the master In the SCADA system, remote terminal units and PLC devises which are located at remote field sites act as slaves.

Remote Terminal Unit: these are designed to support SCADA remote stations, it is a special-purpose data acquisition and control unit. RTU's are used to support remote situations where wire-based communications are unavailable.

Programmable Logic Controller: PLC is a small industrial computer that is designed to perform the logic functions executed by electrical hardware. PLC has the ability to control complex process and they are used in SCADA systems and DCS. PLC's can be used as a field device because they are more economical and flexible.

Intelligent Electronic Device: IED is a smart sensor that has the intelligence to acquire data, communicate to other devices, and it performs local processing and control. Automatic control is possible with the help of IED.

Human-Machine Interface: It can be considered as the combination of the software and hardware which allows operators to check the state of a process if it is under control or not. HMI can be used to modify control settings to change the control objective and it can be used to manually override automatic control operations in case of emergencies. Operators can configure set points or control algorithms with the help of HMI. It can display process, status information, historical information and other information to operators.

Data historian: It is a centralized database for logging all process information within an ICS information that is stored in a database that can be accessed to support various analyses.

Communications gateways: Two dissimilar devices can be communicated by this, it transforms data from a sending system to match the protocol and transmission medium of a destination host.

Field devices: Field devices are sensors transducers and actuators and machinery which directly interface with a controller through a digital or analog input/output module.

I/O server: It is a control component that does the collecting, buffering, and providing access to process information from control sub-components such as PLC, RTU. It can be used to interface with the third party control components such as an HMI and a control server.

2.8 NETWORK COMPONENTS OF ICS

Network components of Industrial Control System are briefly described below.

Fieldbus network: this device can link sensors and other devices to a PLC or other controller. With the help of this, the need for point to point wiring between the controller and the device is eliminated *Control network:* It connects the supervisory control level to lower-level control.

Routers: It is a device that can transfer messages between two networks. LAN and WAN are examples of routers, it can be used as a long-distance network medium.

Firewalls: Devices on a network are protected by a firewall, it can protect the network by monitoring and controlling.

Remote Access Points: They are distinct devices which control system remotely.

MODEMS: Modems are used for long-distance serial communications, digital data can be converted by modem and it can transmit data over a telephone line to allow devices to communicate. Remote communication is possible through the help of MODEMS.

2.9 DIFFERENT OPERATIONAL ZONES IN ICS

Industrial control systems are very complex, they can be used to control the complex and precision processes in real-time with the help of many components. In order to control the operation process, ICSs are divided mainly into three operational zones they are,

Enterprise zone: This zone comprises of business network and enterprise systems. It has many endpoint devices and is upgraded continuously. The business network is commonly operated on the IP protocols and can be connected to external networks including the internet. These networks are usually kept separate from the operational networks of other zones.

Control zones: This zone has a network-based IP protocol just like the enterprise zone including a control room environment. The devices in this zone are not often updated.

Field zone: It has many field devices and networks in charge of control and automation. The field zone devices and networks are comprised of high reliability and safety.

2.10 CHANGING ICS CULTURE

ICS is traditionally the domain of Electrical Engineers. But with the integration of Information Communication Technology (ICT) to ICS systems broke the geographical barriers which requires expertise in advanced hardware and software platforms, internet communication and security protocols, flawless connectivity to corporate networks, physical cyber security, etc. Thus involvement of ICT and cyber security experts becomes unavoidable with modern ICS systems. This introduced conflicting cultures and priorities and differing stances especially on implementing intrusion detection systems, firewalls, authentication, and encryption.

Until recently, there was a view that the very nature of most SCADA systems, they are less vulnerable than IT systems. It is true that control systems are less visible than IT systems and many were not connected to external networks or cyber space. Further their components required detailed technological knowledge to implement and operate. Hence the myth of security through obscurity was a fact until the end of 1999. But the Y2K issue exposed the information of ICS and potential security problems especially to the critical infrastructure. Today manufactures of ICS components provide detailed product information in brochures and Web sites. Further media and Web articles continuously report attacks, threats and vulnerabilities, which make public as well as the attackers aware of SCADA technology.

Open communication systems become a necessity as they bring costs down, but as the name implies these systems are more open to cyber-attack than their proprietary and more closed alternatives. Proprietary systems not only have fewer connections to other systems, they are also less familiar to professional hackers, creating a possible *security through obscurity* defense. On the other hand, communication systems based on Ethernet, TCP/IP protocols, the Internet and widely used operating systems such as Windows invite attack from literally millions of hackers worldwide.

In fact, presently the industrial automation using SCADA is a combined and cooperative effort of power engineers, ICT professionals, and cyber security experts. With the introduction of more and more IEDs with advanced resilience and communication technology, the role of ICT professionals become more predominant in ICS.

2.11 ICS ATTACK PHASES

In the present environment, most of the ICS networks are designed and implemented as air gapped/stand-alone with no connectivity to cyber-space to make it secure. Hence the threat actors usually carried out the attacks to ICS in two phases viz.

- In the first stage the ICS attacker gain access to the ICS network by all means possible, to launch the second stage attack. Then the hackers may try their best to find a foothold into the administrative or business network of the utility, so that a pivot point can be found to jump into the ICS network.

- The main objective of the second stage attack may be to sabotage of the production process or plant functionality. This stage attack includes gaining the access of ICS network, identifying the ICS network topology, creating the backdoors in the applications and devices to exfiltrate the data, and finally carry out the sabotage the plant process.

Summary

Chapter begins with explaining Operational Technology (OT) and its difference with Information Technology (IT). Then it describes the Industrial Control Systems, various types of Industrial Control Systems, control and network components of Industrial Control Systems. The chapter ends with explaining the attack strategies and the two main stages of ICS attack.

CHAPTER THREE
ICS ARCHITECTURE & DESIGN
CONSIDERATIONS

3.1 INTRODUCTION

Various SCADA architectures are adapted today depending on the requirements. It starts with the basic single channel Data Acquisition and Control architecture to the complex multi-channel, real-time, fault tolerant, fail safe system which utilizes many secure communication methodologies with proper End Node Security (ENS). A Stand alone ICS architecture is relatively simple as it has PLCs, RTUs, Servers, and HMI segmented into two or three zones viz. Enterprise Security Zone, Industrial Demilitarised Zone and Process Security Zone. However when comes to Distributed SCADA, the system architecture becomes complex and needs stringent physical-cyber security measures. The following sections elaborate the various ICS architectures with emphasis on Distributed SCADA.

3.2 DCS COMMUNICATION ARCHITECTURE

There are three physical communication architectures which are generally popular and deployed in SCADA systems. In certain cases they are deployed in a combined mode. They are,

1. Point to point,
2. Point to multistations, and
3. Relay Stations.

➤ Point-To-Point Between Two Stations

This is the simplest configuration where data is exchanged between two stations. One station can be setup as the master and one as the slave as shown in Figure 3.1. It is possible for both the stations to communicate in full duplex mode (transmitting and receiving on two separate frequencies) or simplex with only one frequency.

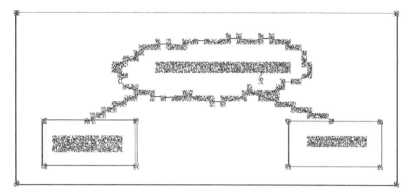

Figure 3.1 Point to Point Master-Slave Communication

➢ **Multipoint or Multiple Stations**

In this configuration, there is generally one master and multiple slaves which is shown in Figure 3.2. Generally data points are efficiently passed between the master and each of the slaves. If two slaves need to transfer data between each other they would do so through the master who would act as arbitrator or moderator. Alternatively, it is possible for all the stations to act in a peer-to-peer communications manner with each other. This is a more complex arrangement requiring sophisticated protocols to handle collisions between two different stations wanting to transmit at the same time.

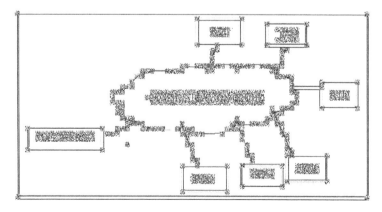

Figure 3.2 Master RTU communicating with multiple station RTUs

Another possibility is the store and forward relay operation. This can be a component of other approaches discussed above where, one station retransmits messages onto another station out of the range of the first station which is shown in Figure 3.3.

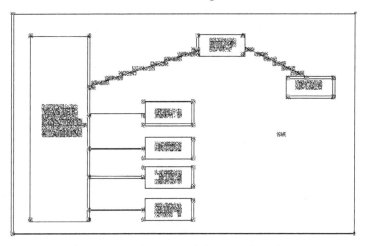

Figure 3.3 Store and forward station

> ➢ **Talk Through Repeaters**

This is the generally preferred way of increasing the range of radio systems. This retransmits a radio signal received simultaneously on another frequency. It is normally situated on a geographically high point.

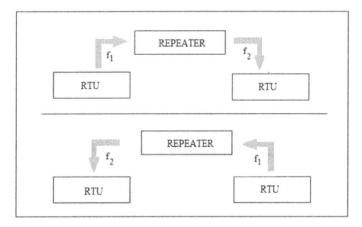

Figure 3.4 Talk through repeaters

The repeater receives on one frequency and retransmits on another frequency simultaneously. This means that all the stations repeating the signal must receive and transmit on the opposite frequencies. It is important that all stations communicate through the talk through repeater. It must be a common link for all stations and thus have a radio mast, high enough to access all RTU sites. It is a strategic link in the communication system; failure would wreak havoc with the entire system. The antenna must receive on one frequency and transmit on a different frequency which is shown in Figure 3.4. This means that the system must be specifically designed for this application with special filters attached to the antennas. There is still a slight time delay in the transmission of data with a repeater. The protocol must be designed with this in mind with sufficient lead-time for the repeater's receiver and transmitter to commence operation.

3.3 COMMUNICATION PHILOSOPHIES

There are two main communication philosophies in practice. These are polled (or master slave) and Carrier Sense Multiple Access/Collision Detection (CSMA/CD). The one of the notable methods accepted for reducing the amount of data that needs to be transferred from one point to another is to use exception reporting.

➢ **Polled or Master Slave**

This is one of the simplest master- slave point to point or point to multipoint configuration where the master polls, the slave in predetermined regular intervals and gather the data which is shown in Figure 3.5. Here the master is in total control of the monitoring, decision making and control of the process. The slaves never initiate the data exchange rather, wait for the master's request and respond. Essentially it is a half-duplex communication. In case the slave fails to respond timely, then the master retries typically two or three times. If the slave still fails to respond, the master then moves to the next slave in the

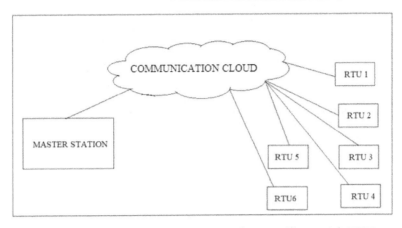

Figure 3.5 Illustration of master-slave polling with RTUs

sequence with a remark that the particular slave is inactive or faulty and requires attention for rectification. The advantages of this approach are,

- Software development is fairly easy and can be made reliable due to the simplicity of the philosophy,

- Link failure between the master and a slave node is detected fairly quickly,

- No collisions can occur on the network, hence the data throughput is predictable and constant, and

- For heavily loaded systems, each node has constant and bulk data transfer requirements giving a predictable and efficient system.

However it has the certain disadvantages which are described below.

- Variations in the data transfer requirements of each slave cannot be handled,

- Interrupt type requests from a slave cannot be entertained as the master may be either attending or processing some other slave request or data,

- Systems, which are lightly loaded with minimum data changes from a slave, are quite inefficient and unnecessarily slow, and

- Communication between the slaves can be achieved only through the master which adds complexity.

Two applications of the polled or master slave, approach are given in the following two implementations. This is possibly the most commonly used technique and is illustrated in the Figure 3.6.

Table 3.1 Polling table with the master station

RTU 1
RTU2
RTU 5
RTU 6
RTU 3
RTU 4

The master station details of priority and sequence. Based on this information it prepares a polling cycle as shown in Table 3.1.

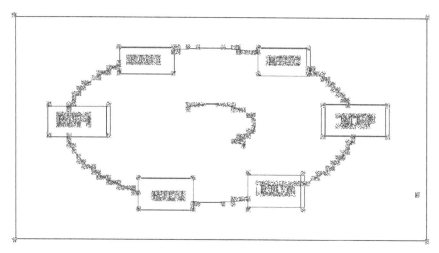

Figure 3.6 Polling cycle as per the polling table

In the scheme of polling, in certain situations, the polling may be modified as,

- if there is no response from a given RTU during a poll, a timeout timer has to be set and three retries (in total) initiated before flagging this station as inactive, and

- if an RTU is to be treated as a priority station it will be polled at a greater rate than a normal priority station. It is important not to put too many RTUs on the priority list, otherwise the differentiation between high and normal priority becomes meaningless.

➢ CSMA/CD SYSTEM (PEER-TO-PEER)

RTU to RTU Communication

In certain situations, especially in DCS an RTU in the SCADA system may need to communicate with another RTU. One of the solutions is, while responding to the master station to the poll, a message carrying a request with the destination address of the RTU can be added. The master station will then examine the destination address field of the message received from the RTU and retransmit onto the appropriate remote station. The only attempt to avoid collisions is to, listen to the medium before transmitting. If a collision occurs, the RTU wait for a random time period, and retransmit the data avoiding the collision. In this style of operation, it is possible for two nodes to try and transmit at the same time, with a resultant collision. In order to minimize the chance of a collision, the source node first listens for a carrier signal before commencing transmission. Unfortunately this does not always work where certain stations which cannot hear each other to try and transmit back to the station simultaneously.

➢ Exception Reporting (Event Reporting)

On many occasions, the status and the RTU may be the same but the polling mechanism gathers the data from the RTU. This unnecessary transfer of data can be minimized or virtually eliminated with a technique called *exception reporting*. This approach is popular with the CSMA/CD philosophy but it could also offer a solution for the polled approach where there is a considerable amount of data to transfer from each slave.

In exception reporting, the remote station reporting devices such as RTUs monitor itself to identify a change of state or data. If there is a change of state, the remote station writes a block of data to the master station when the master station polls the remote. Typical reasons for using polled report by exception include,

- The polling or scanning is performed with a low data rate due the communication channel constraints,

- There is substantial data being monitored at the remote stations, and

- The number of remote devices connected to master station is reasonably high.

Each analog or digital point that reports back to the central master station has a set of exception reporting parameters associated with it. The type of exception reporting depends on the particular environment but could be,

- High and low alarm limits of analog value,

- Percent of change in the full span of the analog signal, and

- Minimum and maximum reporting time intervals.

The main advantages of this approach are quite clearly to minimize unnecessary (repetitive) traffic from the communications system.

➢ Polling Plus CSMA/CD With Exception Reporting

A practical method to combine all the approaches discussed earlier is to use the concept of a slot time and exception reporting. Here each slave station is assigned a specific time slot comprising the following sub-slot assuming that there is no requirement for communication between the slaves.

- A slave transmitting to a master and

- A master transmitting to a slave.

A slot time is calculated as the sum of the maximums of modem up time, plus radio transmit time, plus time for protocol message, plus muting time of transmitter. The master commences operations by polling each slave in turn. Each slave will be in synchronize with the polling and respond to the master with exception reporting if there is a status change, else respond with passive acknowledgement. As a result, the master move on to poll the next slave by overriding the remaining sub-slots. Otherwise it will complete the data exchange and then move to hear from the next slave. The master thus completes the poll cycle.

The previous and present chapter elaborated the building blocks of SCADA systems starting from the RTU, IEDs, communication systems, master stations and the HMI. Utilities have a variety of options available to mix and match the elements to building a cost-effective, efficient, and operator-friendly SCADA system as per their requirements.

Automation of the power systems started as early as the beginning of the twentieth century, and substations and control centers operate at various stages of automation all over the world. There are legacy systems with RTUs, hardwired communication from the field to the RTU, and traditional software functionalities in the control room, and it is not often financially viable to dismantle everything and purchase a completely new automation system.

Hybrid systems are a viable option, where any automation expansion project can be implemented with new devices, like IEDs, data concentrators, and merging units. The new system will coexist with the legacy RTU-based systems and the data integration and if necessary protocol conversion issues will have to be handled while commissioning the project.

If a utility decides to purchase a completely modern system, the latest building block of the SCADA system, viz, IEDs, merging units, and fiber optic communication facility with brand new HMI with situational awareness and analysis tools, can be implemented.

3.4 SYSTEM RELIABILITY AND AVAILABILITY

Real-time system operation demands high level of availability and reliability to ensure error free operations. The real-time process control systems directly control the process, and any system catastrophe or erroneous operation may lead to process damage and may affect the safety of operations. Thus these applications necessitate a high level of system reliability without compromise. Numerically system reliability is defined as the probability that the system will not fail under specified conditions.

Standards and guidelines are available for the development of safe and secure critical systems. Among these standards, the most pertinent is for power system automation and is the NERC CIP standard. These development standards may be used while designing a power system SCADA. In keeping with these guidelines, an analysis must be performed as the early stage of system design in order to assign a system integrity level which allows the utility to define the accepted failure rate of system under consideration. Before discussing the fail safe system, it is better to have a clue of the two classifications of failures namely Common Cause Failures and Common Mode Failure.

Common Cause Failure (CCF): A Common cause failure occurs when two or more items fall within a specified time such that the success of the system mission would be uncertain. Item failures result from a single cause and mechanism.

Common Mode Failure (CMF): A Common-Mode Failure is the result of an event(s) which because of dependencies, causes a coincidence of failure states of components in two or more separate channels of a redundancy system, leading to the defined systems failing to perform its intended function.

> **Fail Safe System (FSS)**

A fail safe system describes a feature or a device which in the event of failure, responds in a way that will cause no harm or minimum harm to other devices or danger to personnel. Fail safe systems are used wherever the highest degree of safety needs to be guaranteed for humans, machines and the environment. A system being fail safe means, not that failure is impossible or improbable, but rather that the system design prevents or mitigates unsafe consequences of the system failure. That is, if and when a fail-safe system fails in any case, accidents and damage as a result of fault must be evaded at all costs. Thus when controlling, dangerous or critical machinery, it is necessary to device and implement a fail-safe strategy to ensure that the machine operates safely even when, the elements of the control hardware or software fail.

The types of failure are many hence a thorough analysis of the failure mode and effects are used for identifying the failure situations and design safety procedures. Some systems can never be made fail safe, as continuous availability is needed. Redundancy, fault tolerance, or recovery procedures are employed in these situations. This also makes the system, less sensitive for the reliability prediction errors or quality induced uncertainty for the separate items. On the other hand, failure detection, correction and avoidance of CCF become increasingly important to ensure system level reliability.

- In industrial automation, usually alarm circuits are normally closed. This ensures that in case of a wire break the alarm will be triggered. If the circuit were normally open, a wire failure would go undetected, while blocking actual alarm signals.

- In control systems, critically important signals can be carried by a complementary pair of wires. Only states where the two signals are opposite (one is high, the other low) are valid. If both are high or both are low, the control system knows that something is wrong with the sensor or connecting wiring. Simple failure modes such as dead sensor cut or unplugged wires, are thereby detected. An example would be a control system reading both the normally open (NO) and normally closed (NC) poles of a SPDT selector switch against common, and checking them for coherency before reacting to the input.

> ### Fault Tolerant System (FTS)

Certain utility or plant operations, once started have to continue as uninterrupted and nonstop operations, even in the case of a hardware or equipment failure. In other way, these are fault tolerant systems which has the ability of preventing a catastrophic let-down, that could result from a single point of failure. A fault-tolerant system is designed from the ground up for reliability by building multiples of all critical components, such as CPUs, memories, disks and power supplies into the same computer. In the event one component fails, another should take over without skipping a single point of operation. A feasible strategy for a fault tolerant system is by anticipating exceptional conditions and design a system to cope with them. The basic aim is that the system should be able to self-stabilize after the fault and converge towards an error free state. The above strategy may not be successful in some cases. In such applications, fault tolerance is implemented by providing redundancy.

> ### Graceful Degradation Systems

Fault tolerance is often used synonymously with graceful degradation, although the latter is more aligned with the more holistic discipline of fault management, which aims to detect, isolate and resolve problems pre-emptively. A fault-tolerant system swaps in backup component to maintain high levels of system availability and performance. But Graceful degradation allows a system to continue operations, with a reduced state of performance.

3.5 DESIGN CONSIDERATIONS OF FAULT TOLERANT SYSTEM

While designing a Fault Tolerant System, one may consider the business continuity requirements, disaster recovery plan, the disaster recovery products presently available in the market, and of course the budget and available manpower for engaging. Nevertheless Fault-tolerant systems are designed to compensate for multiple failures. The failure point has to be specifically identified, and a backup component or an immediate procedure should be taken its place with no loss of service.

The failure point can be computer processor unit, I/O subsystem, memory cards, motherboard, power supply, network components in the cloud, communication servers of the service provider, etc. Hence each and every stage should be thoroughly analyzed and necessary provisions may be envisaged and implemented.

In a software implementation, the Operating System (OS) provides an interface that allows a programmer to checkpoint critical data at predetermined points within a transaction. In a hardware implementation. the programmer need not to be aware of the fault-tolerant capabilities of the machine.

At a hardware level, fault tolerance is achieved by duplexing each hardware component. Disks are mirrored. Multiple processors are lock-stepped together and their outputs are compared for correctness. When an anomaly occurs, the faulty component is determined automatically, and is taken out of service, but the machine continues to function as usual.

➤ High Availability

Fault tolerance is closely associated with maintaining business continuity via highly available computer systems and networks. Fault-tolerant environments are defined as those that restore service instantaneously following a service outage, whereas a high-availability environment strives for setting up of independent servers coupled loosely together to guarantee system-wide sharing of critical data and resources. The loosely coupled clusters monitor each other's health and provide fault recovery, to ensure applications remain available. Conversely, a fault-tolerant cluster consists of multiple physical systems that share a single copy of a computer's OS. Software commands issued by one system are also executed on the other system. Systems with integrated fault tolerance incur a higher cost due to the inclusion of additional hardware.

➤ Critical Functions

If any operation of plant or process is critical, i.e. if the downtime costs are high or cause any human fatality or any expensive hardware destruction, redundancy must be incorporated into the system to eliminate system failures, due to equipment failure. Such functionalities are categorized as mission critical functions. In fact it is the privilege of the critical function to have software and hardware redundancy to be fault tolerant in a SCADA system. In power system SCADA with remote access RTU sites, both system redundancy and channel redundancy must be ensured for critical functions. In such cases RTU with CPU redundancy and communication port redundancy are highly recommended. At the master station end, the routers, firewalls, and servers must be configured to have redundancy for a fault tolerant system. Mission-critical installations often have separate power sources in case of a power failure, and installations in areas prone to natural disasters or the threat of fire, keep the servers in different geographic locations. However, whatever type of disaster recovery is planned for, it is possible to greatly reduce lost data and downtime by planning the proper system design, and by choosing a SCADA system with built-in redundancy. While ensuring system redundancy requirement for critical functions to be fault tolerant, it is highly recommended to consider the following points.

- Dual networks for full LAN redundancy,
- Redundancy can be applied to specific hardware,
- Supports primary and secondary equipment configurations,
- Intelligent redundancy allows secondary equipment to contribute to processing load,
- Automatic changeover and recovery,
- Mirrored disk I/O devices,
- Mirrored alarm servers, and
- File server redundancy.

A typical redundant and fail safe DCS master control station configuration with HA is shown in Figure 3.7 below. The sub components such as DMZ, SCADA Control System LAN, Dispatch Training Simulator, and Fail Safe connectivity to Smart Grid MCC using HA are shown separately in Figure 3.8, Figure 3.9, Figure 3.10

respectively. Here a De Militarized Zone (DMZ) is designed carefully and kept exclusively between two Firewalls of different make. The session from the servers of DMZ to the servers of SCADA zone is strictly made forbidden by appropriately defining the Firewall ruleset.

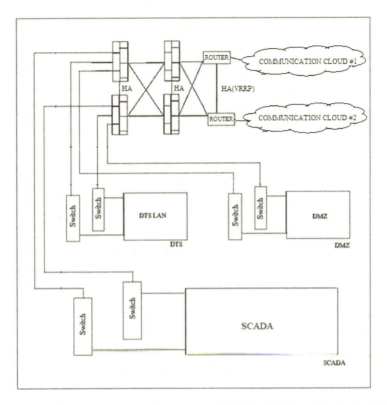

Figure 3.7 Block diagram of a typical DCS MCC with Fail Safe HA connectivity

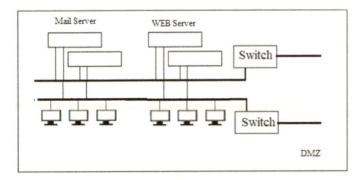

Figure 3.8 De Militarized Zone (DMZ)

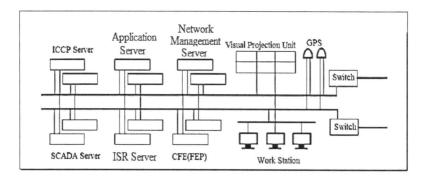

Figure 3.9 SCADA Control System LAN

Dispatcher Training Simulator (DTS) is a subsystem within Distribution Management System (DMS) that operates separately from the real–time system and provides a realistic environment for hands–on dispatcher training under simulated normal, emergency, and restorative operating conditions.

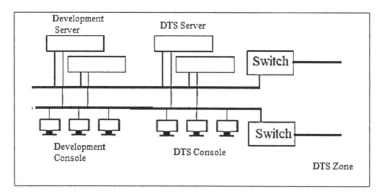

Figure 3.10 Dispatch Training Simulator

The training is based on interactive communication between instructor and trainee. The DMS training simulator serves two main purposes.

- Allowing personnel to become familiar with the DMS system and its user interface without impacting actual substation and feeder operations.

- Allowing personnel to become familiar with the dynamic behavior of the electric distribution system in response to manual and automatic actions by control and protection systems during normal and emergency conditions.

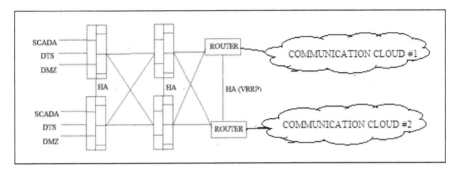

Figure 3.11 Fail Safe connectivity to DCS MCC using HA

The Figure 3.11 describes a Fail Safe connectivity to DCS MCC using HA which is mostly preferred in the Power System SCADA and DCS which control the critical operations.

➢ System Redundancy

Redundancy is the hallmark of fault tolerant systems. It is defined as additional or alternative systems, sub-systems, assets, or processes that maintain a degree of overall functionality in case of loss or failure of another system, sub-system, asset, or process. Normally power system SCADA redundancy, starts from the data capturing units such as RTU or PLC. If the SCADA is a distributed system, then every system component upto the MODEM have to be redundant. Further if the communication to the master control station is by means of unguided media, then system should have antenna redundancy as well. Obviously this adds cost considerably and the implementing agencies/vendors normally find pretexts for compromise which is the general lapse observed in implementing power system SCADA. But this makes the SCADA system unreliable.

Definitely true fault tolerant SCADA systems with redundant hardware are the most costly as the additional components add to the overall system cost. However, fault tolerant systems provide the same processing capacity after a failure as before, and ensures safety.

➢ Channel Redundancy

Most of the power system SCADA is distributed in nature and geographically separated. Hence remote site to site communications are required. This mainly depends on third party communication service providers.

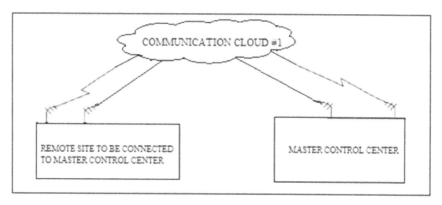

Figure 3.12A Channel redundancy achieved with a resilient and reliable cloud

While selecting the third party communication providers, channel redundancy has to be ensured to have true system redundancy. Mainly this is achieved in two ways which is explained below

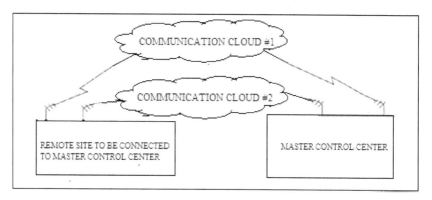

Figure 3.12B Channel redundancy achieved with two different communication clouds

If the third party communication provider is highly reliable and having a true self-healing communication cloud as per the requirement of the utility, then connectivity to the two geographically different nodes is an acceptable solution on economic reasons. However in the strictest sense, true channel redundancy for critical functions ideally demands two different communication providers with active-active or active-standby mode. These are shown in Figure 3.12a and 3.12 b.

> **Design and Configuration Considerations of MCC**

The following aspects are utmost important while designing the Master Control Center of the power system SCADA.

- Sufficient hardware and software redundancy have to be ensured, to achieve the overall system redundancy with High Availability having No Single Point of Failure (NSPF) as the SCADA functions for the power system are critical. This includes communication channel as well,

- The firewall must be properly configured with the appropriate ruleset, after due deliberation with the security policy of the utility. Design with a two layer Firewall configuration, with different make IDS loaded are not a better option but a must, while moving for a DMZ, and

- The CFE or the FEP of the SCADA control center must have high end capabilities with suitable IDS loaded and have cryptographic capabilities. If third party communication media are used, especially using the VPN for data transfer, utmost care must be given for proper VPN termination.

Summary

This chapter begins with describing the communication architecture of basic SCADA and then moves on to describing the common communication philosophies adopted in DCS. As the reliability and availability of DCS functions are the most important, they are briefly introduced, but cater the necessary understanding to computer science and automation engineers and students who are engaged or intend to embark into the DCS, Smart Grid and Microgrid domain. It then explains the concepts of Fault Tolerant Systems, Fail Safe and

Redundant Systems, High Availability, etc. Based on these concepts, this chapter then elaborates the design of a typical SCADA Master Control Center architecture having redundant and HA connectivity.

CHAPTER FOUR
INDUSTRIAL NETWORKING BASICS

4.1 INTRODUCTION

Computer networking which is the underlying technology of the Industrial Networking is one of the most complex but exciting topics in the field of computer science and engineering which involves various mechanisms, devices, software, and protocols that are interrelated and integrated. Day by day the functionality of current technology is improving drastically especially the area of network security which records an exponential growth. To catch up with the pace of these new emerging technologies, automation engineers have to learn and understand the relevant technology to implement and secure the system. It is indispensible for an ICS engineer to configure networking software, protocols, services, and devices which deal with interoperability issues. They also have to install, configure, and interface with telecommunication software and devices, and troubleshoot them effectively. It will be an added advantage if the ICS engineer has the knowledge and capability of understanding these issues and analyze them a few levels deeper to recognize fully where vulnerabilities can arise within each of these components and the mitigation techniques. Obviously it is an overwhelming and challenging task. This chapter elaborates the computer networking fundamentals and concept and structure protocols such as Open Systems Interconnection (OSI) reference model, TCP/IP Model, Enhanced Performance Architecture (EPA), etc.

4.2 TYPES OF TRANSMISSION

There are various transmission classifications depending upon the different technologies employed and they are mainly based on

- Analog and Digital,
- Synchronous and Asynchronous,
- Broadcast, Multicast, and Unicast,

- Simplex, Half Duplex, and Full Duplex, and

- Baseband and Broadband.

As the communication is the key enabler of the modern SCADA, a basic understanding of these terms is most essential for an automation engineer. Hence a brief explanation of these terminologies are given in succeeding chapters.

4.3   LOCAL AREA NETWORKS (LAN) AND NETWORK TOPOLOGIES

*Local Area Networks (LAN):*A group of computers located within a limited area such as a room, a residence, school, laboratory, university campus or office building that are connected to form a single network. Local Area Networks (LANs) allow users to share storage devices, printers, applications, data, and other network resources and locally managed. They are limited to a specific geographical area, usually less than 2 kilometers in diameter. They might use a dedicated backbone to connect multiple subnet works, but they do not use any telecommunication carrier circuits or leased lines except to connect with other LANs to form a Wide Area Network (WAN).A local area network domain is defined as a sub-network that is made up of servers and clients, each of which are controlled by a centralized database. User approval is obtained through a central server or a domain controller. The term *domain* can refer to descriptors for internet sites, which is a site's web address, or to LAN sub-networks.

Domains on the internet are categorized by levels. Top Level Domains (TLD) which include.com, .net, .edu and .org. Domain names are governed by the internet Corporation for assigned names and numbers, which oversees the creation of TLDs as well as their distribution. Domain Name Servers maintain a connection between domain names and IP addresses. The DNS system is used by computers to transmit information online.

Advantages and disadvantages of LAN

Local Area Networks let families, schools, businesses and other entities to connect their computers one another, but they are complex. They make administration simple, and they are customizable. However, they can be difficult to secure appropriately. In many ways, LANs are similar to the internet as a whole. They are built on open standards, and the lack of proprietary software and communication standards means that licenses and other costs are not required. Their technology has been proven to be scalable and durable, and is believed that they will be replaced by other technologies. Their flexibility, however, also makes them complex, and medium and large networks generally require expert maintenance. LAN technology was designed to scale to large networks, and setting it up needs awareness of a number of IT topics which requires significant experience. The technology used in LANs is designed to be open, which sometimes leads to security problems. Generally, all network requests are sent and acknowledged, and the vulnerable computers present within the network can be easily targeted. Hence if any computer on a LAN is not sufficiently protected, the networking infrastructure as a whole becomes vulnerable.

Network Topologies

The physical layout and arrangement of computers and networking devices is known as the network topology. Topology refers to the manner in which a network is physically connected and shows the layout of resources and systems. The logical topology is the grouping of networked systems into trusted collectives. The physical topology is not always the same as the logical topology. A network can be configured as a physical star but work logically as a ring, as in the Token Ring technology. The four basic network topologies are ring, bus, star, and mesh. The best topology for a particular network depends on how nodes are supposed to interact, the protocols used, the types of applications, the reliability, expandability, physical layout of a facility, existing wiring, and the technologies implemented. The wrong topology or combination of topologies can negatively affect the network's performance, productivity, and growth possibilities.

Most networks are very complex and are usually implemented using a combination of topologies.

Ring Topology

A ring topology connects each system as points on a circle as shown in Figure 4.1. The connection medium acts as a unidirectional transmission loop. These links form a closed loop and do not connect to a central system, as in a star topology which is discussed later in this chapter. In a physical ring formation, each node is dependent upon the preceding nodes. In simple networks, if one system fails, all other systems could be negatively affected because of this interdependence.

In ring topology only one system can transmit data at a time. Traffic management is performed by a token. The *token,* which is a special bit pattern, travels around the ring until a system catches it. The system which possess the token can transmit the data. Data and the token are transmitted to a specific destination. As the data travels around the loop, each system checks whether it is the intended recipient of the data. If not, it passes the token else, it reads the data. Once the data is received, the token is released and returns to travels around the loop until another system grabs it. If any one segment of the loop is broken, all communication around the loop ceases.

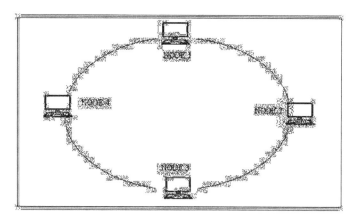

Figure 4.1 Ring Topology

Today, most networks have redundancy or other mechanisms that protects the whole network from being affected by malfunctioning of one workstation. Network engineers generally designs ring topologies incorporating a fault tolerance mechanism, such as dual loops running in opposite directions, to prevent single points of failure.

Bus Topology

A bus topology connects each system to a trunk or backbone cable. All systems on the bus can transmit data simultaneously, which can result in collisions. To avoid this, the systems employ a collision avoidance mechanism that basically *listens* for any other currently occurring traffic. If traffic is observed, the system waits for a few moments and listens again. If traffic is not observed, the system transmits its data. On a bus topology, all systems on the network hear the data which is transmitted. If the data is not addressed to a specific system, that system just ignores the data. The main benefit of a bus topology is that if a single segment fails, communications on all other segments continue uninterrupted. However, the central trunk line remains a single point of failure.

There are two types of bus topologies viz, linear and distributed (tree). A linear bus topology employs a single trunk line which has explicitly two end points as shown in4.2(a). In distributed (tree) topology all the nodes of the network are connected to a common transmission medium which has more than one end point as shown in Figure 4.2(b). The primary reason for a bus is rarely used today is that it must be terminated at both ends and any disconnection can take down the entire network. A fully connected bus topology is having only one linking channel.

In a simple bus topology, a single cable runs the entire length of the network. Nodes are attached to the network through drop points on this cable. Data communications transmit the length of the medium, and each packet transmitted has the capability of being looked at by all nodes. Depending upon the packet's destination address, each node decides to accept or ignore the packet.

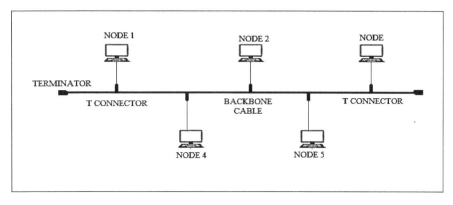

Figure 4.2A Linear bus topology

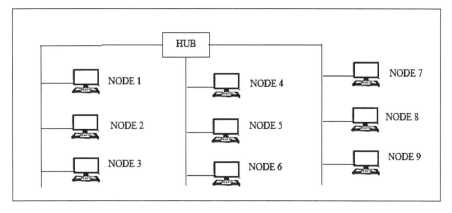

Figure 4.2B Distributed (tree) bus topology

Star Topology

A star topology employs a centralized connection device. This device can be a simple hub or switch. Each node has a dedicated link to the central device as shown in Figure 4.3. The central device needs to provide enough throughput so that it does not turn out to be a detrimental bottleneck for the network as a whole. As a central device is required in star topology, it is a potential single point of failure, redundancy has to be implemented.

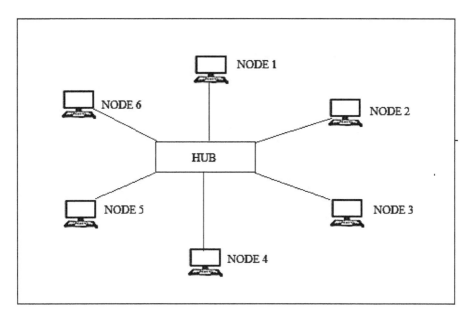

Figure 4.3 Star Topology

If any one segment fails, the other segments can continue to function. However, the central hub is a single point of failure. Generally, the star topology uses less cabling than other topologies and helps the identification of damaged cables easier.

A logical bus and a logical ring can be implemented as a physical star. Ethernet is a bus based technology. It can be deployed as a physical star, but the hub or switch device is actually a logical bus connection device. Likewise, Token Ring is a ring-based technology. It can be deployed as a physical star using a Multistation Access Unit (MAU). MAU allows the cable segments to be deployed as a star while the device makes logical ring connections internally. Presently no networks use true linear bus and ring topologies. A ring topology can be used for a backbone network, but most networks are constructed in a star topology because it enables the network to be more resilient and not as affected if an individual node experiences a problem.

Mesh Topology

A mesh topology connects systems to other systems using numerous paths as shown in Figure 4.4. This arrangement is usually a network of interconnected routers and switches that provides multiple paths to all the nodes on the network. In a full mesh topology, every node is directly connected to every other node, which provides a great degree of redundancy. A partial mesh topology connects many systems to many other systems. A full mesh topology provides redundant connections to systems, allowing multiple segment failures without seriously affecting connectivity. The internet is an example of a partial mesh topology.

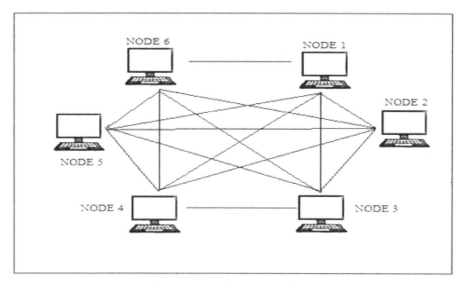

Figure 4.4 Mesh topology

Comparison of Network Topologies

The comparisons of Network Topologies are summarized in Table 4.1 below.

Table 4.1 Comparison of Network Topologies

Topology	Characteristics	Problems	Security
Star	All information passes through the central network connection	The central device is a single point of failure	Denial of service attack
Bus	It is a network topology in which there is a single line (the bus) to which all nodes are connected and the nodes are connected only to this bus. The cable has a small cap installed at the end, called a terminator. The terminator prevents signals from bouncing back and causing network errors.	If one station experiences a problem, it can negatively affect surrounding computers on the same cable	Not secure due to broadcast
Ring	Information goes in one direction around the ring and passes along the ring until it reaches the correct computer	If one station experiences a problem, it can negatively affect the surrounding computers on the same ring	Has the least security as the information intended for one machine must pass through all the others
Mesh	A network topology in which there are at least two nodes with two or more paths between them	Requires more expense in cabling and extra effort to track down cable faults	A mesh needs secure links, routing, and forwarding
Tree	A bus topology with branches of the main cable	Heavily relies on the main bus cable, a break in the main cable will cripple the entire network. Further adding more nodes and segments makes the maintenance difficult.	Low security as it is physically a star but logically a bus

4.4 MEDIA ACCESS METHODS

A media access method refers to the manner a computer gain and controls access to the network's physical medium. In other words it defines how the network places data on the transmission media and how it takes it off. Common media access methods include the following,

- ➢ Contention systems
  - CSMA/CD
  - CSMA/CA
- ➢ Selection systems
  - Token Passing
  - Polling
  - Polling by Exception
- ➢ Reservation systems
  - Frequency Division Multiplexing
  - Time Division Multiplexing
- ➢ Demand Priority

One of the primary concerns with media access is to prevent packets from colliding as a collision occurs when two or more computers transmit signals at the same time. The Media Access Control (MAC) layer in a communication protocol governs the rules which are a sub layer of Data Link Layer.

Contention Systems

In contention, any computer in the network can transmit data at any time. In fact it is a first-come-first-served media access method. In a contention-based access method, a node accesses medium when the network is idle. The main contention methods used are Carrier Sense Multiple Access with Collision Detection (CSMA/CD) and

Carrier-Sense Multiple Access with Collision Avoidance (CSMA/CA). Contention is at the heart of these methods which are used in the IEEE 802.3 and the original Ethernet networks.

1. CSMA/CD: Carrier Sense Multiple Access with Collision Detection

Carrier Sense means that each station on the LAN continually listens to (test) the cable for the pretence of a signal prior to transmitting. *Multiple Access* means that there are many computers attempting to transmit and compete for the opportunity to send data. *Collision Detection* means that when a collision is detected, the station will stop transmitting and wait for a random length of time before transmitting. CSMA/CD works best in an environment where relatively fewer, longer data frames are transmitted. CSMA/CD is used on Ethernet networks. CSMA/CD operates as follows.

- a station that wishes to transmit on the network checks if the cable is free, and if the cable id is free, the station starts transmitting,

- however, another station may have detected a free cable at the same instant and also start transmitting which result in a collision,

- once the collision is detected, all stations immediately stop transmitting, and

- station then wait for a random length of time before checking the cable and then retransmit.

2. CSMA/CA- Carrier Sense Multiple Access with Collision Avoidance

It is similar to CSMA/CD. The difference is that the CD (Collision Detection) is changed to Collision Avoidance (CA). Instead of detecting and reacting to collisions, CSMA/CA tries to avoid them by having each computer signal and understand the intention to transmit before actually transmitting. CSMA/CA is slower than CSMA/CD and is used in Apple networks.

The collision detection logic ensures that more than one message on the channel will be simultaneously detected from both ends and eventually stopped. The system is a probabilistic one, since access to the channel cannot be ascertained in advance.

Selection Systems

1. Token Passing

Collisions are eliminated under token passing because only a computer that possesses a free token (a small data frame) is allowed to transmit. Transmission from a station with higher priority takes precedence over station with lower priority. Token passing works best in an environment where relatively large number of shorter data frames is being transmitted. Token passing is used on Token Ring and ArcNet networks. Token passing works as described below.

- A station that wishes to transmit on the network waits until the token is free.

- The sending station transmits its data with the token.

- The token travels to the recipient without stopping at other stations.

- The receiving station receives the transmitted information.

Networks that use token passing generally have some provision for setting the priority with which a node gets the token. Higher level protocols can specify that a message is important and should receive higher priority.

2. Polling

This is one of the simplest master-slave point to point or point to multipoint configuration where the master polls, the slave in predetermined regular intervals and gather the data. Here the master is in total control of the monitoring, decision making and control of the process. The slaves never initiates the data exchange rather wait for the master's request and respond. Essentially it is a half-duplex communication. In case the slave fails to respond timely, then the master retries typically two or three times. If the slave still fails to respond, the master then moves to the next slave in the sequence with a remark that the particular slave is inactive or faulty and requires attention for rectification.

3. Polling by Exception

On many occasions, the status and the slave may be the same but the polling mechanism gathers the data from the slaves. This unnecessary transfer of data can be minimized or virtually eliminated with a technique called exception reporting. This approach is popular with the CSMA/CD philosophy but it could also offer a solution for the polled approach where there is a considerable amount of data to transfer from each slave. In exception reporting, the remote station reporting slave devices monitor itself to identify a change of state or data. If there is a change of state, the remote station writes a block of data to the master station when the master station polls the remote. Typical reasons for using polled report by exception includes,

- the polling or scanning which is performed with a low data rate due to the channel constraints,

- a substantial data being monitored from the remote stations, and

- the number of remote devices connected to master station is reasonably high.

Reservation systems

1. Frequency Division Multiple Access (FDMA)

Frequency Division Multiple Access (FDMA) is a channel access technique found in multiple-access protocols as a channelization protocol. FDMA permits individual allocation of single or multiple frequency bands, or channels to the users. FDMA, just like any other multiple access system, harmonizes access between multiple users.

Advantages of FDMA

- It allocates dedicated frequencies to different stations. Moreover there are separate bands for both uplink and downlink. Hence stations transmit and receive continuously at their allocated frequencies.

- It is very simple to implement with respect to hardware resources.

- FDMA is efficient when constant traffic is required to be managed with less number of user populations.

Disadvantages of FDM

- In FDMA, frequencies are allocated permanently and hence spectrum will be wasted when stations are not transmitting or receiving.

- Network and spectrum planning is cumbersome and time consuming.

- It uses guard bands to prevent interference. Very useful and scarce frequency resources get wasted.

- It requires RF filters to meet stringent adjacent channel rejection specifications. This increases the cost of the system.

2. Time Division Multiple Access (TDMA)

Time Division Multiple Access (TDMA) is a Channel Access Method (CAM) used to facilitate channel sharing without interference. TDMA allows multiple stations to share and use the same transmission channel by dividing signals into different time slots. Users transmit in rapid succession, and each one uses its own time slot. Thus, multiple stations (like mobiles) may share the same frequency channel but only use part of its capacity.

Disadvantages of TDMA: The users has a predefined time slot. When moving from one cell site to the other, if all the time slots in this cell are full the user might be disconnected. Another problem in TDMA is that it is subjected to multipath distortion.

Demand Priority

This is a new Ethernet media access method that will probably replace popular but older CSMA/CD and by which stations on a 100VG-AnyLan network gain access to the wire for transmitting data. 100VG-AnyLan is a high-speed form of Ethernet based on the IEEE standard 802.12.A 100VG-AnyLan network based on the demand priority access method consists of end nodes (stations), repeaters (hubs), switches, routers, bridges, and other networking devices. A typical 100VG-AnyLan network consists of a number of stations plugged into a cascading star topology of repeaters (hubs). Because of timing, a maximum of five levels of cascading of the physical wiring is permitted. Hubs are connected using uplink ports. Each hub is aware of the stations directly connected to it and the hubs that are uplinked from it. The main features of the demand priority are,

- used with 100 Mbps Ethernet,

- requires a *smart* hub,

- station must require permission from hub before they can transmit,

- stations can transmit and receive at the same time, and

- transmission can be prioritized.

Hubs can be considered of as servers and end nodes as clients. With demand priority, before transmitting data, a client must place a request access to the network media. The server processes this request and decides whether to allow the client to access the media. If the server decides to grant permission to the client to access the media, it sends the client a signal informing the decision. The client then takes over the control of the media and transmits its data.

Demand priority is considered as a contention method, but it operates differently from the CSMA/CD access method used in

Ethernet networks. Cables in a 100VG-AnyLan network are capable of transmitting and receiving data at the same time using all four pairs of twisted-pair cabling in a quartet signalling method.

4.5 ISO OPEN SYSTEMS INTERCONNECTION REFERENCE MODEL

International Standards Organization (ISO) is a worldwide federation that works to provide international standards. In 1984, when the basics of the internet was under developing and implementing, ISO worked to develop a protocol set that would be used by all vendors throughout the world to allow the interconnection of network devices. This movement was fuelled with the hope of ensuring that all vendor products and technologies could communicate and interact across international and technical boundaries. This Open Systems Interconnection Reference Model, as described by ISO standard 7498, provides important guidelines used by vendors, engineers, developers, and others. This protocol set did not catch on as a standard, but the model of this protocol set, was adopted and is used as an abstract framework to which most operating systems and protocols adhere. In general it is believed that the OSI Reference Model arrived at the beginning of the computing age. The Transmission Control Protocol/ internet Protocol (TCP/IP) suite has its own model that it is often used extensively while examining and understanding.

4.6 PROTOCOL

A network protocol is a standard set of rules that determines how systems will communicate across networks. Two different systems that use the same protocol can communicate and understand each other despite their physical differences, similar to how two people can communicate and understand each other by using the same language. In fact protocol is a set of rules or standards that defines the syntax, semantics and synchronization of communication and possible error recovery methods and may be implemented by hardware, software, or a combination of both.

OSI Reference Model

The main concept of OSI is the process of communication between two endpoints in a telecommunication network by segmenting the networking tasks, protocols, and services which are classified into seven different layers. Each layer has its own responsibilities and functionalities regarding how two computers communicate over a network. So in a given message between users, there will be a flow of data down through the layers in the source computer, across the network and then up through the layers in the receiving computer. The functions of different layers are provided by a combination of applications, operating systems, network card device drivers and networking hardware that enable a system to put a signal on a network cable or out over Wi-Fi or other wireless protocol.

The primary objective of the OSI model is to help others to develop products that will work within an open network architecture, which is not owned by any vendor and is not a proprietary. Hence it can easily integrate various technologies without any changes in the system's internal logic. Vendors have used the OSI model as a stepping stone for developing their own networking frameworks. These vendors use the OSI model as a blueprint and develop their own protocols and services to produce functionality which is entirely a new form, or with overlapping layers. Since these vendors use the OSI model as their starting point, integration of other vendor products is an easier task and the interoperability issues become less cumbersome if the vendors had developed their own networking framework from scratch.

The physical transmission of the data happens in the physical layer as electronic signals passed from one computer to another over a communication media. But the computer can communicate through logical channels. Each protocol operating at the same OSI layer on one computer communicating with a corresponding protocol operates at the same operating layer on another computer. This happens through encapsulation which is a method of designing modular communication protocols in which logically separate functions in the network are abstracted from their underlying structures by, inclusion or information hiding within higher level objects. The concept of the encapsulation is explained below.

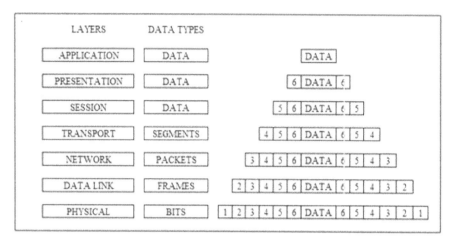

Figure 4.5 OSI Layer Protocol Data Encapsulation

A message is constructed within a program on one computer and is then passed down through the network protocol's stack. A protocol at each layer adds its own information to the message; hence the message grows in size as it goes down the protocol stack. The message is then sent to the destination computer, and the encapsulation is reversed by taking the packets through the same steps used by the source computer that encapsulated it. At the data link layer, only the information pertaining to the data link layer is extracted, and the message is sent up to the next layer. Then at the network layer, only the network layer data are stripped and processed, and the packet is again passed up to the next layer, and so on. This is how the logical communication between computers takes place. The information stripped off at the destination computer informs to interpret and process the packet properly. Data encapsulation is shown in Figure 4.5.

A protocol at each layer has specific responsibilities and control functions it performs, as well as data format syntaxes it expects. Each layer has a special interface (connection point) that allows it to interact with three other layers viz, (1) communications from the interface of the layer above it, (2) communications to the interface of the layer below it, and (3) communications with the same layer in the interface of the target packet address. The control functions, added by the protocols at each layer, are in the form of headers and trailers of the packet.

The benefit of modularizing these layers, and the functionality within each layer, is that various technologies, protocols, and services can interact with each other and provide the proper interfaces to enable communications. This means a computer can use an application protocol developed by Novell, a transport protocol developed by Apple, and a data link protocol developed by IBM to construct and send a message over a network. The protocols, technologies, and computers that operate within the OSI model are considered as open systems. They are capable of communicating with other open systems because they implement international standard protocols and interfaces. The specification for each layer's interface is very structured, while the actual code that makes up the internal part of the software layer is not defined. This makes it easy for vendors to write plug-ins in a modularized manner. Systems are able to integrate the plug-ins into the network stack seamlessly, gaining the vendor-specific extensions and functions.

Understanding the functionalities that take place at each OSI layer and the corresponding protocols that work at those layers helps to understand the overall communication process between computers. An in-depth understanding of each protocol is most essential to explore the full range of options each protocol provides and the security weaknesses embedded into each of these options.

Application Layer

The application layer, layer 7, is the top most layer which works closest to the end users. This layer does not include the actual applications, but rather the protocols that support the applications. Application layer provides network access to the user, where services provides file transmissions, message exchanges, terminal sessions, directory services and much more. Network virtual terminal allows a user to log on to the remote host. The application creates software emulation of a terminal at the remote host. When the user tries to log on to the host, the user's computer talks to the software virtual terminal which in turn talks to the host and vice versa. Then the remote host believes it is communicating with one of its own terminals and allows user to log on. This application allows the user to read the remote host files and edit, manage and control host files, and also sometimes fetch the host files for use in the local computer.

To understand the protocol layering and operation, consider that Gopi wants to send a letter to Jessy. The job of Gopi is to write the letter (the application) which creates the content or message and take it to Post Office (application layer protocol). After putting the content into an envelope, write the address of Jessy on the envelope which corresponds to inserting headers and trailers. At the Post Office the envelope is put into the mailbox (pass it on to the next protocol in the network stack). The envelope then passes through various means and finally delivered to Jessy. And she can open the envelop and receive the content. In a similar fashion the different layer protocols perform their assigned responsibilities one by one in a hierarchical fashion and the data reaches the destination, where the data can be stripped off the headers and trailers. More than 15 protocols are presently used in the application layer, including,

- Simple Mail Transfer Protocol
- File transfer
- Web surfing
- Web chat
- E-mail clients
- Network data sharing
- Virtual terminals
- Various file and data operations

Mail Services: This layer provides the basis for e-mail forwarding and storage.

Network Virtual Terminal: It allows a user to log on to a remote host. The application creates software emulation of a terminal at the remote host. User's computer talks to the software terminal which in turn talks to the host and vice versa. Then the remote host believes it is communicating with one of its own terminals and allows the user to log on.

Directory Services: This layer provides access for global information about various services.

File Transfer, Access and Management (FTAM): It is a standard mechanism to access and manage the files. Users can access files in a remote computer and manage it. They can also retrieve files from a remote computer.

This layer is not the application itself rather it is the set of services an application should be able to make use of directly, although some applications may perform application layer functions. The application layer provides full end-user access to a variety of shared network services for efficient OSI model data flow. This layer has many responsibilities, such as error handling and recovery. It is also used to develop network-based applications. Its major network device or component is the gateway.

Some examples of the protocols working at this layer are the Simple Mail Transfer Protocol (SMTP), Hypertext Transfer Protocol (HTTP), Line Printer Daemon (LPD), File Transfer Protocol (FTP), Telnet, and Trivial File Transfer Protocol (TFTP). Figure 4.6 shows how applications communicate with the underlying protocols through application programming interfaces (APIs).

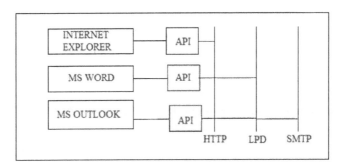

Figure 4.6 Application request through API supporting interface protocol

If a user makes a request to send an e-mail message through the e-mail client Outlook, the e-mail client sends this information to SMTP which adds its information to the user's message and passes it down to the presentation layer. The protocols that work at this layer include,

- Hypertext Transfer Protocol (HTTP),
- File Transfer Protocol (FTP),
- Line Print Daemon (LPD),
- Simple Mail Transfer Protocol (SMTP),
- Trivial File Transfer Protocol (TFTP),
- Electronic Data Interchange (EDI),
- Post Office Protocol version 3 (POP3),
- Internet Message Access Protocol (IMAP),
- Simple Network Management Protocol (SNMP),
- Network News Transport Protocol (NNTP),
- Secure Remote Procedure Call (S-RPC), and
- Secure Electronic Transaction (SET).

Presentation Layer

The presentation layer, the layer 6, receives information from the application layer protocol and take care of the syntax and semantics of the information exchanged in such a way that all computers following the OSI model can understand. This layer provides a common means of representing data in a structure that can be properly processed by the end system. This means that when a user creates a Word document and sends it out to several people, it does not matter whether the receiving computers have different word processing programs so that each of these computers will be able to receive this file and understand and present it to its user as a document. It is the data representation processing that is done at the presentation layer which enables this to take place.

For example, when a Windows 7 computer receives a file from another computer system, information within the file's header indicates the type of file. The Windows 7 operating system has a list of file types it understands and a table describing the programs to be used to open and manipulate each of these files types. For example, the sender could create a Word file in Word 2010, while the receiver uses Open Office. The receiver can open this file because the presentation layer on the sender's system converted the file to American Standard Code for Information Interchange (ASCII), and the receiver's computer knows and it opens these types of files with its word processor, Open Office.

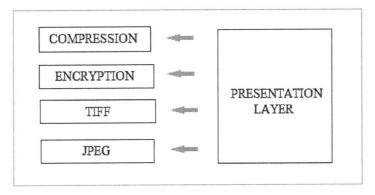

Figure 4.7 Data into standard formats by the Presentation Layer

The presentation layer is not concerned with the meaning of data, but with the syntax and format of those data. It works as a translator, by translating the application format to a standard format which is used for passing message over a network. If a user uses a Corel application to save a graphic, for example, the graphic could be a Tagged Image File Format (TIFF), Graphic Interchange Format (GIF), or Joint Photographic Experts Group (JPEG) format. The presentation layer adds information to inform the destination computer the file type and how to process and present it. In a similar fashion, if the user sends this graphic to another user who does not have the Corel application, the user's operating system can still present the graphic because it has been saved into a standard format. Figure 4.7 illustrates the conversion of a file into different standard file types.

This layer also handles data compression and encryption issues. If a program requests a certain file to be compressed and encrypted before being transferred over the network, the presentation layer provides the necessary information for the destination computer. It provides information regarding the encryption of the file and compression so that the receiving system knows the software and processes which are necessary to decrypt and decompress the file. Suppose a file which is compressed by WinZip is sent to another system which is remotely located. As soon as the system receives this file it looks at the data within the header and comprehends the application which can decompress the file. If the system has WinZip installed, then the file can be decompressed and presented in its original form. If receiving system does not have an application that understands the compression/decompression instructions, the file will be presented with an unassociated icon.

There are no protocols that work at the presentation layer. Network services work at this layer, and when a message is received from a different computer, the service basically informs the application protocol. The following are some of the presentation layer standards.

- American Standard Code for Information Interchange (ASCII)

- Extended Binary Coded Decimal Interchange Mode (EBCDIC)

- Tagged Image File Format (TIFF)

- Joint Photographic Experts Group (JPEG)

- Motion Picture Experts Group (MPEG)

- Musical Instrument Digital Interface (MIDI)

Session Layer

This layer sets up, coordinates and terminates conversations. Services include authentication and reconnection after an interruption. Transfer of data from one destination to another session layer streams of data are marked and are resynchronized properly, so that the ends of the messages are not cut prematurely and data loss is avoided. On the internet, Transmission Control Protocol (TCP) and User Datagram Protocol (UDP) provide these services for most applications.

When two applications need to communicate or transfer data between themselves, a connection may need to be set up between them. The session layer, layer 5, is responsible for establishing a connection between the two applications, maintaining it during the transfer of data, and controlling the release of this connection. A good analogy for the functionality within this layer is a telephone conversation. When Jessy wants to call a friend, she uses the telephone. The telephone network circuitry and protocols set up the connection over the telephone lines and maintain that communication path, and when Jessy hangs up, they release all the resources they were using to keep that connection open.

Similar to how telephone circuitry works, the session layer works in three phases viz. connection establishment, data transfer, and connection release. It provides session restarts and recovery, if necessary and provides the overall maintenance of the session. When the conversation is over, this path is broken down and all parameters are set back to their original settings. This process is known as dialog management. Figure 4.8 depicts the three phases of a session. Some protocols that work at this layer are Structured Query Language (SQL), NetBIOS, and Remote Procedure Call (RPC).

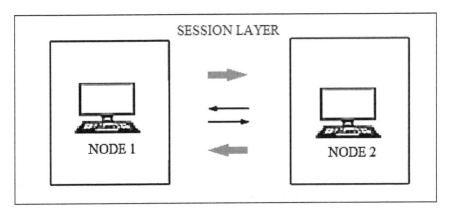

Figure 4.8 The three phases of a Session Layer

It can enable communication between two applications to happen in three different modes and they are,

- Simplex communication which takes place in one direction,

- Half-duplex communication which takes place in both directions, but only one application can send information at a time, and

- Full-duplex communication which takes place in both directions, and both applications can send information at the same time.

Many people have difficulty in understanding the difference between what is happening at the session layer versus the transport layer because their similarity in definitions. Session layer protocols control application-to-application communication, whereas the transport layer protocols handle computer-to-computer communication.

It provides interprocess communication channels, which allow a piece of software on one system to call upon a piece of software on another system without the programmer having to know the specifics of the software on the receiving system. The programmer of a piece of software can write a function call, that calls upon a subroutine. The subroutine could be local to the system or be on a remote system. If the subroutine is on a remote system, the request is carried over a session layer protocol. The result that the remote system provides is then returned to the requesting system over the same session layer protocol. A piece of software can execute components that reside on another system which is the core of distributed computing.

One security issue common to Remote Procedure Call (RPC) is the lack of authentication or the use of weak authentication. Secure RPC can be implemented, which requires authentication to take place before two computers located in different locations can communicate with each other. Authentication can take place using shared secrets, public keys, or Kerberos tickets, session layer protocols need to provide secure authentication capabilities.

Session layer protocols are the least used protocols in a network environment. Thus, many of them should be disabled on systems to decrease the chance of getting exploited. RPC and similar distributed computing need to take place within a network only. Hence, firewalls should be configured so that this type of traffic is not allowed into or out of a network. Firewall filtering rules should be in place to stop this type of unnecessary and dangerous traffic. Some of the protocols that work at this layer include,

- Network File System (NFS),

- NetBIOS,

- Structured Query Language (SQL), and

- Remote Procedure Calls (RPC).

Transport Layer

When two computers communicate through a connection-oriented protocol, they will first agree on the quantum of information each computer will send at a time, the technique to verify the integrity of the data once received, and the methodology to determine whether a packet was lost along the way. The two computers agree on these parameters through a handshaking process at the transport layer, layer 4. The agreement on these issues before transferring data helps provide more reliable data transfer, error detection, correction, recovery, and flow control, and it optimizes the network services needed to perform these tasks. The transport layer provides end-to-end data transport services and establishes the logical connection between two communicating computers.

The functionality of the session and transport layer is similar so far as both of them set up some type of session or virtual connection for communication. The difference is, protocols that work at the session layer set up connections between applications, whereas protocols that work at the transport layer set up connections between computer systems. For example, one can have three different applications on a computer communicating to three applications on another computer. The session layer protocols keep track of these different sessions.

The transport layer protocol can be considered as a bus. It does not know or care the type of applications which are communicating each other. It just provides the mechanism to get the data from one system to another.

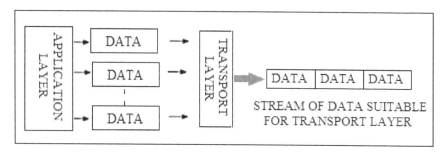

Figure 4.9 TCP formats data into a stream suitable for transmission

The transport layer receives data from different applications and assembles the data into a stream to be properly transmitted over the network. The main protocols that work at this layer are TCP, UDP, Secure Socket Layer (SSL), and Sequenced Packet Exchange (SPX). Information is passed down from different entities at higher layers to the transport layer, which assembles the information into a stream, as shown in Figure 4.9. The stream is made up of the various data segments passed to it. Just like a bus can carry variety of people, the transport layer protocol can carry a variety of application data types. In fact functionalities of the transport layer can be summarized as follows,

> *Segmentation and Reassembling:* A message is divided into segments. Each segment contains sequence number, which enables transport layer to reassemble the message. Message is reassembled correctly upon arrival at the destination and replaces packets which were lost in transmission.

> *Connection Control:* It includes Connectionless Transport Layer and Connection Oriented Transport Layer.

> *Connectionless Transport Layer:* Each segment is considered as an independent packet and delivered to the transport layer at the destination machine.

Connection Oriented Transport Layer: Before delivering packets, connection is made with transport layer at the destination machine.

Flow Control: In this layer, flow control is performed end to end.

Error Control: Error Control is performed end to end in this layer to ensure that the complete message arrives at the receiving transport layer without any error. Error Correction is done through re-transmission. The following are some of the protocols that work at this layer.

- Transmission Control Protocol (TCP)

- User Datagram Protocol (UDP)

- Secure Sockets Layer (SSL)/Transport Layer Security (TLS)

- Sequenced Packet Exchange (SPX)

Network Layer

The main responsibilities of the network layer, layer 3, are to insert information into the packet's header so it can be properly addressed and then route the packets to their proper destination. In a network, many routes can lead to one destination. The protocols at the network layer must determine the best path for the packet to take. Routing protocols build and maintain their routing tables. These tables are maps of the network, and when a packet must be sent from computer A to computer M, the protocols check the routing table, add the necessary information to the packet's header, and send it on its way.

The protocols that work at this layer do not ensure the delivery of the packets. They depend on the protocols at the transport layer to catch any problems and resend packets if necessary. IP is a common protocol working at the network layer, although other routing and routed protocols work there as well. Some of the other protocols are the Internet Control Message Protocol (ICMP), Routing Information Protocol (RIP), Open Shortest Path First (OSPF), Border Gateway

Protocol (BGP), and internet Group Management Protocol (IGMP). A packet can take many routes but reaches the correct destination as the network layer enters routing information into the header. The Figure 4.10 shows how a network layer takes the most efficient path for each packet to take.

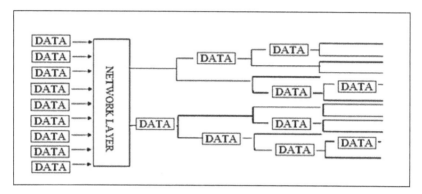

Figure 4.10 The most efficient path by the Network Layer

The network layer deliver packets from source to destination across multiple links (networks). If two computers are connected on the same link then there is no need for a network layer. It routes the signal through different channels to the other end and acts as a network controller. It also divides the outgoing messages into packets and to assemble incoming packets into messages for higher levels. Functionalities of network layer are summarized below.

The main function of network layer is that it translates logical network address into physical address. When concerned with the computer networks, message or packet switching, routers and gateways operate in the network layer. Mechanism is provided by Network Layer for routing the packets to final destination. Connection services are provided including network layer flow control, network layer error control and packet sequence control. The following are some of the protocols that work at this layer.

- Internet Control Message Protocol (ICMP),
- Routing Information Protocol (RIP),
- Open Shortest Path First (OSPF),

- Border Gateway Protocol (BGP),

- Internet Group Management Protocol (IGMP),

- Internet Protocol (IP),

- Internet Protocol Security (IPSec),

- Internetwork Packet Exchange (IPX),

- Network Address Translation (NAT), and

- Simple Key Management for Internet Protocols (SKIP).

Data Link layer

Data link layer which is close to the physical layer where the actual transmission channel is defined is the most reliable node to node delivery of data. It forms frames from the packets suitable to the LAN or wide area network (WAN) technology binary format that are received from network layer and gives it to physical layer for proper line transmission. It also synchronizes the information which is to be transmitted over the data.

LAN and WAN technologies can use different protocols, Network Interface Cards (NICs), cables, and transmission methods. Each of these components has a different header data format structure, and they interpret electric voltages in different ways. The Data link layer determines the format of the data frame to be transmitted properly over Token Ring, Ethernet, ATM, or Fiber Distributed Data Interface (FDDI) networks. If the network is an Ethernet network, for example, all the computers will expect packet headers to be a certain length, the flags to be positioned in certain field locations within the header, and the trailer information to be in a certain place with specific fields. Compared to Ethernet, Token Ring network technology has different frame header lengths, flag values, and header formats. The responsibilities of Data link layer are,

- *Framing:* Frames are the streams of bits received from the network layer into manageable data units. This division of stream of bits is done by Data link layer.

- *Physical Addressing:* The Data link layer adds a header to the frame in order to define physical address of the sender or receiver of the frame, if the frames are to be distributed to different systems on the network.

- *Flow Control:* A mechanism to avoid a fast transmitter from running a slow receiver by buffering the extra bit is provided by flow control. This prevents traffic jam at the receiver side.

- *Error Control:* Error control is achieved by adding a trailer at the end of the frame. Duplication of frames is also prevented by using this mechanism. Data link layers add mechanism to prevent duplication of frames.

- *Access Control:* Protocols of this layer determines the devices that have control over the link at any given time, when two or more devices are connected to the same link.

The data link is divided into two functional sub-layers viz, the Logical Link Control (LLC) and the Media Access Control (MAC). The LLC, defined in the IEEE 802.2 specification, communicates with the protocol immediately above it, the network layer. The MAC will have the appropriately loaded protocols to interface with the protocol requirements of the physical layer.

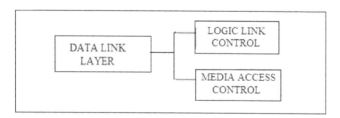

Figure 4.11 Two sub-layers of the Data Link Layer

As data is passed down the network stack, it has to go from the network layer to the data link layer. The protocol at the network layer is not aware of the underlying network which may be Ethernet, Token Ring, or ATM. The protocol at the network layer just adds its header and trailer information to the packet and it passes it on to the next layer, which is the LLC sub-layer. The LLC layer takes care of flow control and error checking. Data coming from the network layer passes down through the LLC sub-layer and goes to MAC. The technology at the MAC sub-layer knows if the network is Ethernet, Token Ring or ATM, as it knows how to put the last header and trailer on the packet before it *hits the wire* for transmission.

The IEEE MAC specification for Ethernet is 802.3, Token Ring is 802.5, wireless LAN is 802.11, and so on. A reference to an IEEE standard, such as 802.11, 802.16, or 802.3, refers to the protocol working at the MAC sub-layer of the data link layer of a protocol stack.

Some of the protocols that work at the data link layer are the Point-to-Point Protocol (PPP), ATM, Layer 2 Tunnelling Protocol (L2TP), FDDI, Ethernet, and Token Ring. Figure 4.11 shows the two sub-layers that make up the data link layer.

Each network technology such as Ethernet, ATM, FDDI, etc. defines the compatible physical transmission type (coaxial, twisted pair, fiber, wireless) that is required to enable network communication. Each network technology also has defined electronic signalling and encoding patterns. For example, if the MAC sub-layer received a bit with the value of 1 that needed to be transmitted over an Ethernet network, the MAC sub-layer technology would tell the physical layer to create 0.5 volts of electricity. In the *language of Ethernet* this means that 0.5 volts is the encoding value for a bit with the value of 1. If the next bit the MAC sub-layer receives is 0, the MAC layer would tell the physical layer to transmit 0 volts. The different network types will have different encoding schemes. So a bit value of 1 in an ATM network might actually be encoded to the voltage value of 0.85V. It is just a sophisticated Morse code system. The receiving end will know when it receives a voltage value of 0.85V that a bit with the value of 1 has been transmitted.

Network cards bridge the data link and physical layers. Data is passed down through the first six layers and reaches the network card driver at the data link layer. Depending on the network technology being used (Ethernet, Token Ring, FDDI, and so on), the network card driver encodes the bits at the data link layer, which are then turned into electricity states at the physical layer and placed onto the wire for transmission. Some protocols that work at this layer include the following.

- Address Resolution Protocol (ARP)
- Reverse Address Resolution Protocol (RARP)
- Point-to-Point Protocol (PPP)
- Serial Line Internet Protocol (SLIP)
- Ethernet
- Token Ring
- FDDI
- ATM

Physical Layer

The electrical and mechanical specifications of the network termination equipment and the transmission medium are defined at this layer which is referred to as layer 1 in the OSI reference model where everything ends up as electrical signals. These include the type of cable and connectors used, the pin assignments for the cable and connectors and the format for the electrical signals. Cable may be coaxial, twisted pair, or fiber optic and the types of connectors depend on the type of cable. Pin assignments depend on the type of cable and also on the network architecture being used, and the encoding scheme used to signal 0 and 1 values in a digital transmission or particular values in an analog transmission depend on the network architecture being used.

Signals can be transmitted as electrical signals, optical signals, or electromagnetic waves. Devices and network components that are associated with the physical layer, are antenna, amplifier, plug and socket for the network cable, the repeater, the transceiver, the T-bar and the terminator. At the physical layer of the communication process, the user data which has been segmented by the transport layer, is placed into packets by the network layer, and further encapsulated as frames by the data link layer. It is then converted to the electrical, optical, or microwave signal that represents the bits in each frame. These signals are then sent on the media one at a time. At the receiving end, the job of the physical layer is to retrieve these individual signals from the media, restore them to their bit representations, and pass the bits up to the data link layer as a complete frame.

Signals and voltage schemes have different meanings for different LAN and WAN technologies. If a user sends data through his dial-up software and transmits out from the modem onto the telephone line, the data format, electrical signals, and control functionality are much different than if that user sends data through the NIC and onto an Unshielded Twisted Pair (UTP) wire for LAN communication. The mechanisms that control this data going onto the telephone line, or the UTP wire, work at the physical layer. This layer controls synchronization, date rates, line noise, and transmission techniques. Specifications for the physical layer include the timing of voltage changes, voltage levels, and the physical connections for electrical, optical, and mechanical transmission. At the destination, the physical layer converts the electrical signals into a series of bit values. These values are grouped into packets and passed up to the data link layer. The following are some of the standard interfaces of Physical layer.

- EIA-422, EIA-423, RS-449, RS-485,

- 10BASE-T,10BASE2,10BASE5,100BASE-TX,100BASE-FX, 100BASE-T,

- 1000BASE-T, 1000BASE-SX,

- Integrated Services Digital Network (ISDN),

- Digital subscriber line (DSL), and

- Synchronous Optical Networking (SONET).

Attacks on Different Layers

In the different layers of this network model, there can be specific attack types. One concept to understand at this point is that a network can be used as a channel for an attack or the network can be the target of an attack. If the network is a channel for attack, it means the attacker is using the network as a resource. Here, when an attacker sends a virus from one system to another system, the virus travels through the network channel. If an attacker carries out a Denial of Service (DoS) attack, which sends a large amount of bogus traffic over a network link to bog it down, then the network itself is the target. Hence it is important to understand how and where the attacks take place so that appropriate countermeasures can be taken.

4.7 TCP/IP MODEL

The most widely used protocol suite is TCP/IP model, but it is not just a single protocol, rather, it is a protocol suite comprising dozens of individual protocols. It is a hierarchical protocol which implies that the lower level protocols support the upper level protocols.

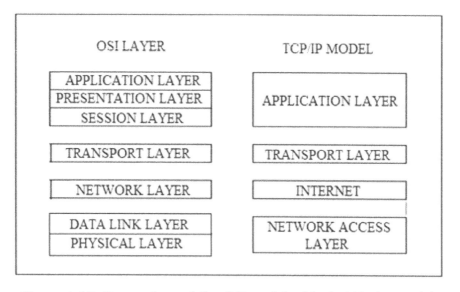

Figure 4.12 Comparison of the OSI model with the TCP/IP model

TCP/IP consists of only four layers, as opposed to the OSI Reference Model's seven. The four layers of the TCP/IP model are application, transport, internet, and link or network access layer. The application layer is similar to the combination of session, presentation, and application layers of OSI. Figure 4.12 shows the comparison to the seven layers of the OSI model. TCP/IP is a platform-independent protocol based on open standards. TCP/IP can be found in just about every available operating system, but it consumes a significant amount of resources and is relatively easy to hack into because it was designed for ease of use rather than for security. The TCP/IP protocol suite was developed before the OSI Reference Model was created. The designers of the OSI Reference Model took care to ensure that the TCP/IP protocol suite fit their model because of its established deployment in networking. In fact TCP/IP is a suite of protocols that is the de facto standard for transmitting data across the internet. TCP is a reliable, connection-oriented protocol, while IP is an unreliable, connectionless protocol.

The TCP/IP model's Application layer corresponds to layers 5, 6, and 7 of the OSI model. The TCP/IP model's transport layer corresponds to layer 4 from the OSI model. The TCP/IP model's internet layer corresponds to layer 3 from the OSI model. The TCP/IP model's link layer corresponds to layers 1 and 2 from the OSI model. It has become a common practice to call the TCP/IP model layers by their OSI model layer equivalent names. The TCP/IP model's application layer is already using a name borrowed from the OSI, so that one is a snap. The TCP/IP model's host-to-host layer is sometimes called the transport layer. The TCP/IP model's internet layer is sometimes called the network layer. And the TCP/IP model's Link layer is sometimes called the data link or the network access layer. Since the TCP/IP model layer names and the OSI model layer names can be used interchangeably, it is important to know the model used in various contexts. The four layers of protocol and its components are shown in Figure 4.13.

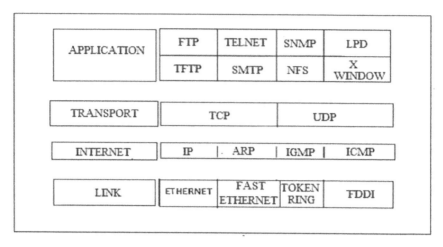

Figure 4.13 Four layers of TCP/IP and its component protocols

TCP/IP can be secured using VPN links between systems. VPN links are encrypted to add privacy, confidentiality, and authentication and to maintain data integrity. Protocols used to establish VPNs are Point-to-Point Tunnelling Protocol (PPTP), Layer 2 Tunnelling Protocol (L2TP), and Internet Protocol Security (IPSec). Another method to provide protocol-level security is to employ TCP wrappers. A *TCP wrapper* is an application that can serve as a basic firewall by restricting access to ports and resources based on user IDs or system IDs. Using TCP wrappers is a form of port-based access control. A brief description of the TCP/IP layers is given below.

Physical and Data Link Layers (Host-to-Network)

The network access layer includes the function of the data link and physical layers of the OSI model. It converts packets into bits for transmission over the physical medium and is responsible for error-free delivery of frames. IEEE 802.2 Logical Link Control (LLC) manages data link communications between devices and performs error checking on frames received. EIA-422-B (RS422) is the Electronic Industry Association standard that defines the electrical characteristic of a balanced interface circuit that is designed to for high common-mode noise rejection and data rates less than 0.5Mbps.

Internet (Network Layer)

Internet layer is the second layer of the four layer TCP/IP model. The position of internet layer is between Network Access Layer and transport layer. Internet protocol assigns IP addresses of the sender and recipient to data packets to be used in routing the message to its intended receiver. IP does not guarantee reliable delivery of data packets. Internet Control Message Protocol (ICMP) is a management protocol used to determine transmission routes from a source to a destination host and to check the availability of a host to receive messages. One of the ICMP utilities is PING, which is used to check the connection of host to the network. ARP is another protocol, which determines the MAC hardware address of a destination host from its IP address. PPP is a full duplex, encapsulation protocol for sending IP messages over Point-to-Point links.

Transport Layer

Transport layer is the third layer of the four layer TCP/IP model. The position of the Transport layer is between application layer and internet layer. Transport layer defines the level of service and status of the connection used when transporting data. The two primary Transport layer protocols of TCP/IP are TCP and UDP. TCP is a full duplex connection-oriented protocol, whereas UDP is a simplex connectionless protocol. When a communication connection is established between two systems, it is done using ports. TCP and UDP each have 65536 ports (ports are explicated in the next section). Since port numbers are 16-digit binary numbers, the total number of ports is 216, or 65536, numbered from 0 through 65535. A port (also called a socket) is little more than an address number that both ends of the communication link agree to use when transferring data. Ports allow a single IP address to support multiple simultaneous communications, each using a different port number. The first 1,024 of these ports (0–1,023) are called the well-known ports or the service ports. This is because they have standardized assignments as to the services they support. For example, port 80 is the standard port for web (HTTP) traffic, port 23 is the standard port for Telnet, and port 25 is the standard port for SMTP.

Application Layer

Application layer is present on the top of the transport layer. It provides applications the capability to access the services of the other layers and defines the protocols that applications use to exchange data. Application layer defines TCP/IP application protocols and helps the host programs for interfacing with Transport layer services in using the network. It includes all the higher-level protocols like Domain Naming System, HTTP, Telnet, SSH, File Transfer Protocol, Trivial File Transfer Protocol, SNMP, SMTP, Dynamic Host Configuration Protocol, X Windows, Remote Desktop Protocol etc.

The TCP layer requires a *port number* to be assigned to each message. Similar way it can determine the type of service being provided. It is important to note that whenever *ports* are referred in computer networking, they are not the ports that are used in serial and parallel devices, or ports used for computer hardware control. These ports are merely reference numbers used to define a service. For instance, port 23 is used for telnet services, and HTTP uses port 80 for providing web browsing service. There is a group called the Internet Assigned Numbers Authority (IANA) that controls the assigning of ports for specific services. There are some ports that are assigned, some reserved and many unassigned which may be utilized by application programs. Port numbers are straight unsigned integer values which range up to a value of 65535.

4.8 PORTS AND PORT NUMBERS

Ports 1024 to 49151 are known as the registered software ports. These are ports that have one or more networking software products specifically registered with the Internet Assigned Numbers Authority (IANA) in order to provide a standardized port-numbering system for clients attempting to connect to their products. Ports 49152 to 65535 are known as the random, dynamic, or ephemeral ports because they are often used randomly and temporarily by clients as a source port. These random ports are also used by several networking services when negotiating a data transfer pipeline between client and server outside the initial service or registered ports, such as performed by common FTP.

The IANA recommends that ports 49152 to 65535 be used as dynamic*c and/or private ports. However, not all Operating Systems abide by this, especially, the Berkeley Software Distribution (BSD) which uses ports 1024 through 4999. Many Linux kernels use 32768 to 61000. Microsoft uses the range 1025 to 5000 in Windows Server 2003. Windows Vista, Windows 7, and Windows Server 2008 use the IANA range. Transmission Control Protocol (TCP) operates at layer 4 (the Transport layer) of the OSI model. It supports full-duplex communications, is connection oriented, and employs reliable sessions. TCP is connection oriented because it employs a handshake process between two systems to establish a communication session. Upon completion of this handshake process, a communication session that can support data transmission between the client and server is established.

4.9 TCP/IP VULNERABILITIES

TCP/IP's vulnerabilities are numerous. Improperly implemented TCP/IP stacks in various operating systems are vulnerable to buffer overflows, SYN flood attacks, various DoS attacks, fragment attacks, oversized packet attacks, spoofing attacks, man-in-the middle attacks, hijack attacks, coding error attacks, etc. TCP/IP (as well as most protocols) is also subject to passive attacks via monitoring or sniffing. Network monitoring is the act of monitoring traffic patterns to obtain information about a network. Packet sniffing is the act of capturing packets from the network in hopes of extracting useful information from the packet contents. Effective packet sniffers can extract usernames, passwords, email addresses, encryption keys, credit card numbers, IP addresses, system names, and so on.

4.10 ENHANCED PERFORMANCE ARCHITECTURE (EPA)

Since all the seven layers of the OSI model are not always necessary, IEC has introduced a reduced form of the OSI seven layer model which is a three layer model called the Enhanced Performance Architecture (EPA). The three layers are,

- Physical layer
- Data Link layer, and
- Application layer.

Obviously the physical and data link layer are the hardware layers and the Application layer is the software layer. EPA when used over a network adds a pseudo transport layer to assist network communication.

Physical layer: It is the bottom layer of the EPA model. This converts each frame into a bit stream to be sent over the physical media and keeps track of transmission of one bit at a time. The physical layer provides a physical medium between sender and receiver for sending and receiving information. The connection topology could be point to point, multi-drop, hierarchical, or with multiple masters. The communication can be half duplex or full duplex.

Data Link layer: It deals with the message frame which is the group of bit stream appropriately formed from the bits of data through the physical layer. An acknowledgement is sent for the receipt of data, for reliable and secure transmission.

Pseudo Transport layer: This does the combined function of network and transport layer of the OSI model. Network function is concerned with the routing and data flow over the network from sender to receiver. Transport function includes proper delivery of the message from sender to receiver, message sequencing, and error correction. This function of the transport layer is limited when compared to the OSI layer.

Application Layer: This layer serves the end user directly and will add meaning to the data received from the process. It helps the user to do functions like file transfer and network access. The Figure 4.14 gives a comparison of the EPA model with the OSI model.

OSI MODEL	EPA MODEL
APPLICATION LAYER	APPLICATION LAYER
PRESENTATION LAYER	
SESSION LAYER	
TRANSPORT LAYER	PSEUDO TRANSPORT LAYER
NETWORK LAYER	
DATA LINK LAYER	DATA LINK LAYER
PHYSICAL LAYER	PHYSICAL LAYER

Figure 4.14 Comparison of the EPA model with the OSI model

Summary

The advancement of ICT innovates the four major areas in industry viz. Data Acquisition Systems (DAS), computer and communication, cyber-security and the pertinent ICS applications. The present domain of the automation engineers require in depth knowledge of secure M2M communication. This chapter begins with explaining the common terminologies of industrial networking and then moves on to explain the different network topologies. The OSI reference model has been explained in detail, followed by the TCP/IP and EPA models. The TCP/IP vulnerabilities and attack vectors to different layers and concept of port are also explained.

CHAPTER FIVE
INDUSTRIAL COMMUNICATION

5.1 INTRODUCTION

The key enabler for the ICS and DCS is the availability of secure and preferably bi-directional data communications and the proper amalgamation of distributed intelligence and communication technologies. Thus, the design and implementation of a modern, reliable communications infrastructure is a fundamental and important requirement for making the ICS or DCS smarter.

The medium by which data is transmitted is known as a communication channel or communication media. The transfer of data takes place in the form of analog signals and it is measured in the form of bandwidth, the higher the bandwidth the more the data that will be transferred. Communication media are broadly classified into two categories, namely, guided media (wired) and unguided media (wireless). Both are used for short distance (LANs, MANs) and long distance (WANs) communication. This chapter elaborates various guided and unguided media used in communication, its merits and demerits, and practical considerations to be taken care while selecting the media for different applications. The chapter also explains the various communication technologies currently available for the deployment in ICS and DCS. Before that, it is better to be familiar with certain terminologies which are briefly explained below.

5.2 TYPES OF TRANSMISSION

There are various transmission classifications depending upon the different technologies employed and they are mainly based on

- Analog and digital,
- Synchronous and Asynchronous,
- Broadcast, Multicast, and Unicast,

- Simplex, Half Duplex, and Full Duplex, and

- Baseband and Broadband.

As the communication is the key enabler of the modern SCADA, a basic understanding of these terms become most essential for an automation engineer. Hence brief explanation of these terminologies is given below.

Analog and Digital

Two types of communication technologies are in practice and they are Analog and Digital. Analog communications occur with a continuous signal that varies in frequency, amplitude, phase, voltage, and so on. The variances in the continuous signal produces a wave shape as opposed to the square shape of a digital signal. Digital communications occur through the use of a discontinuous electrical signal and a state change or *on-off* pulses. In other words the information is encoded digitally as discrete signals and transmitted electronically to the recipients. Digital signals are more reliable than analog signals over long distances or when interference is present. This is because of a digital signal's definitive information storage method employing direct current voltage where voltage *on* represents a value of 1 and voltage *off* represents a value of 0. These *on-off* pulses create a stream of binary data. Analog signals become altered and corrupted because of attenuation over long distances and interference. Since an analog signal can have an infinite number of variations used for signal encoding as opposed to digital's two states, unwanted alterations to the signal make extraction of the data more difficult as the degradation increases. A brief comparison between these two technologies is summarized below.

- *Bandwidth:* This factor creates the key difference between analog and digital communication. Analog signal requires less bandwidth for the transmission while digital signal requires more bandwidth for the transmission.

- *Power Requirement:* Power requirement for digital communication is less when compared to analog communication as the bandwidth requirement in digital systems is more.

- *Fidelity:* Fidelity is a factor which creates a crucial difference between analog and digital communication. Fidelity is the ability of the receiver which receives the output exactly in coherence with that of transmitted input. Digital communication offers more fidelity as compared to analog communication.

- *Noise Distortion and Error Rate:* Analog systems are affected by noise while, digital systems are immune from noise and distortion. Error rate is another significant difference which separates analog and digital communication. In analog instruments, there is an error due to parallax or other kinds of observational methods.

- *Synchronization:* Digital communication system offers to synchronize which is not effective in analog communication. Thus, synchronization also creates a key difference between analog and digital communication.

- *Cost:* Digital communication equipments are costly and digital signal require more bandwidth for transmission.

- *Hardware Flexibility and Portability:* The hardware of analog communication system is not as flexible as digital communication. Analog systems are less portable as components are heavy while digital systems are more portable as they are compact equipments.

Synchronous and Asynchronous

Communications are either synchronous or asynchronous. Some communications are synchronized with some sort of clock or timing activity and referred to as synchronous communications. It relies *on* timing or clocking mechanism based on either an independent clock or a time stamp embedded in the data stream. Synchronous communications are typically able to support very high rates of data transfer. On the other hand, asynchronous communications rely on a *stop* and *start* delimiter bit to manage the transmission of data. Because of the use of delimiter bits and the stop and start nature of its transmission, asynchronous communication is best suited for smaller amounts of data. Public Switched Telephone Network (PSTN) modems are good examples of asynchronous communication devices.

Unicast, Broadcast and Multicast

Unicast, Broadcast and Multicast technologies determine the number of destinations a single transmission can reach.

Unicast: Unicast technology supports only a single communication to a specific recipient. In this case there is just one sender, and one receiver. Unicast transmission, in which a packet is sent from a single source to a specified destination, is still the predominant form of transmission on LANs and within the internet. All LANs and IP networks support the unicast transfer mode, and most users are familiar with the standard unicast applications such as HTTP, SMTP, FTP and telnet, which employ the TCP transport protocol.

Broadcast: Broadcast technology supports communications to all possible recipients. In this case there is just one sender, but the information is sent to all connected receivers. Broadcast transmission is supported on most LANs, and may be used to send the same message to all computers on the LAN like in the Address Resolution Protocol (ARP) uses this to send an address resolution query to all computers on a LAN. Network layer protocols also support a form of broadcast that allows the same packet to be sent to every system in a logical network (in IPv4 this consists of the IP network ID and an all 1's host number). Typical example of an application which may use multicast is a video server sending out networked TV channels. Simultaneous delivery of high quality video to a large number of delivery platforms will exhaust the capability of even a high bandwidth network with a powerful video clip server. This poses a major scalability issue for applications which requires sustained high bandwidth. One of the methods to significantly ease scaling to larger groups of clients is to employ multicast networking.

Multicast: Multicast networking technology supports simultaneous communications to multiple specific recipients. In this case there may be one or more senders, and the information is distributed to a set of receivers. IP multicast provides dynamic many-to-many connectivity between a set of senders (at least 1) and a group of receivers. The format of IP multicast packets are identical to that of unicast packets and are distinguished only by the use of a special class of destination address, which, denotes a specific multicast group. Since TCP supports only the unicast mode, multicast applications should use the UDP transport protocol.

Unlike broadcast transmission, multicast clients receive a stream of packets only if they have previously elected to do so. The routers in a multicast network find the sub-networks which have active clients. Each multicast group attempts to minimize the transmission of packets across parts of the network for which there are no active clients.

The multicast mode is useful if a group of clients require a common set of data at the same time, or when the clients are able to receive and store (cache) common data until needed. Where there is a common need for the same data required by a group of clients, multicast transmission may provide significant bandwidth savings up to 1/N of the bandwidth compared to N separate unicast clients.

The majority of installed LANs are able to support the multicast transmission mode. Shared LANs inherently support multicast, since all packets reach all the Network Interface Cards (NIC) connected to the LAN. The earliest LAN network interface cards had no specific support for multicast and introduced a big performance penalty by forcing the adaptor to receive all packets and perform software filtering to remove all unwanted packets. Most modern network interface cards implement a set of multicast filters, relieving the host of the burden of performing excessive software filtering.

Simplex, Half Duplex and Full Duplex

In a communication system, there will be a transmitter and a receiver. In between the transmitter and the receiver, there is a transmission medium of the data/information, usually referred to as the communication channel. Although the required information for transmission originates from a single source, there may be more than one destination or receivers. This depends upon the number of receiving stations which are linked to the channel and the quantity of energy that the transmitted signal possesses. If the channel length is more and the transmission power is less, the receiver situated at a long distance cannot receive the data properly. In a digital communications channel, the information can be represented by a stream of bits called bytes. A collection of bytes can be grouped to form a frame or other higher-level message unit. These types of multiple levels of encapsulation facilitate the handling of messages in a complex data communications network. If any communications channel is considered, it has a direction associated with it.

Simplex Channel: It is conventional that the message source is the transmitter, and the destination is the receiver. A channel whose direction of transmission is unchanging is called as a simplex channel. In other words, a type of data transmission, where message transmission is taking place only in one direction, typical example is the radio station which is a simplex channel because it always transmits the signal to its listeners and never allows them to transmit back. Another example is the television. The advantage of simplex mode of transmission is, since the data can be transmitted only in one direction, the entire band width can be used.

Half Duplex Channel: A half duplex channel can be considered as a single physical channel in which the direction may be reversed. Messages can flow in two directions in a halfduplex type, but never at the same time. In other words it can be said that at a single time, the transmission of data are done in only one direction. For example, in a telephone call, one party speaks while the other listens. After a pause, the other party speaks and the first party listens. Speaking simultaneously will result in a garbled sound that cannot be understood. The main difficulty of half-duplex mode of transmission is since two channels are used, the band width of the channel would be decreased.

Full Duplex Channel: A full duplex channel can be used for bi-directional communication. In fact, message can be transmitted simultaneously in both directions. It comprises of two simplex channels, a forward channel and a backward (reverse) channel, linking at the same points. The transmission rate of the reverse channel will be very slow if it is used only for flow control of the forward channel. The main problem of the full duplex mode of transmission is, since two channels are required, the band width would be decreased.

Baseband and Broadband

The number of channels that can be pushed into a single wire simultaneously over a cable segment depends on whether the customer uses baseband technology or broadband technology. Baseband technology can support only a single communication channel. In analog transmission the data is transmitted as waves while in digital transmission the data is moved as discrete electric pulses. Baseband uses a direct current applied to the cable. A current that is at a higher level represents the binary signal of 1, and a current that is at a lower level represents the binary signal of 0. Baseband is a form of digital signal. Ethernet is a baseband technology.

Broadband technology divides the communication channel into individual and independent sub-channels so that different types of data can be transmitted simultaneously. Broadband uses frequency modulation to support numerous channels, each supporting a distinct communication session. Broadband is suitable for high throughput rates, especially when several channels are multiplexed. Broadband is a form of analog signal. As an example, a Coaxial Cable TV (CATV) system is a broadband technology that delivers multiple television channels over the same cable. This system can also provide home users with internet access, but these data are transmitted at a different frequency spectrum than the TV channels. A Digital Subscriber Line (DSL) uses one single phone line and constructs a set of high-frequency channels for internet data transmissions. A cable modem uses the available frequency spectrum that is provided by a cable TV carrier to move internet traffic to and from a customer premise. Mobile broadband devices implement individual channels over a cellular connection, and Wi-Fi broadband technology moves data to and from an access point over a specified frequency set. Characteristics of baseband and broadband are summarized below.

Baseband:

- Digital signals are used
- Frequency division multiplexing is not possible
- Baseband is bi-directional transmission
- Short distance signal travelling
- Entire bandwidth of the cable is consumed by a single signal in a baseband transmission.

Broadband:

- Analog signals are used
- Transmission of data is unidirectional
- Signal travelling distance is long
- Frequency division multiplexing is possible
- Multiple frequency signals are sent simultaneously in broadband transmission.

5.3 GUIDED MEDIA

Guided media are more commonly known as wired media or bounded media, or those media in which electrical or optical signals are transmitted through cables or wires. In fact it needs a physical material medium to propagate and the electrical signals are confined within the cable or wire which transmits them. Typical forms of guided media include copper co-axial cables, fiber-optic cables and twisted-pair copper cables, which can be shielded or unshielded. Transmission of digital data through either guided or unguided communication involves the coding of the data at the sender's end, the modulation of the carrier signal, the demodulation of the signal on the receiving end and the decoding of the binary signal.

Twisted Pair

It is the most widely deployed media type across the world, as the last mile telephone link connecting every home with the local telephone exchange is made of twisted pair copper. It is also used as last mile connectivity to access the internet from home. They are also used in Ethernet LAN cables within homes and offices. They support low to High Data Rates (in order of Giga bits). However, they are effective only up to a maximum distance of a few kilometers, as the signal strength is lost significantly beyond this distance.

They come in two variants, namely UTP (unshielded twisted pair) and STP (Shielded Twisted Pair). Within each variant, there are multiple sub-variants, based on the thickness of the material (like UTP-3, UTP-5, UTP-7 etc.). Twisted-pair cabling has insulated copper wires surrounded by an outer protective jacket. If the cable has an outer foil shielding, it is referred to as *shielded twisted pair (STP),* which adds protection from radio frequency interference and electromagnetic interference. Twisted-pair cabling, which does not have this extra outer shielding, is called *unshielded twisted pair (UTP).* Twisted-pair cable is cheaper and easier to work with.

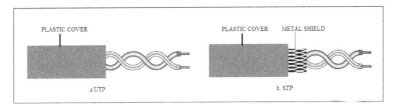

Figure 5.1 Twisted Pair Copper

The twisted-pair cable contains copper wires that twist around each other, as shown in Figure 5.1. This twisting of the wires protects the integrity and strength of the signals they carry. Each wire forms a balanced circuit, because the voltage in each pair uses the same amplitude, just with opposite phases. The tighter the twisting of the wires, the more resistant the cable is to interference and attenuation. UTP has several categories of cabling, each of which has its own unique characteristics. The twisting of the wires, the type of insulation used, the quality of the conductive material, and the shielding of the wire determine the rate at which data can be transmitted. The UTP ratings indicate which of these components were used when the cables were manufactured. Some types are more suitable and effective for specific uses and environments. Table 5.1 lists the cable ratings.

Table 5.1 UTP cable ratings

UTP Category	Characteristics	Usage
Category 1	Voice grade telephone cable for up to 1 Mbps transmission rate.	Not recommended for network use, but modems can communicating over it.
Category 2	Data transmission up to 4 Mbps	Used in mainframe and minicomputer terminal connections, but not recommended for high-speed installations.
Category 3	10 Mbps for Ethernet and 4 Mbps for Token Ring	Used in 10 Base-T network installations.
Category 4	16 Mbps	Usually used in Token Ring networks.
Category 5	100 Mbps: has high twisting and thus low crosstalk.	Used in 100 Base-TX, CDDI, Ethernet, and ATM installations: most widely used in network installations.
Category 6	10 Gbps	Used in new network installations requiring high speed transmission. Standard for Gigbit Ethernet.
Category 7	10 Gbps	Used in new network installations requiring high speed transmission.

Copper cable has been around for many years. It is inexpensive and easy to use. A majority of the telephone systems today use copper cabling with the rating of voice grade. Twisted-pair wiring is the preferred network cabling, but it also has its drawbacks. Copper actually resists the flow of electrons, which causes a signal to degrade after it has travelled a certain distance. That is why cable lengths are recommended for copper cables; if these recommendations are not followed, a network could experience signal loss and data corruption. Copper also radiates energy, which means information can be monitored and captured by intruders. UTP is the least secure networking cable compared to coaxial and fiber. If a company requires higher speed, higher security, and cables to have longer runs than what is allowed in copper cabling, fiber-optic cable may be a better choice.

Co-axial

Co-axial copper cables have an inner copper conductor and an outer copper shield, separated by a di-electric insulating material, to prevent signal losses as shown in Figure 5.2. This is encased within a protective outer jacket. The term coaxial comes from the inner conductor and the outer shield sharing a geometric axis. Compared to twisted-pair cable, coaxial cable is more resistant to electromagnetic interference (EMI), provides a higher bandwidth (the bandwidth is 80 times more than twisted pair cable.), and supports the use of longer cable lengths.

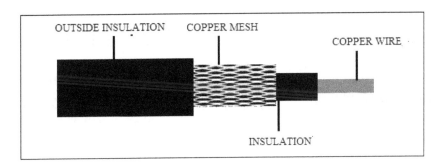

Figure 5.2 Co-axial copper cable

It is primarily used in cable TV networks and as trunk lines between telecommunication equipments.

- It serves as an internet access line from the home.

- It supports medium to High Data Rates

- It has much better immunity to noise and hence signal strength is retained for longer distances than in copper twisted pair media.

There are two main types of coaxial cables viz. thinnet and thicknet. Thinnet, also known as 10Base2, was commonly used to connect systems to backbone trunks of thicknet cabling. Thinnet can span distances of 189 meters and provide throughput up to 10 Mbps. Thicknet, also known as 10Base9, can span 900 meters and provide throughput up to 10 Mbps (megabits per second). The most common problems with coax cable are as follows.

- Bending the coax cable past its maximum arc radius and thus breaking the center conductor.

- Deploying the coax cable in a length greater than its maximum recommended length (which is 189 meters for 10Base2 or 900 meters for 10Base9)

- Not properly terminating the ends of the coax cable with a 90 ohm resistor

Fiber Optical Cables

Here, information is transmitted by propagation of optical signals (light) through fiber optic cables and not through electrical/electromagnetic signals. Due to this, fiber optics communication supports longer distances as there is no electrical interference. As the name indicates, fiber optic cables are made from glass (silica) and are as very thin as the human hair. They are coated with plastic also known as jacket.

As they support very high data rates, fiber optic lines are used as WAN backbone and trunk lines between data exchange equipments. They are also used for accessing internet from home through FTTH (Fiber-To-The-Home) lines. Additionally, they are used even for LAN environment with different LAN technologies like Fast Ethernet, Gigabit Ethernet etc. using optical links at the physical layer.

Fiber-optic cabling has higher transmission speeds that allow signals to travel over longer distances. Fiber cabling is not as affected by attenuation and EMI when compared to cabling that use copper. It does not radiate signals, as does UTP cabling, and is difficult to eavesdrop on; therefore, fiber-optic cabling is much more secure than UTP, STP, or coaxial.

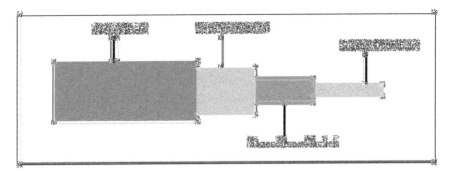

Figure 5.3 Fiber Optic Cable

Optical fiber consists of a core and a cladding layer, selected for total internal reflection due to the difference in the refractive index between the two which is shown in Figure 5.3. In practical fibers, the cladding is usually coated with a layer of acrylate polymer. This coating protects the fiber from damage but does not contribute to its optical waveguide properties. Individual coated fibers (or fibers formed into ribbons or bundles) then have a tough resin buffer layer and/or core tube(s) extruded around them to form the cable core. Several layers of protective sheathing, depending on the application, are added to form the cable. Rigid fiber assemblies sometimes put light-absorbing (dark) glass between the fibers, to prevent light that leaks out of one fiber from entering another. This reduces cross-talk between the fibers, or reduces flare in fiber bundle imaging applications. For indoor applications, the jacketed fiber is generally enclosed, with a bundle of flexible fibrous polymer *strength members* like aramid , in a lightweight plastic cover to form a simple cable. Each end of the cable may be terminated with a specialized optical fiber connector to allow it to be easily connected and disconnected from transmitting and receiving equipment.

For use in more strenuous environments, a much more robust cable construction is required. In *loose-tube construction* the fiber is laid helically into semi-rigid tubes, allowing the cable to stretch without stretching the fiber itself. This protects the fiber from tension during laying and due to temperature changes. Loose-tube fiber may be *dry block* or gel-filled. Dry block offers less protection to the fibers than gel-filled, but costs considerably less. Instead of a loose tube, the fiber may be embedded in a heavy polymer jacket, commonly called tight buffer construction. Tight buffer cables are offered for a variety of applications, but the two most common are Breakout and Distribution. Breakout cables normally contain a ripcord, two non-conductive dielectric strengthening members (normally a glass rod epoxy), an aramid yarn, and 3 mm buffer tubing with an additional layer of Kevlar surrounding each fiber. The ripcord is a parallel cord of strong yarn that is situated under the jacket(s) of the cable for jacket removal. Distribution cables have an overall Kevlar wrapping, a ripcord, and a 900 micrometer buffer coating surrounding each fiber. These *fiber units* are commonly bundled with additional steel strength members, again with a helical twist to allow stretching.

A critical concern in outdoor cabling is to protect the fiber from contamination by water. This is accomplished by use of solid barriers such as copper tubes, and water-repellent jelly or water-absorbing powder surrounding the fiber. Finally, the cable may be armored to protect it from environmental hazards, such as construction work or gnawing animals. Undersea cables are more heavily armored in their near-shore portions to protect them from boat anchors, fishing gear, and even sharks, which may be attracted to the electrical power that is carried to power amplifiers or repeaters in the cable. Modern cables come in a wide variety of sheathings and armor, designed for applications such as direct burial in trenches, dual use as power lines, installation in conduit, lashing to aerial telephone poles, submarine installation, and insertion in paved streets.

Cabling Considerations

Cables are extremely important within networks, and when they experience problems, the whole network can become problematic. This section addresses some of the common cabling issues that many networks experience.

Noise

Noise on a line is usually caused from the adjoining devices or from the environment. Noise can be produced by motors, computers, copy machines, fluorescent lighting, and microwave ovens. This background noise can combine with the data being transmitted over the cable and distort the signal.

Cabling Connection Types

Cables follow standards, for interoperability and connectivity between common devices and environments. The standards are developed and maintained by the Telecommunications Industry Association (TIA) and the Electronic Industries Association (EIA). The TIA/EIA standards enable the design and implementation of structured cabling systems for commercial buildings. The majority of the standards define cabling types, distances, connections, cable system architectures, cable termination standards and performance characteristics, cable installation requirements, and methods of testing installed cable. The following are commonly used physical interface connection standards.

- RJ-11 is used for terminating telephone wires,
- RJ-45 is used for terminating twisted-pair cables in Ethernet LAN, and
- BNC (British Naval Connector) is used for terminating coaxial cables.

Attenuation

Attenuation is the loss of signal strength while it propagates through the medium. The attenuation is more for a longer cable which causes the data signal to deteriorate. That is why standards suggest cable-run lengths. The effects of attenuation increase with higher frequencies. This means that cable used to transmit data at higher frequencies should have shorter cable runs to ensure attenuation does not become an issue.

Basically, the data are in the form of electrons, and these electrons have to swim through a copper wire. However, this is more like swimming upstream, because there is a lot of resistance on the electrons working in this media. After a certain distance, the electrons start to slow down and their encoding format loses form. If the form gets too degraded, the receiving system cannot interpret them any longer. If a network administrator needs to run a cable longer than its recommended segment length, network administrator needs to insert a repeater that will amplify the signal and ensure it gets to its destination in the right encoding format. Attenuation can also be caused by cable breaks and malfunctions. If a cable is suspected of attenuation problems, cable testers can inject signals into the cable and confirm the fault.

Crosstalk

Crosstalk is a phenomenon caused by the electric or magnetic fields of one communication channel spill over to the signals of adjacent channel. When the different electrical signals mix, the integrity of the signals degrades and data may get corrupted. In a telephone circuit, crosstalk can result in disturbing the hearing part of a voice conversation. It can occur in microcircuits within computers, audio equipment and within network circuits. UTP is much more vulnerable to crosstalk than STP or coaxial, because it does not have extra layers of shielding to protect against crosstalk.

Fire-rated and Flame-retardant Cables

Fire-resistive or fire-rated cable is a cable that will continue to operate in the presence of a fire. This is commonly known as circuit integrity (CI) cable. Some cables produce hazardous gases when on fire that would spread throughout the building quickly. Network cabling that is placed in these types of areas, referred as plenum space, must meet a specific fire rating to ensure it will not produce and release harmful chemicals in case of a fire.

Flame-retardant cable is a cable that will not convey or propagate a flame as defined by the flame-retardant or propagation tests. Flame-retardant tests measure flame propagation for both horizontal and vertical applications. There are also plenum cable flame tests when it is used in ducts, plenums or other spaces.

A flame-retardant cable is not a fire-rated cable. There are certain but specific differences between flame-retardant cables and fire-resistive cables. Flame-retardant cables resist the spread of fire into a new area, whereas fire-resistive cables maintain circuit integrity and continue to work for a specific time under defined conditions. These circuit integrity cables continue to operate in the presence of a fire and are sometimes called 1-hour or 2-hour fire-rated cables. CI cables are needed when it is most essential and critical for life safety or to prevent a plant shut down.

Depending upon the situation, while setting up a network, it is important to select the appropriate types of wire. Cables should be installed in unexposed areas so they are not easily tripped over, damaged, or eavesdropped upon. The cables should be strung behind walls and in the protected spaces as in dropped ceiling. In environments that require extensive security, wires are encapsulated within pressurized conduits so if someone attempts to access a wire, the pressure of the conduit will change, causing an alarm to sound and a message to be sent to the security men.

Note: A plenum is the air return path of a central air handling system. It can be either ductwork or open space over a suspended ceiling or raised floor.

5.4 UNGUIDED MEDIA

Unguided media are more commonly known as wireless media or unbounded media, in which data is transferred into electromagnetic waves and sent through free space without guiding any specific direction. Hence the name unguided media and are classified as wireless transmission which is a quickly expanding field of technology for networking. These are microwave, cellular radio, radio broadcast and satellite. As wireless technologies continue to proliferate, the organization's security efforts must go beyond locking down its local network. Security should be an end-to-end solution that addresses all forms, methods, and techniques of communication.

Different types of unguided communication are classified based on the frequency spectrum used for communication, the distance between the end stations and the type of encoding used for the communication. Broadband wireless signals occupy frequency bands that may be shared with microwave, satellite, radar, and ham radio use. Unguided communication allows electromagnetic signals to travel between antennas, some of which are on satellites. Antennas can provide point-to-point communication or can send their signals in all directions. These technologies are used for television transmissions, cellular phones, satellite transmissions, spying, surveillance, and garage door openers. The different unguided medias which are employed in distributed SCADA system are briefly explained below.

Microwaves Communication

In this kind the data is transferred via air. The waves travel in a straight line. The data is received and transferred via microwave stations. The speed at which data is transferred is 190 Mbps. The two main microwave wireless transmission technologies are satellite (ground to orbiter to ground) and terrestrial (ground to ground). They are widely used by telephone and cable companies.

Terrestrial communication

This type of communication is limited to line-of-sight (LOS) transmission. This means that microwaves are transmitted in a straight line and that no obstructions can exist, such as buildings or mountains, between microwave stations as shown in Figure 5.4. To avoid possible obstructions, microwave antennas often are positioned on the tops of buildings, towers, or mountains. It finds applications in long-distance telecommunication service. It requires fewer amplifiers or repeaters than coaxial cable but it is line-of-sight transmission. Short point-to-point links, Data link between local area network, closed-circuit TV, etc.

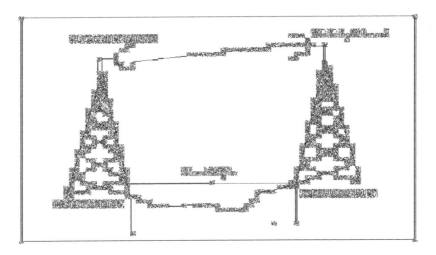

Figure 5.4 Terrestrial communication

Satellite communication

The satellites are located at a distance of 22300 miles above the earth as shown in Figure 5.5. The signals are received from earth stations. Devices like GPS and PDAs also receive signals from these earth based stations. The process of transferring and receiving data takes place within few seconds. The data is transferred at a speed of 1 Gbps. They are used for purposes like weather forecast, military communication, radio transmission, satellite TV, data transmission, etc.

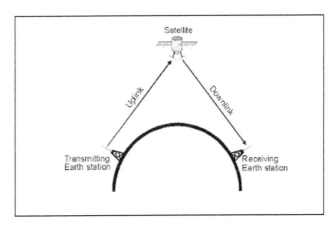

Figure 5.5 Satellite communication

Today the cost of satellite launching has brought down significantly with advanced and reusable launching modules. This made extensive use of satellite communication to provide wireless connectivity between different locations. But for two different locations to communicate via satellite links, they must be brought within the satellite's line-of-sight and area covered by the satellite called footprint. The information or data is appropriately modulated by the ground station and is transmitted to the satellite. A transponder on the satellite receives this signal, amplifies it, and relays it to the receiver. The receiver at the ground station must have an antenna, usually a circular dish like structure normally placed on top of buildings. The antenna contains one or more microwave receivers, depending upon how many satellites it is accepting data from. Satellites provide broadband transmission. If a user is receiving radio or TV data, then the transmission is set up as a one-directional network. If a user is using this connection for internet, then the transmission is set up as a bi-directional network. The available bandwidth depends upon the antenna, terminal type and the service rendered by the service provider.

As the satellites are kilometers above the Earth, time-critical applications may experience delay as the signal has to traverse to and from the satellite. Hence these types of satellites are placed into a low Earth orbit, keeping the distance between the ground stations and the satellites is less when compared to other types of satellites. Further, smaller receivers can be used for reception of signals, which makes low-Earth-orbit satellites ideal for cellular communication, radio and TV stations, Internet, etc.

Mobile communication

High frequency radio frequency (RF) waves are used for the transmission of data in mobile communication. Here one can receive and make calls and also access the internet. Earlier, when Gopi wanted to call Jessy, they had to depend on the telephone which had a physical connection. The telephone would only reach as far as the telephone cord that it was attached to, and the handset was also physically connected. So they actually had to sit in one place to carry out a conversation. This model worked for almost 100 years, but once mobile phones were materialized and available to everyone at a low price, there was no going back. Today mobile wireless communication has exploded with its popularity and capabilities.

Mobile phone is a device that can send voice and data over wireless radio links. It connects to a cellular network, which is connected to the Public-Switched Telephone Network (PSTN). So instead of a physical cord and connection that connects the phone and the PSTN, one should have a device which connects indirectly to the PSTN. Radio is the transmission of signals via electromagnetic waves within a certain frequency range. A cellular network distributes radio signals over delineated areas, called cells. Each cell has at least one fixed-location transceiver at base station, and is joined to other cells to provide connections over large geographic areas. So as somebody is talking on his mobile phone and he move out of range of one cell, the base station in the original cell sends his connection information to the next base station so that his call is not dropped and he can continue his conversation.

This switching from one cell to another cell, does not arise the requirements of an infinite number of frequencies to work with. Lots of people around the world may be using their cell phones simultaneously. All of these calls take place with a set of frequencies. An elementary representation of a cellular network is shown in Figure 5.6.

Individual cells can use the same frequency range, as long as they are not next to each other. So the same frequency range can be used in every other cell, which drastically decreases the amount of ranges required to support simultaneous connections. The communication service providers have to come up with different ways to allow millions of consumers to use this finite frequency range in a flexible manner.

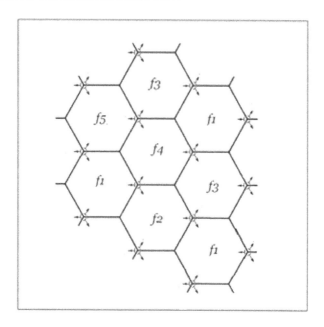

Figure 5.6 Non-adjoint cells can use the same frequency ranges

Presently, mobile wireless communication has been gradually made up of complex and powerful multiple access technologies, which are mentioned below.

- Frequency division multiple access (FDMA)

- Time division multiple access (TDMA)

- Code division multiple access (CDMA)

- Orthogonal frequency division multiple access (OFDMA)

The characteristics of each of these technologies are briefly described below as they are the foundational constructs of the various cellular network generations.

When the useful bandwidth of the medium exceeds the required bandwidth of a signal, Frequency division multiple access (FDMA) is a better solution. Here a number of signals can be carried simultaneously by modulating the signals into different carrier frequency with sufficient separation between them. In 3G FDMA, the available frequency range is divided into sub-bands called channels, and one channel is assigned to each cell phone. The subscriber has exclusive use of that channel while the call is made, or until the call is terminated, no other calls or conversations can be made on that channel during that call. Using FDMA, multiple users can share the frequency range without the risk of interference between the simultaneous calls. FMDA was used in the 1G.

When the achievable bit rate of the medium, exceeds the required data rate of a digital signal, Time Division Multiple Access (TDMA) is a better solution. TDMA increases the speed and efficiency of the cellular network by taking the RF spectrum channels and dividing them into time slots. In TDMA systems, time is divided into frames and each frame is divided into slots. TDMA requires information regarding starting and ending time of each slot which is known to both the source and the destination. Mobile communication systems such as Global System for Mobile Communication (GSM), Digital AMPS (D-AMPS), and Personal Digital Cellular (PDC) use TDMA.

As the term implies, CDMA is a form of multiplexing, which allows numerous signals to occupy a single transmission channel, optimizing the use of available bandwidth. It assigns a unique code to each voice call or data transmission to uniquely identify it from all other transmissions sent over the cellular network. In a CDMA spread spectrum network, calls are spread throughout the entire frequency band. CDMA permits all users of the network to simultaneously use every channel in the network. At the same time, a particular cell can simultaneously interact with multiple other cells. These features make CDMA a very powerful technology, for the mobile cellular networks that presently dominate the wireless space. It has improved voice and data communication capability and is more secure.

Orthogonal Frequency Division Multiple Access (OFDMA) is a combination of FDMA and TDMA. In former implementations of FDMA, the different frequencies for each channel were widely spaced to allow analog hardware to separate the different channels. In OFDMA, each of the channels is subdivided into a set of closely spaced orthogonal frequencies with narrow bandwidths (subchannels). Each of the different subchannels can be transmitted and received simultaneously in a Multiple Input and Output (MIMO) manner. The use of orthogonal frequencies and MIMO allows signal processing techniques to reduce the impacts of any interference between different subchannels and to correct for channel impairments, such as noise and selective frequency fading. Mobile wireless technologies have gone through a whirlwind of confusing generations. The first generation (1G) dealt with analog transmissions of voice-only data over circuit-switched networks. This generation provides a throughput of around 19.2 Kbps. The second generation (2G) allows for digitally encoded voice and data to be transmitted between wireless devices, like cell phones.

Mobile communication

The third-generation (3G) networks became available by incorporating FDMA, TDMA, and CDMA. In 3G, circuit switching is replaced by packet switching is the major achievement. The flexibility to support a great variety of applications and services are the other advantages of 3G. The modular design allows expandability, backward compatibility, and interoperability among mobile systems, global roaming, and internet services. 3G with more enhancements, referred to as 3.9G or mobile broadband, is taking place under the title of Third Generation Partnership Project (3GPP). 3GPP has a number of new technologies such as Enhanced Data Rates for GSM Evolution (EDGE), High-Speed Downlink Packet Access (HSDPA), CDMA2000, and Worldwide Interoperability for Microwave Access (WiMax). There are two competing technologies that fall under the umbrella of 4G, which are Mobile WiMax and Long-Term Evolution (LTE). A 4G system does not support traditional circuit-switched telephony service as 3G does, but works over a purely packet based network. 4G devices are IP-based and are based upon OFDMA.

Communication engineers and scientists have developed Fifth-Generation (5G) mobile communication. The standard requirements and implementation are expected to begin from 2020 onwards. Each of the different mobile communication generations has taken advantage of the improvement of hardware technology and processing power. The increase in hardware has allowed for more complicated data transmission between customers as more customers want to use mobile communications.

Table 5.2 illustrates some of the main features of the 1G through 5G networks. It is important to note that this table does not and cannot easily cover all the aspects of each generation. Earlier generations of mobile communication have considerable variability between countries. The variability was due to country-sponsored efforts before agreed-upon international standards were established. Various efforts between the ITU and countries have attempted to minimize the differences.

Table 5.2　Different characteristics of Mobile Technology

5.5　SCADA COMMUNICATION TECHNOLOGIES

SCADA communication technologies broadly classified into two viz. wired (guided) or wireless (unguided).

Wired or Guided Media Technologies

Wired or guided media technologies used in industrial SCADA and power system SCADA are Copper UTP, Coaxial, Optical Fiber, Power

Line Carrier Communication (PLCC), Broadband over Power line (BPL) and HomePlug. A brief description of these technologies is given below.

Copper UTP

Unshielded Twisted Pair (UTP) is a popular type of cable that consists of two unshielded wires twisted around each other which has been explained earlier in this chapter. Low cost makes it attractive, and is used extensively for local-area networks (LANs) and telephone connections. UTP cabling does not offer as high bandwidth or good protection from interference when compared to coaxial or fiber optic cables, but easier to work with.

Optical Fiber

Fiber cables offer several advantages over traditional long-distance copper cabling. The bandwidth for an optical fiber which has the same thickness that of a copper cable is much higher. Fiber cables rated at 10 Gbps, 40 Gbps and even 100 Gbps are standard. As light can travel much longer distances in a fiber cable without attenuation, the need for signal boosters are less. Further fiber is less susceptible to interference. Traditional copper network cable requires shielding to protect it from electromagnetic interference. Though shielding helps to prevent interference, it is not always sufficient especially, when many cables are strung together in close proximity to each other. But fiber optic cables which are made up of glass or silica avoid most of these problems.

Fiber to the home (FTTH)

Fiber to the Home (FTTH) broadband is one of the fine solutions for providing connectivity and presently it is generally referred as fiber optic cable connections to individual houses. It can deliver a large number of digital information including voice, video, and data with more efficiently and economically than coaxial cable. FTTH depend on both active and passive optical networks to provide connectivity. FTTH technology is supposed to be an apt standard which can provide connectivity without much web traffic congestion.

Hybrid Fiber Coax (HFC)

A hybrid fiber coaxial (HFC) network is a guided media technology where optical fiber cable and coaxial cable are used in different portions of a communication network to carry broadband information such as video, data, and voice. Using HFC, service providers install fiber optic cable as the backbone from the cable distribution center to the serving nodes located close to customers. Then using coaxial cables, connections are provided to the customers by connecting to the nodes of the fiber optic backbone. The main advantage of using HFC as backbone is that some of the features of fiber optic cable such as high bandwidth, improved noise immunity and interference susceptibility, etc. can be brought close to the customer premises without the replacement of the existing coaxial cable if it exists already.

Power Line Carrier Communication (PLCC)

Power-line carrier communication (PLCC) is a communication method that uses electrical wiring to simultaneously carry both data and electric power. Although many power utilities use this for longer distances to send data, it is very rarely used within the buildings. But recently PLCC is used to achieve load shedding in Advanced Metering Infrastructure (AMI). As it uses the existing power lines, there is no additional investment on cables and structural alterations to the building. It is an economical and a reliable technique to achieve bi-directional communications which is one of the prime requirements in Smart Grid.

Different PLCC technologies are required for different applications, ranging from home automation to internet access which is often called broadband over power lines (BPL). Most PLCC technologies limit themselves to one type of wire but some can cross between the distribution network and customer premises wiring. Typically transformers prevent propagating the signal, which requires multiple technologies to form very large networks. Various data rates and frequencies are used in different situations. But the main drawback is low bandwidth and point-to-point communication. Although long distance communication is possible, it poses significant challenges, especially in developing countries where the disturbances on transmission lines cause issues.

Broadband over Power Line (BPL)

PLCC can be broadly grouped as narrow band PLCC and broadband PLCC, also known as low frequency and high frequency respectively. There are four basic forms of PLCC and they are,

- Narrowband internal applications where home wiring is used for home automation and intercoms but with low bit rate,

- Narrowband outdoor applications which are mainly used by the power distribution utilities for AMR,

- Broadband in-house mains power wiring can be used for high speed data transmission for home networking, and Broadband over Power Line which uses outdoor mains power wiring and can be used to provide broadband internet.

Broadband PLCC works at higher frequencies. High data rates (up to 100s of Mbps) are used in shorter-range applications. In fact BPL is a system to transmit two-way data over existing AC medium voltage electrical distribution wiring, between transformers, and AC low voltage wiring between transformer and customer outlets. This makes it suitable for indoor as well as outdoor applications. This avoids the expense of a dedicated network of wires for data communication, and the expense of maintaining a dedicated network of antennas, radios and routers in wireless network.

HomePlug

HomePlug is a Power line networking which uses power line communications. The specification of Homeplug is defined by the home networking technology that connects devices to each other through the power lines within a home. HomePlug certified products connect PCs and other devices that use Ethernet, USB and 802.11 Wi-Fi technologies to the power line via a HomePlug bridge or adapter. Some products have HomePlug technology built-in. It is one of the cheapest forms of home networking and has a low start-up cost and minimal IT workload. It also will not have an adverse effect on home electric bills.

As consumers need to connect more devices, the need for high throughput connectivity has tremendously amplified. HomePlug technology enables electrical wires of homes to distribute broadband Internet, Ultra High Definition video streaming, virtual reality, digital music and smart energy applications. HomePlug hybrid networking products are used by consumers and service providers worldwide to provide both wired home networking connectivity and Wi-Fi extension throughout the home in dead spots and areas furthest from the router. Growing smart home trends will also continue to increase the strain on home networks and the need for a singular network for both entertainment and IoT products.

HomePlug adapters are available for advertising physical rates of 200Mbps, 900Mbps and 1Gbps. This claims more bandwidth than an ordinary broadband connection, and perfect for streaming HD videos, downloading large files and online gaming. One benefit of this high capacity is the ability for multiple simultaneous communication streams. In SCADA, PLCC is mainly used in PSS for tele-protection and tele-monitoring between electrical substations through power lines at high voltages, such as 110 kV, 220 kV, and 400 kV. But this can also be used by utilities for Energy Management Systems (EMS), fraud detection and network management, Advanced Metering Infrastructure (AMI), Demand Side Management (DSM), load control, and demand response (DR) etc.

Wireless or Unguided Media Technologies

Presently, the unguided or wireless technology has become the most thrilling area in communications and M2M networking. The advancement of wireless communication has revolutionized Industrial SCADA networks as well. Some of the wireless technologies which find applications in DCS and Smart Grid are Frequency Hopping Spread Spectrum (FHSS), 3G Cellular, Wi-Fi, WiMax, ZigBee, ZWave, and VSAT which are briefly described below.

IEEE and Wireless Standards

Standards are developed so that many different vendors can create various products that will work together seamlessly. Standards are usually developed on a consensus basis among the different vendors in a specific industry. The Institute of Electrical and Electronics Engineers (IEEE) develops standards for a wide range of technologies and wireless being one of them.

The 802.11 standard outlines how wireless clients and Access Points communicate, lays out the specifications of their interface, dictates how signal transmission should take place, and describes how authentication, association, and security should be implemented. IEEE created several task groups to work on specific areas within wireless communications. Each group had its own focus and was required to investigate and develop standards for its specific section. The letter suffixes indicate the order in which they were proposed and accepted. As an example, one of the members of the 802.11 family which specifies Wi-Fi is succinctly described below.

802.11b High Rate or Wi-Fi is an extension to 802.11 which applies to wireless LANS and provides 11 Mbps transmission in the 2.4 GHz band. 802.11b uses only Direct Sequence Spread Spectrum (DSSS). 802.11b is ratification to the original 802.11 standard, allowing wireless functionality comparable to Ethernet.

Wireless LAN products are being developed following the stipulations of this 802.11i wireless standard. Customers should review the certification issued by the Wi-Fi Alliance before buying wireless products as it assesses the systems against the 802.11i proposed standard.

Frequency Hopping Spread Spectrum (FHSS)

Frequency-hopping spread spectrum (FHSS) transmission is the repeated switching of frequencies during radio transmission to reduce interference and avoid interception. It is one of the better methods to counter eavesdropping, and to block jamming of telecommunications.

It also has the capability to minimize the effects of unintentional interference. In FHSS, the transmitter hops between available narrowband frequencies within a specified broad channel in a pseudo-random sequence known to both sender and receiver. A short burst of data is transmitted on the current narrowband channel, and then transmitter and receiver tune to the next frequency in the sequence for the next burst of data. In most systems, the transmitter will hop to a new frequency more than twice per second. As no channel is used for a long time, and the possibility of any other transmitter being in the same channel at the same time are low, FHSS is often used as a method to allow multiple transmitter and receiver pairs to operate in the same space, in the same channel, at the same time. Direct Sequence Spread Spectrum (DSSS) is a related technique. It also spreads a signal across a wide channel, but it does so, all at once, instead of in discrete bursts separated by hops. The spreading code has a higher chip rate, which results in a wideband time continuous scrambled signal. DSSS has certain advantages such as having the best discrimination against multipath signals, capability of effectively avoiding intentional interference like jamming, and better noise immunity than FHSS system.

The frequency hopping spread spectrum over a fixed-frequency transmission method has following primary advantages.

- The method is very resistant to narrow band interference since the spread signal causes the interfering signal to recede into the background.

- The signals are very difficult to intercept. FHSS signals seem like there has been an increase in background noise when a narrow band receiver detects them. In order to intercept the signal, the pseudorandom transmission hopping sequence has to be known.

- FHSS transmissions can share frequency bands with a number of other types of conventional transmissions without causing significant interference. Each of these signals causes minimal interference and allows the bandwidth to be used more effectively.

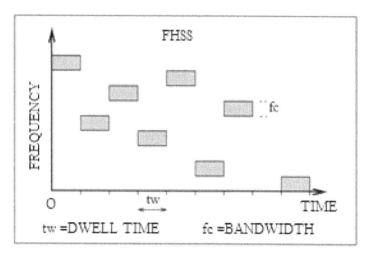

Figure 5.7 Changing carrier frequency at random

However FHSS faces certain disadvantages as it requires greater bandwidth than when a single carrier frequency is used. Also, one of the most problematic aspects of this technology is to initially synchronize the transmitter and receiver. Further significant time is required to master the process of synchronizing the transmitter and receiver.

Wi-Fi

Wi-Fi is based on IEEE 802.11 standard, a trademark for the open standards, is a popular Radio Frequency (RF) wireless networking technology to provide high-speed Internet and network connections. One can attain bandwidth from 9 to 94Mbps. The limited distance of 100 to 290m and poor reception in buildings are the main disadvantages. Wi-Fi networks have no physical wired connection between sender and receiver as it uses Radio Frequency technology. RF being a member of the electromagnetic spectrum associated with radio wave propagation (2.9GHz for 802.11b or 11g, 9GHz for 802.11a). The RF current supplied to an antenna creates an electromagnetic field which makes radio waves to propagate through space. The keystone of any wireless network is an Access Point (AP). The primary job of an AP is to broadcast a wireless signal that computers can detect and tune into. In order to connect to an AP and join a wireless network, computers and devices must be equipped with wireless network adapters.

Wi-Fi Alliance: Wi-Fi is supported by many applications and devices which include mobile phones, video game consoles, home area networks, PDAs, major operating systems, and many consumer electronic products. Any products that are tested and approved as *Wi-Fi Certified* by the Wi-Fi Alliance are interoperable each other, even if they are from different make and model. This implies, a consumer with a Wi-Fi Certified product can use any brand of access point with any other brand of client hardware which also Wi-Fi Certified. Products that pass this certification are required to carry an identifying seal on their packaging that states Wi-Fi Certified and indicates the radio frequency band used.

WiMax

WiMax stands for Worldwide Interoperability for Microwave Access, follows IEEE 802.16d communication standard. One can get up to 70 Mbps bandwidth over 70 to 80 kilometers. This bandwidth is a savoir when an environmental disaster strikes a densely populated area and all smart meters start communicating the outages at same time. WiMax can handle this increased traffic and because of this, WiMax can be an ideal backhaul medium for in-premise Wi-Fi and ZigBee devices. Higher cost and poor market adoption are major constraints at the moment and is not a replacement for Wi-Fi or wireless hotspot technologies. However, all-in-all, it can be cheaper to implement WiMax instead of standard wired hardware like with DSL.

WiMax equipment exists in two basic forms viz. base stations, installed by service providers to deploy the technology in a coverage area; and receivers, installed in clients. WiMax is developed by an industry consortium, overseen by a group called the WiMax Forum, who certifies WiMax equipment to ensure that it meets technology specifications. Its technology is based on the IEEE 802.16 set of wide-area communications standards. Presently deployments of WiMax are in fixed locations, but development of mobile version is underway.

WiMax can be installed faster than other internet technologies because it can use shorter towers and less cabling, supporting even non-line-of-sight (NLoS) coverage across an entire city or country. WiMax isn't just for fixed connections either, like at home. One can also subscribe to a WiMax service for his mobile devices since USB dongles, laptops and phones can have the technology built-in. In addition to internet access, WiMax can provide voice and video transferring capabilities as well as telephone access. Since WiMax transmitters can span a distance of several miles with data rates reaching up to 30-40 Megabits per Second (Mbps), it's easy to see its advantages, especially in areas where wired internet is impossible or too costly to implement.

However it has certain disadvantages as WiMax is wireless by nature, and they are briefed below.

1. WiMAX technology offering long distance data range which is 70 kilometer and high bit rate which is 70Mbit/s. But both features don't work together. Increasing the distance range will decrease the bit rate and increasing bit rate will reduce the distance range,

2. Any user closer to the tower can get high speed while user at the cell edge from the tower gets much diminished speed of connectivity,

3. Functionality could go down with sharing of bandwidth. if more than one user exists in a single sector and a range of 2- to 8 or 12 Mbps services cannot be ensured, then additional radio cards are added to the base station to boost the capability,

4. Susceptible to weather conditions like rain which could interrupt the signal and the wireless equipment could cause interference, and

5. WiMAX is very power intensive technology and requires strong electrical support.

ZigBee

It is a low cost and low power technology and uses unlicensed spectrum which covers only short distance. ZigBee is gaining popular in the home energy market and multiple ZigBee enabled products are available in the market. ZigBee enables the smart meter to communicate with home appliances which helps to shed the load. ZigBee technology enables the coordination of communication among thousands of tiny sensors, which can be scattered throughout the offices, farms, factories, picking up information about the operations and process. They are designed to consume very little energy because it will be left in place for five to ten years and their batteries need to last. ZigBee devices communicate efficiently, passing data over radio waves from one to the other like a human chain. At the end of the line, the data can be dropped into a computer for analysis or picked up by another wireless technology like Wi-Fi or WiMax.

ZigBee is constituted of mesh technology and this makes it more robust. ZigBee alliance has come up to ensure interoperability among home appliances but the limited distance and inability to penetrate concrete walls are major constraints. Further the low power consumption limits transmission distances to 10–100 meters line-of –sight, depending on power output and environmental characteristics. ZigBee devices can transmit data over long distances by passing data through a mesh network of intermediate devices to reach more distant ones. ZigBee is typically used in low data rate applications that require long battery life and secure networking. ZigBee networks are secured by 128 bit symmetric encryption keys. ZigBee has a defined rate of 290 kbit/s, best suited for intermittent data transmissions from a sensor or input device. ZigBee is an ideal solution for Personnel Area Netwoks. However, ZigBee is not for situations with high mobility among nodes. Hence, it is not suitable for tactical ad hoc radio networks in the battlefield, where high data rate and high mobility is present and needed.

ZWave

ZWave is a low cost, low power RF signalling and control protocol used for communication among devices preferably in home area networks. It is developed by a private company named Zensys, Inc. a start-up company based in Denmark. It's technology is based on the concepts of ZigBee. However ZWave attempts to build simpler and less expensive devices than ZigBee. Presently, Zensys is acquired by Sigma Designs of Milpitas, Camay manufacturers make ZWave compatible products, mostly for the building automation and HVAC. ZWave operates at 908.42 MHz in the US and 868.42 MHz in Europe using a mesh networking topology. A ZWave network can contain up to 232 nodes, although reports exist of trouble with networks containing over 30-40 nodes. ZWave operates using a number of profiles, but the manufacturer claims they interoperate. One should be careful when selecting products as some products from certain manufacturers are not compatible with other manufacturers' products.

ZWave uses GFSK modulation with Manchester channel encoding. A network controller, at the center monitors and controls the ZWave network. Each product in the home must be included to the ZWave network before it can be controlled via ZWave. Each ZWave network is identified by a Network ID and each device is further identified by a Node ID. The Network ID is the common identification of all nodes belonging to one logical ZWave network. Network ID has a length of four bytes and is assigned to each device by the primary controller when the device is added into the network. Nodes with different Network ID's cannot communicate with each other. The Node ID is the address of the device / node existing within network. The Node ID has a length of one byte. ZWave uses a source-routed mesh network topology and has central controller. Devices can communicate to one another by using intermediate nodes to route around and circumvent household obstacles or radio dead spots that might occur though a message called healing. A ZWave network can consist of up to 232 devices with the option of bridging networks if more devices are required.

ZWave Alliance: The ZWave Alliance was established as a consortium of companies that make connected appliances controlled through apps on smart phones, tablets or computers using ZWave wireless mesh networking technology. The alliance is a formal association focused on both the expansion of ZWave and the continued interoperability of any device that utilizes ZWave.

ZWave Security: Recently, ZWave Alliance announced stronger security standards for devices receiving ZWave Certification. The security standards are known as Security 2 (S2), it provides advanced security for devices to be connected to ZWave gateways and hubs. Encryption standards for transmissions between nodes, and mandates new pairing procedures for each device, with unique PIN on each device are established. The new layer of authentication is intended to prevent hackers from taking control of unsecured or poorly secured devices.

VSAT

This is widely used today for remote monitoring and control of transmission and distribution substations. It is a proven technology for quick implementation but relatively expensive. Major disadvantage is that severe weather will impacts its reliability. VSAT systems provide high speed, broadband satellite communications for Internet or private network communications. VSAT is ideal for remote monitoring and control such as off- shore wind farms, mining industry, vessels at sea, oil and gas camps or any application that requires a broadband Internet connection at a remote location.

Technically, a VSAT is a two-way satellite ground station with a dish antenna that is smaller than 3.8 meters. The majority of VSAT antennas range from 79cm to 1.2m. Data rates, usually, range from 4 Kbit/s up to 16 Mbit/s. VSATs access satellites in geosynchronous orbit or geostationary orbit to relay data from small remote Earth stations to other stations in mesh topology or master Earth station *hubs* in star topology. VSATs can be used to transmit both narrowband data and broadband data. It also uses portable, phased array antennas or mobile communication infrastructures.

5.6 SECURITY IN WIRELESS COMMUNICATIONS

Wireless communication is a rapidly expanding field of technologies for networking, connectivity, communication, and data exchange. There are literally thousands of protocols, standards, and techniques that can be labelled as wireless. These include cell phones, Bluetooth, cordless phones, and wireless networking. As wireless technologies continue to proliferate, the organization's security efforts must go beyond locking down its local network. Security should be an end-to-end solution that addresses all forms, methods, and techniques of communication. While managing network security with filtering devices such as firewalls and proxies is important, one must not overlook the need for endpoint security. Endpoints are the ends of a network communication link. One end is often at a server where a resource resides, and the other end is often a client making a request to use a network resource. Even with secured communication protocols, it is still possible for abuse, misuse, oversight, or malicious action to occur across the network because it originated at an endpoint. All aspects of security from one end to the other, often called *end-to-end security*, must be addressed. Any unsecured point will be discovered eventually and abused. Endpoint security is the security concept that encourages administrators to install firewalls, malware scanners, and IDS on every host.

➢ Endpoint Threat Detection and Response (ETDR)

Endpoint security is the concept that each individual device must maintain local security whether it is a network or telecommunications channels. In a modest way it can be referred as the protection of an organization's network when accessed via remote devices such as laptops or other wireless or mobile devices. Sometimes this is expressed as the end device which is responsible for its own security. However, a clearer perspective is that any weakness in a network, whether on the border, on a server, or on a client, presents a risk to all elements within the organization. Traditional security has depended on the network border sentries, such as appliance firewalls, proxies, centralized virus scanners, and even IDS/IPS/IDP solutions, to provide security for all of the interior nodes of a network. This is no longer considered best business practice because threats exist from internal and external. A network is secure as the security of the weakest element. Lack of internal security is even more problematic when remote access services, including dial-up, wireless, and VPN, might allow an external entity (authorized or not) to gain access to the private network without having to go through the border security gauntlet. Endpoint security should therefore be viewed as an aspect of the effort to provide sufficient security on each individual host. Every system should have an appropriate combination of a local host firewall, antimalware scanners, authentication, authorization, auditing, spam filters, and IDS/IPS services.

Endpoint Threat Detection and Response (ETDR) mainly focus on the endpoint threats. It includes incident response and collection of tools mainly used for detection and incident response.

Transparency

Just as the name implies, transparency is the characteristic of a service, security control, or access mechanism that ensures that it is unseen by users. Transparency is often a desirable feature for security controls. The more transparent a security mechanism is, the less likely a user will be able to circumvent it or even be aware that it exists. With transparency, there is a lack of direct evidence that a feature, service, or restriction exists, and its impact on performance is minimal. In some cases, transparency may need to function more as a configurable feature than as a permanent aspect of operation, such as when an administrator is troubleshooting, evaluating, or tuning a system's configurations. A security boundary can be the division between two secured areas, or it can be the division between a secured area and an unsecured area. But both must be addressed in a security policy. In the simplest sense a transparent device should perform the exact function for which it is designed but not carry out any other functions.

Redundancy in SCADA

In order to make the industrial SCADA systems most reliable, it is necessary to have redundancy built into the SCADA. Satellite Communications not only provide a feasible means for distributed SCADA communication but also for redundancy for SCADA as a whole. Given the rate at which the cost for satellite communications is dropping and the available bandwidth is increasing, satellite communications infrastructure can be deployed along with conventional broadband technologies which are used in urban areas. Also, given the fact that satellite communications may not be used most of the time in urban areas, except for times when the main infrastructure goes down.

Satellite communications is found very useful in providing redundancy in SCADA especially when employed in Power System SCADA. One of the advantages is that it does not require much terrestrial equipment. The only equipment required to establish communications are the VSATs and modems. The main advantage of employing the satellite communication is that even during the adverse weather conditions or disasters like floods, systems like cable and Wi-Fi fail because of wires or repeaters being knocked down, satellite communications would still continue to function. This is especially important since utilities might need to know the field conditions of the distributed plant or process during such times, to find faults or problems in the industry and fix the solutions.

VSATs can be run on backup batteries, if the main source of its power goes down and still continue to relay information to the utilities. In this respect satellite communications is the only technology that can efficiently deliver the results during times of disasters and rough weather conditions. One of the fears in the past is the poor satellite communications connectivity during thick cloud cover or during rains or heavy snow.

Summary

This chapter has focused on various communications technological aspects of the industrial SCADA with an emphasis on DCS. It begins with discussing various types of transmission technology in very modest way so that it is very apt and most essential for a power engineer who is engaged in the design and implementation of SCADA and Smart Grid. The chapter then discusses the guided and unguided media used today for communication in such a manner that it is very useful for a practicing communication professional, which includes the various cabling issues as well. Various but most relevant communication technologies, which find space not only in industrial SCADA but also in other smart automation technologies today, are discussed comprehensively. Finally the chapter focused on the security issues of the wireless communication technology.

CHAPTER SIX
ICS AND SCADA PROTOCOLS

6.1 INTRODUCTION

To obtain full functionality in ICS, especially in Distributed Control System it needs appropriate protocols for transmitting data between its components effectively and securely. SCADA, being the heart and brain of the Industrial Automation and Smart Grid, standardized and interoperable SCADA protocols are very much needed for their efficient and smooth operation. The old SCADA communication protocols such as Modbus RTU, Profibus and Conitel are though widely adopted and used; they are vendor specific. Standard protocols which are becoming prevalent today are IEC 61850, IEC 60870-5-101 or 104, and DNP3. These communication protocols are standardized and adopted by almost all major SCADA vendors. Many of these protocols are now considerably modified and contain extensions to operate over TCP/IP as well. However it is a good security engineering practice to avoid connecting SCADA systems to the Internet so that the attack surface can be considerably reduced. RTUs and other automatic controller devices were being developed before the advent of industry wide standards for interoperability. This results in multitude of control protocols. This chapter is dedicated to explain various protocols which are relevant to SCADA and DCS environment with an emphasis on cyber-security.

6.2 EVOLUTION OF SCADA PROTOCOLS

SCADA protocols evolved out of the need to send and receive data and control information locally and over distances in deterministic time. Deterministic in this context refers to the ability to predict the amount of time required for a transaction to take place when all relevant factors are known and understood. To accomplish communication in deterministic time for applications in ICS and DCS systems, manufactures developed their own protocols and communication bus structure. Profibus of Siemens and Modbus of Modicon which is presently owned by Schneider Electric are typical examples. Since all the protocols are proprietary, interoperability became a major challenge. This made the control industries and standards organizations to develop open SCADA protocols for control systems which would be non-proprietary and not exclusive to one manufacturer. Further as the Internet gained popularity, manufactures started incorporating the protocols and tools which are developed Internet such as TCP/IP series of protocols and Internet browsers. In addition, manufactures and open standards organizations modified the highly popular and efficient Ethernet LAN technology for use in implementing data acquisition and control networks.

De jure standards are developed by national and International standards development organizations such as ANSI, IEEE, NIST, IEC, etc. Many de facto industrial standards are made de jure, after appropriate evaluation. Modbus is one of the typical such SCADA communication protocol extensively deployed today. The following sections discuss a few of the popular communication protocols used in DCS scenario. ICCP (IEC 60870-6) is the international standard for one control center to communicate with another control center of Power System SCADA. For communication from master stations to substations DNP3 is used in North America and IEC T-101 serial and T-104 (TCP/IP) are used in Europe. For communication between field equipment, IEC 61850, DNP3 (IEEE1815) and Modbus are developed.

6.3 SCADA COMMUNICATION PROTOCOLS

As explained above, the use of international open protocol standards are now recognized throughout the industry especially in electric utility as a key to successful integration of the various parts of the electric utility enterprise. Benefits of open systems include longer expected system life, investment protection, upgradeability and expandability, and readily available third-party components. The following sections elaborate some of the important communication protocols which are presently used by many industries and power utilities.

Distributed Network Protocol (DNP) 3.0

DNP3 is extensively used in many industries in automation like electricity, oil and gas, and water. It is popular and extensively used in the United States of America, Canada, South America, Australia, and parts of Asia and Africa. It is a set of an open SCADA protocol that is used for serial or IP communication between control devices and initially developed by Westronics in Calgary, Alberta, Canada. DNP3 is mainly used between components in process automation systems especially in SCADA systems employed in electric and water companies, but usage in other industries is not common. It has larger data frames and can carry larger RTU messages, and is very much useful for communications between various types of data logging and control devices such as Remote Terminal Units (RTUs), Data Concentrators and Intelligent Electronic Devices (IEDs). It is specifically designed to achieve reliability and efficiency when used in real-time data transfer. Another feature is that it supports time-stamped data communications between a master station and RTUs or IEDs or Phasor Measurement Units (PMU).

DNP3 faces the similar cyber-security problems as IEC 60870-5-104[T-104] is explained in subsequent sections. Scrutiny made by security engineers for integrity in DNP3 revealed that it lacks authentication and encryption. The DNP3 function codes and data types are well known, hence it can be easy to manipulate and compromise a DNP3 communication session.

Protocol Architecture of DNP3

DNP3 is based on the Enhanced Performance Architecture (EPA) and uses the frame format FT3 specified by IEC 60870-5. The lower layers of physical and data link defining the communication between devices are similar to IEC 60870-5-101 and the higher levels of data units and functionality are different. DNP3 uses cyclic redundancy check for error detection.

The DNP3 protocol structure uses the basic three layer EPA model with some added functionality. It adds an additional layer named the pseudo-transport layer. The pseudo-transport layer is a combination of network and transport layer of the Open Systems Interconnection (OSI) model and also includes some functions of the data link layer. Network function is concerned with the routing and data flow over the network from sender to receiver. Transport function includes proper delivery of the message from sender to receiver, message sequencing, and corresponding error correction. This function of a transport layer is limited when compared to the OSI layer, and hence the name pseudo-transport layer, as shown in Figure 6.1.

OSI MODEL	DNP3 (Distributed Network Protocol 3.0)
	USER DEFINED PROCESS APPLICATION FUNCTIONS
APPLICATION LAYER	APPLICATION LAYER (ASDUs)
SESSION LAYER	
PRESENTATION LAYER	
TRANSPORT LAYER	PSEUDO-TRANSPORT LAYER
NETWORK LAYER	
DATA LINK LAYER	DATA LINK LAYER
PHYSICAL LAYER	PHYSICAL LAYER

Figure 6.1 DNP3 and OSI model layers

Modbus

Modbus is a request-response serial communications protocol implemented using a master-slave relationship. In a master-slave relationship, communication always occurs in pairs. Which means one device (the slave) must initiate a request and then wait for a response, and the initiating device (the master) is responsible for initiating every interaction is shown in Figure 6.2. Typically, the master is a Human Machine Interface (HMI) or SCADA server and the slave is a sensor, RTU, PLC, or Programmable Automation Controller (PAC). The content of these requests and responses, and the network layers, across which these messages are sent, are defined by the different layers of the protocol.

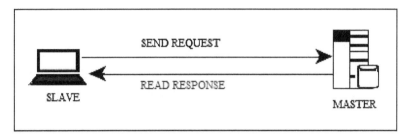

Figure 6.2 A Master-Slave Networking Relationship

Modbus is originally published by Modicon which is presently owned by Schneider Electric for use in their PLCs. Modbus being simple and robust, become a de facto standard communication protocol. It is now commonly available and used for connecting industrial electronic devices in ICS. The main reasons for the use of Modbus in the industrial environment are,

1. developed with industrial applications in mind,

2. openly published and royalty-free,

3. easy to deploy and maintain, and

4. moves raw bits or words without placing many restrictions on vendors.

Modbus enables communication among many devices connected to the same network, for example, a system that measures temperature and humidity and communicates the results to a computer. Modbus is often used to connect a supervisory computer with RTUs in SCADA systems. Many of the data types are named from its use in driving relays: a single-bit physical output is called a coil, and a single-bit physical input is called a discrete input or a contact.

The development and update of Modbus protocols has been managed by the Modbus organization, since Schneider Electric transferred rights to that organization. The Modbus organization is an association of users and suppliers of Modbus-compliant devices that seek to drive the adoption and evolution of Modbus. The different versions of the Modbus protocol which are presently used are,

1. Modbus RTU

2. Modbus ASCII

3. Modbus TCP/IP or Modbus TCP,

4. Modbus over UDP,

5. Modbus over TCP/IP or Modbus over TCP or Modbus RTU/ IP ,

6. Modbus over UDP Modbus Plus (Modbus+, MB+ or MBP) ,

7. Pemex Modbus , and

8. Enron Modbus.

Among these Modbus RTU, Modbus ASCII, and Modbus TCP/IP or Modbus TCP are the most popular versions. A brief description and the frame format of these versions are summarized below.

1. *Modbus RTU:* This is the most common implementation available for Modbus and is used in serial communication by making use of a compact, binary representation of the data for protocol communication. The RTU format follows the commands/data with a Cyclic Redundancy Check (CRC) checksum as an error check mechanism to ensure the reliability of data. A Modbus RTU message must be transmitted continuously without inter-character hesitations. Modbus messages are framed (separated) by idle (silent) periods. A Modbus frame is composed of an Application Data Unit (ADU), which encloses a Protocol Data Unit (PDU).

    1. ADU = Address + PDU + Error check,

    2. PDU = Function code + Data.

Modbus RTU frame format (primarily used on 8-bit asynchronous lines like EIA-485) and can be represented as shown below.

Start	Address	Function	Data	CRC	End
28 bits	8 bits	8 bits	n x 8 bits	16 bits	28 bits

2. *Modbus ASCII:* This is used in serial communication and makes use of ASCII characters for protocol communication. The ASCII format uses a longitudinal redundancy checksum. Modbus ASCII frame format (primarily used on 7- or 8-bit asynchronous serial lines) is given below.

Start	Address	Function	Data	LRC	End
8 bits	16 bits	16 bits	n x 2 bits	16 bits	16 bits

3. *Modbus TCP/IP or Modbus TCP:* This is a Modbus variant used for communications over TCP/IP networks, connecting over port 502. It does not require a checksum calculation, as lower layers already provide checksum protection. Modbus TCP frame format is given below.

Transaction identifier	Protocol identifier	Length field	Unit identifier	Function code	Data bytes
16 bits	16 bits	16 bits	8 bits	8 bits	n bits

One of the other Modbus variants gaining popularity is the Modbus plus. It is a proprietary to Schneider Electric and unlike the other variants, it is a high speed peer to peer network protocol based on token passing communication. It requires a dedicated co-processor to handle fast HDLC-like token rotation. It uses twisted pair at 1 Mbit/s and includes transformer isolation at each node, which makes it transition/edge-triggered instead of voltage/level-triggered. Special hardware is required to connect Modbus Plus to a computer, typically a card made for the ISA, PCI or PCMCIA bus.

In Modbus, data transactions are traditionally stateless, making them highly resistant to disruption from noise. It requires minimal recovery information at either end. Programming operations, on the other hand, expect a connection-oriented approach. This was achieved on the simpler variants by an exclusive login token, and on the Modbus Plus variant by explicit Program Path capabilities which maintained a duplex association until explicitly broken down. The main reason why the connection-oriented TCP/IP protocol is used is to keep control of an individual transaction by enclosing it in a connection, which can be identified, supervised, and cancelled without requiring specific action on the part of the client and server applications. This gives the mechanism of wide tolerance to network performance changes, and allows security features such as firewalls and proxies to be easily added. The other versions of Modbus are briefly explained below.

1. *Modbus over UDP:* Modbus over UDP on IP networks removes the overheads required for TCP.

2. *Enron Modbus:* This is another extension of standard Modbus developed by Enron Corporation with support for 32-bit integer and floating-point variables and historical and flow data. Data types are mapped using standard addresses.

3. *Pemex Modbus:* This is an extension of standard Modbus with support for historical and flow data. It was designed for the Pemex oil and gas company for use in process control but never gained widespread adoption.

Data model and function calls are identical for the Modbus RTU, Modbus ASCII, Modbus TCP/IP, and Modbus over UDP variants, but the encapsulation is different. However the variants are not interoperable.

Modbus Limitations

1. Modbus protocol does not provide any security against unauthorized commands.

2. Modbus was designed and developed initially for the communication with the PLC. Hence the number of data types was limited to those which understood by PLCs at that time.

3. No standard way exists for a node to find the description of a data object, such as determining whether a register value represents a temperature between T_1 and T_2 degrees.

4. Since Modbus is a master-slave protocol, there is no way for a field device to *report by exception*. As a result the master node must routinely poll each field device and look for changes in the data. This consumes considerable bandwidth and network time in applications.

5. Modbus is restricted to addressing 254 devices on one data link, which limits the number of field devices that may be connected to a master station.

6. Modbus transmissions must be contiguous, which limits the types of remote communications devices to those that can buffer data to avoid gaps in the transmission.

Attacks on the DNP3 and Modbus

As the original focus while developing these protocols was not security rather efficiency, Modbus and DNP3 virtually have no security measures incorporated. The lack of authentication in Modbus means that remote terminals accept commands from any machine that appears to be a master. The lack of integrity checking or encryption allows messages to be intercepted, changed and forwarded. In fact it is susceptible to Man In The Middle attack (MITM) which is most perilous in ICS and DCS which control critical infrastructure. For DNP3, message from an outstation can easily be spoofed, making it appear to be unavailable to the master. It is also common that passwords may be sent across the network in clear text. Though the DNPSecure has been developed, deployment is difficult as most of the systems using DNP3 are in the Critical Infrastructure domain, where downtime is very crucial and almost not feasible.

Modbus protocol is highly vulnerable to attacks like response and measurement injection, and command injection. A scrutiny on Modbus protocol with various levels of injection attacks ranging from naïve injection to complex injections targeting specific fields and values based on domain knowledge. Possible consequences are irregular sensor measurements, altered system control schemes and altered circuit breaker status. This can result in partial communication disruption to complete shutdown of the device

Profibus

Profibus is an open standard, serial, smart field-bus technology widely used in time-critical control and data acquisition systems. It can provide data transmission rates of 31 Kbps, 1Mbps, and 2,5 Mbps in the physical layer. It provides determinism for real-time control applications and supports multimaster communication networks.

Profibus uses the bus topology. In this topology, a central line, or bus, is wired throughout the system. Devices are attached to this central bus. One bus eliminates the need for a full-length line going from the central controller to each individual device. In the past, each Profibus device had to connect directly to the central bus. Technological advancements, however, have made it possible for a new *two-wire* system. In this topology, the Profibus central bus can connect to a ProfiNet Ethernet system. In this way, multiple Profibus buses can connect to each other.

Profibus devices which are connected to a central line can communicate information in an efficient manner which can go beyond the automation messages. Profibus devices can also participate in self-diagnosis and connection diagnosis. At the most basic level, Profibus benefits from superior design of its OSI layers and basic topology. There are three versions of Profibus, which are summarized below.

Profibus Process Automation (PA)

Profibus PA is a protocol designed for Process Automation. In fact, Profibus PA is a type of Profibus DP (Decentralized Peripherals) application profile. It connects data acquisition and control devices on a common serial bus and support reliable, intrinsically safe implementations. It also provides power to field devices through the bus. Profibus PA standardizes the process of transmitting measured data. It does hold a very important unique characteristic. Profibus PA was designed specifically for use in hazardous environments. Profibus uses the basic functions and extensions available in Profibus DP.

In most environments, Profibus PA operates over RS485 twisted pair media. This media, along with the PA application profile supports power over the bus. In explosive environments, though, that power can lead to sparks that induce explosions. To handle this, Profibus PA can be used with Manchester Bus Powered technology (MBP). The MBP media was designed specifically to be used in Profibus PA. It permits transmission of both data and power. The stepping down of power, reduces, or nearly eliminates, the possibility of explosion. Buses using MBP can reach 1900 meters and can support branches.

Profibus Factory Automation (Decentralized Peripherals-DP)

The second type of Profibus is more universal which is referred as Profibus DP, for Decentralized Periphery, this new protocol is much simpler and faster. Profibus DP is most popular and has an overwhelming majority of Profibus application today. It uses different physical layer standards than those employed by Profibus PA. Application profiles allow users to combine their requirements for a specific solution. Profibus DP itself has three separate versions. Each version, from DP-V0 to DP-V1 and DP-V2, provides newer, more complicated features such as diagnostics, alarm messaging, and parameterization.

Profibus Fieldbus Message Specification (FMS)

The initial version of Profibus was Profibus FMS, Fieldbus Message Specification. Profibus FMS was designed to communicate between Programmable Controllers and PCs, sending complex information between them. Unfortunately, being the initial effort of Profibus designers, the FMS technology was not as flexible as needed. This protocol was not appropriate for less complex messages or communication on a wider and complicated network. Though it offers a large number of functions and is, generally, more complicated to implement than Profibus PA or Profibus DP. New types of Profibus would satisfy those needs. Profibus FMS is still in use today, though the vast majority of users find newer solutions to be more appropriate.

A comparison of the three Profibus versions is given in Figure 6.3 below.

Profibus PA	Profibus DP	Profibus FMS
Intrinsic safety, Reliable, Bus Powered, Process Applications	High speed, Decentralized Applications	General Automation, Large number of Application

Figure 6.3 Profibus Versions

Communication Architecture of Profibus

Figure 6.4 illustrate the communication architecture of the Profibus versions and shows their relationships in the OSI seven layer model.

OSI MODEL	Profibus PA	Profibus DP	Profibus FMS
Application Layer	application layer not used	application layer not used	application layer field bus message specification
Session Layer			
Presentation Layer			
Transport Layer			
Network Layer			
Data Link Layer			
Data Link Layer	data link layer IEC interface	data link layer fieldbus data link	data link layer fieldbus data link
Physical Layer	physical layer IEC 61158-2	physical layer eia-485, fiber optics, radio waves	physical layer EIA-485, fiber optics, radio waves

Figure 6.4 Profibus PA, DP, and FMS layered protocols

Profibus systems can have three types of physical media. The first is a standard twisted-pair wiring system, in this case RS485. Two more advanced systems are also available. Profibus systems can now operate using fiber-optic transmission in cases where that is more appropriate. A safety-enhanced system called Manchester Bus Power, or MBP, is also available in situations where the chemical environment is prone to explosion. The physical layers can also use either the EIA-485 standard or the IEC 61158-2 standard. If desired, all three Profibus versions can use the same bus line if they employ EIA-485 in the physical layer. However, if the application requires intrinsically safe circuitry, IEC 61158-2 operates at 31.25Kbps.

IEC 60870-5-101/103/104

IEC 60870 was introduced by the IEC Technical Committee 57 and widely used in ICS and DCS communication. It is mainly popular in Europe and China and suitable for controlling electric power transmission grids and other geographically widespread ICS. This is an open protocol originally written for serial communication and was released in 1995. The IEC 60870-5-104 standard, released in 2000, present a combination of the application layer of IEC 60870-5-101 and the transport functions provided by TCP/IP. Presently this is widely used in SCADA and DCS communication protocol especially for monitoring and controlling of remote field locations of DCS especially in electrical grids. The structure of IEC 60870-5 standard is hierarchical and has six parts, each having different sections, and has four companion standards. Main part of the standard defines the fields of application, whereas the companion standards elaborate the information regarding the application field by specific details. These companion standards may be referred as T-101, T-102, T-103, and T-104, where T stands for Telecontrol. The five documents specify the base IEC 60870-5 Tele-control equipment and systems. The six sections of Part 5 of the IEC 60870-5 are described below.

1. IEC 60870-5-1 Transmission Frame Formats

2. IEC 60870-5-2 Data Link Transmission Services

3. IEC 60870-5-3 General Structure of Application Data

4. IEC 60870-5-4 Definition and Coding of Information Elements

5. IEC 60870-5-5 Basic Application Functions

6. IEC 60870-5-6 Guidelines for conformance testing for the IEC 60870-5 companion standards

7. IEC TS 60870-5-7 Security extensions to IEC 60870-5-101 and IEC 60870-5-104 protocols (applying IEC 62351)

IEC 60870-5-101 [T-101]

An Enhanced Performance Architecture (EPA) based architecture released by IEC in the beginning of 90s, which found extensive acceptance in power system SCADA. It is a master slave communication for multi-drop or bus topology. It polls data by cyclic polling technique using the data link layer and use parity check as well as checksum error detection techniques. The data error is decreased by these checks in IEC 60870 protocols. This standard is widely used in power system communications for telecontrol, teleprotection, and associated telecommunications. The application function of T-101 includes station initiation, parameter loading, data acquisition, cyclic data transmission, clock synchronization, etc. for a remote substation. This is completely compatible with IEC 60870-5-1 to IEC 60870-5-5 standards and uses standard asynchronous serial telecontrol channel interface between master and slave. The standard is suitable for multiple configurations like point-to-point, star, multidropped etc. The specific features of IEC 608705-101 are described below.

1. Both master initiated and master/slave initiated modes of data transfer are available,

2. It functions based on Link address and Application Service Data Unit (ASDU) bit,

3. ASDU addresses are provided for classifying the end station,

4. Data can be classified into different information objects and each information object is provided with a specific address,

5. Capability to assigning priority to the data before transmitting the data,

6. Option of classifying the data into 16 different groups to get the data according to the group by issuing specific group interrogation commands from the master,

7. Capability for time synchronization, and

8. Various schemes for data transfer are available which is very much useful in IED's to transfer the SoE and disturbance files for fault analysis.

IEC 60870-5-103 [T-103]

This is a master-slave standard protocol based on the EPA architecture and is mainly used to couple the central unit to several protection devices and is primarily used in the energy sector. The standard is especially designed for the communication with protection devices and therefore difficult to adapt it to other applications. It defines a companion standard that enables interoperability between protection equipment and devices of a control system in a substation. It handles protection functions as status indications of circuit breakers, types of fault, trip signals, auto-reclosure, relay pickup, etc. The device complying with this standard can send the information using two methods for data transfer - either using the explicitly specified ASDU or using generic services for transmission of all the possible information. The standard supports some specific protection functions and provides the vendor a facility to incorporate its own protective functions on private data ranges. IEC 60870-5-103 is mostly used for comparatively slow transmission media with RS232 and RS485 interfaces. Connection via optical fiber is also covered by the standard. The transmission speed in general is specified with a maximum of 19200 Baud.

IEC 60870-5-104 [T-104]

IEC 60870-5-104 [T-104] protocol is a standard for telecontrol equipment and systems with coded bit serial data transmission in TCP/IP based networks for monitoring and controlling geographically widespread processes. It is an extension of IEC 101 protocol suitable for networked circumstances with the changes in transport, network, link and physical layer services to suit the complete network access. The standard uses an open TCP/IP interface to network to have connectivity to the Local Area Network (LAN) and routers with different facility used to connect to the Wide Area Network (WAN). Within TCP/IP various network types can be utilized including X.25, Frame Relay, ATM, ISDN, Ethernet and serial point to point (X.21), Application layer of IEC 104 is preserved same as that of IEC 101 with some of the data types and facilities which are not used. There are two separate link layers defined in the standard, which is suitable for data transfer over Ethernet and serial line Point-to-Point Protocol (PPP). The control field data of IEC104 contains various types of mechanisms for effective handling of network data synchronization.

Unfortunately, by design itself the security of IEC 104 is problematic, same as many of the other contemporary SCADA protocols developed. IEC Technical Committee (TC) 57 have published a security standard IEC 62351, which implements end-to-end encryption which would prevent such attacks as replay, man-in-the-middle and packet injection. However due to the increase in complexity and cost, vendors are reluctant to include this security features on their ICS networks.

Protocol Architecture of IEC 60870-5

Protocol Architecture of IEC 60870 is based on Enhanced Performance Architecture (EPA) model. The EPA model has three layers viz. Physical, Data Link and Application layers. An user layer is added to the top of the EPA model to provide the interoperability between equipments in a telecontrol system. This four layer model is used for T-101, and T-103 companion standards. For companion standard T-104, which is the network adaptation, some additional layers are included from the OSI model. These are network and transport layers that are essential for the networked architecture. This networked architecture is useful for the transportation of data and messages over the network. Thus a non networked version is used for T-101, T-103, and the networked version for T-104, as shown in Figure 6.5. It may be noted that the lower four layers of T-104 are now the TCP/IP suite for networking applications.

OSI model	T-101, T-103 (EPA with user defined process functions)	T-104- EPA with network and transport with user defined process functions
	User defined process application functions	User defined process application functions
Application layer	Application layer (ASDUs)	Application layer (ASDUs)
Session layer		
Presentation layer		
Transport layer		TCP/IP transport and network protocol suite
Network layer		TCP/IP transport and network protocol suite
Data link layer	Data link transmission procedures and frame formats	TCP/IP transport and network protocol suite
Physical layer	Physical interface specification	

Figure 6.5 Communication layers of IEC 60870-5

Attacks on IEC 60870-5

SCADA StrangeLove is an independent group of cyber-security engineers founded in 2012, focused exclusively on security assessment of ICS and SCADA. They could successfully prove detection of an IEC 60870 device on a SCADA network. They also released python scripts which can identify and return the common address of an IEC 60870 device. The common address is an address used for all data contained within the IEC 60870-5 packet, used to identify the physical device. With the help of these existing scripts it is possible to scan an ICS/DCS network for any specific IEC 60870 hosts. Once investigation became successful, the scripts could be used to detect possible targets for a Man in the Middle (MITM) attack. Further improperly terminated VPN running on IEC 60870-5 protocols is highly susceptible to DoS attacks, hence end node security issue has to be sorted out with utmost care, else can be catastrophic.

IEC 61850

Multiple protocols exist for electrical substation automation, which include many proprietary protocols with custom communication links. Interoperation of devices from different vendors is a need of the hour in power system automation, as it would be indeed an advantage to the designers of substation automation. This brought a need for a robust interoperable standard to serve the power system SCADA. This requirement has been attended by a group of about 60 members from different countries worked in three IEC working groups from 1995 and created IEC 61850 which accomplished the following objectives.

1. A single protocol for complete substation automation considering all different data transfer requirement,

2. Definition of basic services required to data transfer,

3. Provide high inter-operability between systems from different vendors,

4. A common method/format for storing complete data, and

5. Define complete testing required for the equipment which conforms to the standard.

IEC 61850 is a layered architecture standard with full OSI layers that separates the functionality required for electric utility applications from the lower level networking tasks. The layered architecture illustrating the separation of functions is shown in Figure 6.6.

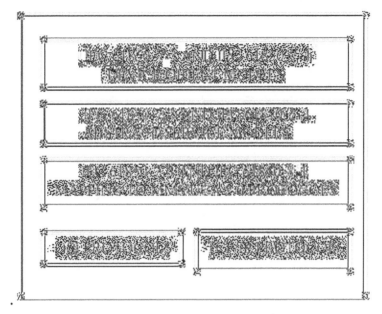

Figure 6.6 IEC 61850 Layered Architecture

IEC 61850 is an object oriented substation automation standard which defines how to describe the devices in an electrical substation and how to exchange the information about these devices. The information model of IEC 61850 is based on two main levels of modelling. The breakdown of physical device into logical device, and the breakdown of logical device into logical nodes, data objects and data attribute. The approach of IEC 61850 is to decompose the application function into the smallest entities which are used to exchange information.

While implementing the PSS, the data exchange between the process level devices and substation is necessary. In order to achieve this all participating devices must be compatible with this protocol. As the IEC 61850 standard has been developed with a clear vision to fully incorporate the IED interoperability, irrespective that the IEDs belong to different vendors. In fact the IEC 61850 compliance of devices takes the substation automation to a next level. IEC 61850 offers three types of communication models.

1. Client/server type communication services model,

2. A publisher subscriber model, and

3. Sample Value model for multicast measurement values.

Generic Object Oriented Substation Events: Generic Object Oriented Substation Events (GOOSE) is a controlled model mechanism in which any format of data like Status Values (SVs) is grouped into a data set and transmitted within a time period of 4 milliseconds. The message structure of GOOSE supports the exchange of a wide range of possible common data organized by a dataset. Being the GOOSE message a multicast, it is received by all the IEDs which have been connected and configured to subscribe it. GOOSE message usually carries the information of a status changed and time of the last status change. In other way, GOOSE time stamped events from IEDs are appropriately communicated. The message frame consists of the destination/source Media Access Control (MAC), addresses, tag protocol identifies, length, two reserved fields and application protocol data unit.

Comparison of DNP3 vs. IEC- 61850 GOOSE

IEC 61850 is not just a communication protocol as it not only defines how the data is transmitted and received but also describes how data is executed and stored. This makes data model of IEC61850 very different to the OSI reference model. This difference in the data model requires IEC61850 to work over a real set of communication protocols such as DNP3 or IEC T[101/3/4], requiring the data model of IEC 61850 to be mapped on to one of the above mentioned protocols. It's more advantageous to use only within a substation and it's specification states that connection to the remote control centers such as remote MCC is beyond its scope. The use of IEC 61850 would be most appropriate if it is used in a substation environment where a number of IEDs interact with the SCADA master. In fact it is referred as substation protocol.

Attacks on IEC 61850 Protocol

Though IEC 61850 based automated substations can provide various advantages over traditional substations, the power distribution utilities are very much cautious about its implementation due to security concerns. Security Engineers have identified a number of security vulnerabilities and flaws in the IEC 61850 protocol such as the lack of encryption used in the GOOSE messages, lack of Intrusion Detection System (IDS) implementation in IEC 61850 networks, and no firewall implementation inside IEC 61850 substation network. If these vulnerabilities are deviously exploited, a number of security attacks can be launched on IEC 61850 substation network.

One of the vulnerabilities within the GOOSE communication of IEC 61850 that can be exploited is by sending GOOSE frames containing higher status numbers. It prevents genuine GOOSE frames from being processed. This effectively causes a hijacking of the communication. This attack could be used to implement a Denial of Service (DoS) attack. This weakness in GOOSE can be exploited to insert spoofed messages with incorrect data between each valid message. This can be used to demonstrate using Scapy, which is a Python program that enables the user to sniff, dissect, forge, and send network packets. This attack is possible due to unencrypted and unauthenticated nature of the GOOSE message.

ICCP TASE 2(IEC 60870-6)

The Inter Control Center Communications Protocol (ICCP or IEC 60870-6/TASE.2) is the protocol used by various power utilities throughout the world to provide data exchange over Wide Area Networks (WANs) between utility control centers, utilities, power pools, regional control centers, and Non-Utility Generators. In fact today ICCP is the international standard adopted by IEC as ICCP Telecontrol Application Service Element 2 (TASE.2) and is an essential protocol in PSS. Usually a typical national power grid includes a hierarchy of control centers to manage the generation, transmission, and distribution of power throughout the grid. The grid is controlled by one or more hierarchical control centers, which are responsible for scheduling of power generation to meet customer demand, and for managing major network outages and faults, are briefly described below.

ICCP Functionalities

The basic functionality of the ICCP is to establish an appropriate link between the other control centres by managing and configuring it for proper information exchange. Generally ICCP establish link with the following control centers.

1. Generation control centers, responsible for managing the operation of generating plants such as coal-fired, natural gas, nuclear, solar, wind, etc. and for adjusting the power generated according to the requirements of the system control center,

2. Transmission control centers, responsible for the transmission of power from generating stations to network distributors, and

3. Distribution control centers, responsible for the distribution of power from the transmission networks to individual consumers.

Protocol Architecture of ICCP TASE 2

At present, the ICCP TASE 2 protocol is the internationally recognized standard for communications between electrical utility control centers. ICCP uses the Manufacturing Messaging Specification (MMS) for the messaging service needed by ICCP. It is based on client / server principles. Consequently data transfers initiated with a request from one control center (client) to another control center (server). Control centers may be both clients and servers. ICCP TASE 2 operates at the application layer in the OSI model. Any physical interfaces transport and network services that fit this model are supported. However TCP/IP over Ethernet seems to be the most common. ICCP may operate over a single point-to-point link between two control centers. The logical connections or *associations* between control centers are completely general. A client can establish association with more than one server and a client can also establish more than one association with the same server. Multiple associations with same server can be established at different levels of quality of service so that high priority real-time data is not delayed by lower priority or non-real-time data transfers.

Implementation Issues and Interoperability

ICCP is a standard real-time data exchange protocol. It provides numerous features for the delivery of data, monitoring of values, program control and device control. All the protocol specifics needed to ensure interoperability between different vendor's ICCP products have been included in the specifications. The ICCP specifications, however, do not attempt to specify other areas that will need to be implemented in an ICCP software product but that do not affect interoperability. These areas are referred to as local implementation issues in the specification. Some of the local implementation issues in the specification are listed below.

1. The API through which local applications interface to ICCP to send or receive data,

2. A user interface to ICCP for user management of ICCP data links,

3. Management functions for controlling and monitoring ICCP data links,

4. Failover schemes where redundant ICCP servers are required to meet stringent availability requirements, such as those typically experienced in an EMS/SCADA system environment, and

5. How data, programs or devices will be controlled or managed in the local SCADA/EMS to respond to requests received via an ICCP data link.

The wide acceptance of ICCP by the utility industry has resulted in several ICCP products are available on the market. Extensive interoperability testing between products of some of the major vendors has been a feature of ICCP protocol development. An ICCP purchaser must define functionality required in terms of conformance blocks and the objects within those blocks. Application profiles for the ICCP client and server conformances must match if the link is to operate successfully. Interoperability among ICCP of different vendors for the power grid is crucial for achieving the benefits of standardization such as application evolution, open architecture and scalability, plug and play capability of components and services, reliability and service orientation.

ICCP-Product Differentiation

ICCP is a real-time data exchange protocol providing features for data transfer, monitoring and control. For a complete ICCP link there need to be facilities to manage and configure the link and monitor its performance. The ICCP standard does not specify any interface or requirements for these features that are necessary but nevertheless do not affect interoperability. Similarly failover and redundancy schemes and the way the SCADA responds to ICCP requests is not a protocol issue, so is not specified. These non-protocol specific features are referred in the standard as local implementation issues. ICCP implementers are free to handle these issues as per their requirements. Local implementation means that developers have to differentiate their product in the market with added features and values. The money spent for a product with appropriately developed maintenance and diagnostic tools will be valued, during its life expectancy, only if the ICCP connection grow and adapt the changes.

ICCP- Product Configurations

Commercial ICCP products are generally available for one of three configurations viz.

1. as a native protocol embedded in the SCADA host,

2. as a networked server, and

3. as a gateway processor.

As an embedded protocol the ICCP management tools and interfaces are all part of the complete suite of tools for the SCADA. This configuration offers maximum performance because of the direct access to the SCADA database without requiring any intervening buffering. This approach may not be available as an addition to a legacy system. The ICCP application may be restricted to accessing only the SCADA environment in which it is embedded. A networked server making use of industry standard communications networking to the SCADA host may provide, performance approaching that of an embedded ICCP application. On the application interface side the ICCP is not restricted to the SCADA environment but is open to other systems such as a separate data historian or other databases. Security may be easier to manage with the ICCP server segregated from the operational real-time systems. The gateway processor approach is similar to the networked server except it is intended for legacy systems with minimal communications networking capability and so has the lowest performance. In the most minimal situation the ICCP gateway may communicate with the SCADA host via a serial port in a similar manner to the SCADA RTUs. Certain other Standards which are deployed in Smart Grid and under development are briefly described below.

6.4   OTHER ICS PERTINENT STANDARDS

Some of the protocols which are relevant and important especially in Power System SCADA (PSS) and DCS are briefly introduced below.

IEEE C37.118.1 Synchrophasor Standard

This standard defines synchrophasor measurements. It also defines a data communication protocol, including message formats for communicating the data in real-time. Mainly intend to take measurements at substations, real-time data sent to control center and collect and align data, for sending on to applications or higher level processing.

A little more elaborated, this standard defines synchrophasors, frequency, and Rate of Change of Frequency (ROCOF) measurement under all operating conditions. It specifies methods for evaluating these measurements and requirements for compliance with the standard under both steady-state and dynamic conditions. Time tag and synchronization requirements are included. Performance requirements are confirmed with a reference model, provided in detail. This document defines a phasor measurement unit (PMU), which can be a stand-alone physical unit or a functional unit within another physical unit. This standard does not specify hardware, software, or a method for computing phasors, frequency, or ROCOF.

IEC 61968 standard

IEC 61968 is a series of standards that will define standards for information exchanges between electrical distribution systems. These standards are being developed by Working Group 14 (WG 14) of Technical Committee 57(TC 57) of the IEC. IEC 61968 is intended to support the inter-application integration of a utility enterprise that needs to collect data from different applications that are legacy or new and each has different interfaces and run-time environments. IEC 61968 defines interfaces for all the major elements of interface architecture for Distribution Management Systems (DMS) and is intended to be implemented with middleware services that broker messages among applications.

IEC 61970 standard

The IEC 61970 series of standards deals with the application program interfaces for energy management systems (EMS). The series provides a set of guidelines and standards to facilitate the following.

1. The integration of applications developed by different suppliers in the control center environment,

2. The exchange of information to systems external to the control center environment, including transmission, distribution and generation systems external to the control center that need to exchange real-time data with the control center,

3. The provision of suitable interfaces for data exchange across legacy and new systems.

IEC 62325 standard

IEC 62325 is a set of standards related to deregulated energy market communications, based on the Common Information Model (CIM). IEC

62325 is a part of the IEC Technical Committee 57 (TC57) reference architecture for electric power systems, and is the responsibility of Working Group 16(WG16) which works on Standards related to energy market communications.

IEC 62325-301 specifies the common information model for energy market communications. The Common Information Model (CIM) is an abstract model that represents all the major objects in an electric utility enterprise typically involved in utility operations and electricity market management. By providing a standard way of representing power system resources as object classes and attributes, along with their relationships, the CIM facilitates the integration of Market Management System (MMS) applications developed independently by different vendors, between entire MMS systems developed independently, or between an MMS system and other systems concerned with different aspects of market management, such as capacity allocation, day-ahead management, balancing, settlement, etc.

Note: *IEC Technical Committee 57(TC 57) is one of the technical committees of the IEC. TC 57 is responsible for development of standards for information exchange for PSS, distribution automation and teleprotection.*

IEC 61508 standard

IEC 61508 is an international standard published by the IEC and is titled Functional Safety of Electrical/Electronic/Programmable Electronic Safety-related Systems. This protocol is intended to be a basic functional safety standard applicable to all kinds of industry. It defines functional safety as part of the overall safety relating to the Equipment Under Control (EUC) and the EUC system which depends on the correct functioning of the E/E/PE safety-related systems, other technology safety-related systems and external risk reduction facilities. The standard covers the complete safety life cycle, and may need interpretation to develop sector specific standards. It has its origins in the process control industry. The safety life cycle of IEC 61508 has 16 phases which can be categorized into three groups as follows.

1. Phases 1-5 address analysis,

2. Phases 6-13 address realization, and

3. Phases 14-16 address operation.

All phases are concerned with the safety function of the system.

IEC 61508:2010 sets out the requirements for ensuring that systems are designed, implemented, operated and maintained to provide the required Safety Integrity Level (SIL). Four SILs are defined according to the risks involved in the system application, with SIL-4 is meant to protect against the highest risks. The standard specifies a process that can be followed by all links in the ICS so that information about the system can be communicated using common terminology and system parameters. The standard is in eight parts which are described below.

1. IEC 61508-0, Functional safety and IEC 61508

2. IEC 61508-1, General requirements

3. IEC 61508-2, Requirements for E/E/PE safety-related systems

4. IEC 61508-3, Software requirements

5. IEC 61508-4, Definitions and abbreviations

6. IEC 61508-5, Examples and methods for the determination of safety integrity levels

7. IEC 61508-6, Guidelines on the application of IEC 61508-2 and IEC 61508-3

8. IEC 61508-7, Overview of techniques and measures

IEC 61508 has been adopted in the UK as BS EN 61508, with the EN indicating adoption also by the European electrotechnical standardization organization CENELEC. Other standards are being produced for the application of the 61508 approach to particular sectors. Sector specific standards related to IEC 61508 include,

1. IEC 61511 Process industries,
2. IEC 61513 Nuclear power plants,
3. IEC 62061 Machinery sector, and
4. IEC 61800-5-2 Power drive systems.

IEC 62351 security standard

IEC 62351 is an industry standard developed for improving security in automation systems especially in the PSS domain. It comprises provisions to ensure the integrity, authenticity and confidentiality for different protocols used in PSS.

IEC 62351 is developed by WG15 (which works on Data and Communication Security) of IEC TC57 mainly for handling the security of TC 57 series of protocols including IEC 60870-5 and its derivatives, IEC 60870-6 (TASE.2), and IEC 61850. In addition, security through network and system management has to be addressed. These security standards have been developed in such a way that it should meet different security objectives for the different protocols, which vary depending upon how they are used. Some of the security standards can be used across a few of the protocols, while others are very specific to a particular profile. The different security objectives include authentication of data transfer through digital signatures, ensuring only authenticated access, prevention of eavesdropping, prevention of playback and spoofing, and intrusion detection.

IEC 62056 Electricity Metering Data Exchange Standard

IEC 62056 is a set of standards for Electricity metering data exchange by International Electrotechnical Commission. The IEC 62056 standards are the International Standard versions of the DLMS/COSEM specification. DLMS or Device Language Message Specification (originally Distribution Line Message Specification), is the suite of standards developed and maintained by the DLMS User Association (DLMS UA) and has been adopted by the IEC TC13 WG14 into the IEC 62056 series of standards. The DLMS UA maintains a liaison with IEC TC13 WG14 responsible for international standards for meter data exchange and establishing the IEC 62056 series. In this role, the DLMS

UA provides maintenance, registration and compliance certification services for IEC 62056 DLMS/COSEM.

COSEM or Companion Specification for Energy Metering includes a set of specifications that defines the Transport and Application Layers of the DLMS protocol. The DLMS UA defines the protocols into a set of four specification documents namely Green Book, Yellow Book, Blue Book and White Book. The Blue book describes the COSEM meter object model and the OBIS object identification system, the Green book describes the Architecture and Protocols, the Yellow book treats all the questions concerning conformance testing, the White book contains the glossary of terms. If a product passes the Conformance Test specified in the Yellow book, then a certification of DLMS/COSEM compliance is issued by the DLMS UA.

The IEC TC13 WG14 groups the DLMS specifications under the common heading: *Electricity metering data exchange-The DLMS/ COSEM suite.* DLMS/COSEM protocol is not confined to electricity metering; rather it is used for gas, water and heat metering.

IEC 62056-21

IEC 61107 is the current IEC 62056-21, is an international standard for a computer protocol to read utility meters. It is designed to operate over any media, including the Internet. A meter sends ASCII or High level Data Link Control (HDLC) data to a nearby Hand-Held Unit (HHU) using a serial port. The physical media are usually either modulated light, sent with an LED and received with a photodiode, or a pair of wires, usually modulated by a 20mA current loop. The protocol is usually half-duplex.

6.5   SECURE COMMUNICATION (sCOMMUNICATION)

The main difference between DCS networks and IT networks is mainly the control part and which is not at all a surprise. As an example a compromised power system SCADA is an unacceptable threat to the reliability of the Bulk Electric System (BES). All software can be hacked, including firewalls, hence why best-practice and unconditional security standards are recommended. Obviously ICCP communication also meets all of these requirements. ICCP does not provide authentication or encryption. These services are normally provided by lower protocol layers. ICCP uses Bilateral Tables to control access. A Bilateral Table represents the agreement between two control centers connected with an ICCP link. The agreement identifies data elements and objects that can be accessed via the link and the level of access permitted. Once an ICCP link is established, the contents of the Bilateral Tables in the server and client provide complete control over what is accessible to each party. There must be matching entries in the server and client tables to provide access to data and objects.

6.6 SELECTING THE RIGHT PROTOCOL FOR SCADA

As there are so many protocols available as both proprietary and open, many factors are to be considered when choosing the protocol for SCADA. The following points are useful while designing the SCADA.

1. Determine the system area with which may become concerned, e.g.

    - the protocol from a SCADA master control station to the SCADA RTUs,

    - a protocol from substation IEDs to an RTU or a PLC, or a LAN in the substation.

2. As the technology is changing so fast that the timing of utility installation can have a great impact on the protocol which is selected. Hence the installation period must be determined most appropriately.

    If new IEDs are implemented in the substation and scheduled to be in service within six months, Protocols may be selected accordingly as Modbus and Modbus Plus are suitable at present in Indian scenario. But if the period of installation and intended applications is for a long time, then consider IEC 61850 and UCA2 MMS as the protocol.

    If the timeframe is around one year, make protocol choices from implementing agency that acts as the industry initiatives and incorporates this technology into their product's migration paths. This helps to protect the investment from becoming obsolete by allowing incremental upgrades to new technologies.

In the design phase, protocol choices differ with the application areas. Different application areas are in different stages of development. An awareness of development stages will help to determine realistic plans and schedules for specific projects. Earlier when SCADA were designed, information and system security was not a priority. Most of the SCADA were designed as proprietary, stand-alone systems, and their security resulted from their physical and logical isolation and controlled access to them.

With the advancement of Information and Communication Technology (ICT), SCADA and DCS began to accept open standards and advanced networking technologies especially the Internet technology. Suppliers acquired the capability to implement Web-based applications to perform monitoring, control, and remote diagnostics. Obviously this introduces control system cyber-vulnerabilities. In addition to traditional IT vulnerabilities, SCADA specific vulnerabilities become the real threat which triggers unique cyber-security requirements to protect ICS against these SCADA specific attacks and vulnerabilities. Further it is a fact that present day technology may become obsolete tomorrow as the pace of the technological advancement is so fast, it seems the time between the present and the future is shrinking. Hence it is most important that one must evaluate not only the vendor's or implementation agencies present products but also their future product development and implementation strategies.

Summary

This chapter begin with the evolution of communication protocols and then move on to explain the various communication protocols used today such as DNP3, Modbus, Profibus, IEC 60870, IEC 61850, and ICCP TASE2 (IEC 60870-6). Other relevant power system SCADA protocols such as IEEE C37.118.1 Synchrophasor Measurement Standard, IEC 61968 standard, IEC 61970 standard, IEC 62325 standard, IEC 61508, IEC 62351, IEC 62056 and IEC 62056-21 are also fleetingly presented. Finally the important points to select the right protocols are discussed.

CHAPTER SEVEN
ESSENTIAL CRYPTOGRAPHY

7.1 INTRODUCTION

Cryptography especially the Public Key Encryption is being used increasingly in industrial automation as more and more industrial assets are being connected internet and to other digital smart devices. Cryptography enhances the levels of data security during transmission, storage and processing. Mathematicians and computer scientists have developed a series of algorithms to ensure confidentiality, integrity, authentication, and nonrepudiation. While cryptographers spent time developing strong encryption algorithms, hackers, utilities and governments alike devoted significant resources to undermining them. This results in the development of the extremely sophisticated algorithms. This chapter looks at the need for cryptography, history of cryptography, the basics of cryptographic communications, methods of encryption, symmetric cryptography, asymmetric or Public Key Infrastructure (PKI) and the hashing algorithms and uses.

7.2 CRYPTOGRAPHY COMPONENTS

Cryptography is a method of storing and transmitting data by appropriately encoding in a non-readable form to achieve security but can process and read the encoded information by only those it is intended for. In fact it is the science and art of securing and protecting information by encoding it into an unreadable format. It is presently the best method of transmitting data through an untrusted communication media. *Cryptanalysis* is the technique of decoding the encoded messages from a non readable format back to a readable format without knowing how they were initially converted format to non readable format. *Cryptology* can be defined as a combination of cryptography and cryptanalysis. A *cryptosystem* encompasses all of the necessary components for encryption and decryption to take place. A cryptosystem is made up of at least the following components.

- Software

- Protocols

- Algorithms

- Keys

Another term to be familiarized is *steganography* is an ancient technique that has been used for thousands of years as a primitive for secrecy systems and secret communications.

➢ Need for Cryptography

The main goal of cryptography is to hide and transmit the information from unauthorized access. But hackers, with enough time, resources, and motivation, break most algorithms and reveal the encoded information. So today the realistic goal of cryptography is to make the decoding too work-intensive and time-consuming for the attacker to steal the information.

The previous generation of computers, devices and the applications mainly of the pre-internet era virtually had no or little security. With the advancement of internet, communication technology revolutionize the world and trusted information passing becomes an inevitability. As a result various areas of security become important and following mechanisms has been implemented.

- All users are provided with an user identification and password, and use that information for authenticating an user.

- The information stored in the database is encrypted, so that it is not visible to users who do not have the right to access.

Today organizations realized the importance of the physical-cyber security and security mechanisms, without which the whole business can be crumbled. The most unfortunate thing is that the attacker can be from anywhere in the world and independent of the nations jurisdiction. Hence cannot be extradited even if he is traced in most of the cases.

➢ Evolution of Cryptography

Cryptography has an interesting history and has undergone many revolutions through the centuries. Encryption was adapted as a tool to use in warfare, commerce, government, and other fields in which secrets needed to be safeguarded. With the arrival of the Internet, encryption has gained new heights as a vital tool in everyday transactions. As a result, the encryption algorithms and the devices that use them have increased in complexity and computing power, new techniques and algorithms have been continually developed, and encryption has become an integrated part of the computing world.

The earliest cryptography methods involved a person carving messages into wood or stone, which was then delivered to the intended individual, who had the necessary means to decipher the messages. Around 100 BC, Julious Ceasar was known to use a form of encryption to convey secret messages to his army generals posted in the war front. During the 16th century, Vignere designed a cypher that was believed as the first cipher which used an encryption key. At the start of 19thcentuary when everything became electric, Hebern designed an electro mechanical contraption which was called the Hebern rotor machine. The Enigma machine was invented by German engineer Arthur Scherbius of the end of World War I and was heavily used by the German forces during the World War II. IBM in early 1970s designed a cipher called Lucifer was eventually accepted by NIST and was called DES or the Data Encryption Standard. In 2000, NIST accepted Rindael, and named it as AES or the Advanced Encryption Standard.

➢ Concepts and Definitions

Cryptology is the science of secure communications while Cryptography creates messages whose meaning is hidden. Cryptanalysis is the science of breaking encrypted messages (recovering their meaning). Many use the term cryptography in place of cryptology: It is important to remember that cryptology encompasses both cryptography and cryptanalysis. A cipher is a cryptographic algorithm. A plaintext is an unencrypted message. Encryption converts the plaintext to a ciphertext. Decryption turns a ciphertext back into a plaintext.

Information Assurance (IA) refers to the steps involved in protecting information systems, like computer systems and networks. There are commonly five terms associated with the definition of information assurance and they are,

- Integrity
- Availability
- Authentication
- Confidentiality
- Non-repudiation

A concise description of these terms is given below.

➤ **Confidentiality**

Cryptography can provide confidentiality and integrity. it is important to note that it does not directly provide availability. Cryptography can also provide authentication. Confidentiality of information is about protecting the information from disclosure to unauthorized parties. Information has value, especially in today's world. Everyone has certain information they wish to keep a secret. Protecting such information is a very major part of information security. A key component of protecting information confidentiality is encryption. Encryption ensures that only the authorised people can read the information. Encryption is very widespread in today's environment and can be found in almost every major protocol in use. A typical example is SSL/TLS. It is a security protocol for communications over the internet that has been used in conjunction with a large number of internet protocols to ensure security. Other ways to ensure information confidentiality include enforcing file permissions and access control list to restrict access to sensitive information.

➢ Integrity

Integrity of message refers to protecting the information from being modified or altered in unauthorized means. Information that has been tampered could be an expesive loss. If Hari sends an online money transfer for Rs100/~, but the information was tampered in such a way that Hari sent Rs10,000/~, it could prove to be very costly. As with data confidentiality, cryptography plays a very major role in ensuring data integrity. Commonly used methods to protect data integrity includes hashing the data that receive and comparing it with the hash of the original message. However, this means that the hash of the original data must be provided to the reciepient in a secure fashion.

➢ Authentication

Authentication is to prove that a message actually originates with its claimed originator. The following are the main needs for authenticating an information.

- Authentication is used by a server when the server needs to know exactly who is accessing their information or site.

- Authentication is used by a client when the client needs to know that the server is system it claims to be.

- In authentication, the user or computer has to prove its identity to the server or client.

- Usually, authentication by a server entails the use of a user name and password. Other ways to authenticate can be through cards, retina scans, voice recognition, and fingerprints.

- Authentication by a client usually involves the server giving a certificate to the client in which a trusted third party such as Verisign or Thawte states that the server belongs to the entity (such as a bank) that the client expects it to.

- Authentication does not determine what tasks the individual can do or what files the individual can see. Authentication merely identifies and verifies who the person or system is.

> ## Non-Repudiation

Non-repudiation prevents an originator from denying credit or blame for creating or sending a message. It is a process that, once completed, makes it extremely difficult for someone to deny that they were involved in the process. It's a method of ensuring that someone sent a file or encrypted a file without *reasonable doubt* that they did so. Protocols for accomplishing this goal are a bit complicated, but the traditional non-digital world has familiar means of accomplishing the same goal through signatures, notarization, and presentation of photo ID.

> ## Availability

Availability of information refers to ensuring that authorized parties are able to access the information when needed. When a system is regularly non-functioning, information availability is affected and significantly impacts users. In addition, when data is not secure and easily available, information security is affected. Another factor affecting availability is time. If a computer system cannot deliver information efficiently, then availability is compromised. Further information only has value if the right people can access it at the right times. Denying access to information has become a very common attack nowadays. Almost every week one can find news about high profile websites being taken down by DDoS attacks. The primary aim of DDoS attacks is to deny users of the website access to the resources of the website. Such downtime can be very costly. Other factors that could lead to lack of availability to important information may include accidents such as power outages or natural disasters such as floods. Regularly doing off-site backups can limit the damage caused by damage to hard drives or natural disasters. For information services that is critical, redundancy might be appropriate. Having a off-site location ready to restore services in case anything happens to the primary data centers will heavily reduce the downtime in case of anything happens.

> ## Confusion, Diffusion, Substitution, and Permutation

Diffusion means the order of the plaintext should be "diffused" (or dispersed) in the ciphertext. Confusion means that the relationship between the plaintext and ciphertext should be as confused (or random) as possible. These terms were first defined by Claude Shannon, the father of information security. Cryptographic substitution replaces one character for another; this provides diffusion.

As an example, the word *security* can be encrypted into *hvxfirgb*. This is an example of a *substitution cipher*, because each character is replaced with another character. This type of substitution cipher is referred to as a *monoalphabetic substitution cipher* because it uses only one alphabet, whereas a *polyalphabetic substitution cipher* uses multiple alphabets. Permutation often called transposition provides confusion by rearranging the characters of the plaintext, anagram-style. *ATTACKATDAWN* can be rearranged to *CAAKDTANTATW*. Substitution and transposition are often combined. These techniques were used in the past and they are still used in combination in modern ciphers such as the Advanced Encryption Standard (AES). Strong encryption destroys patterns. If a single bit of plaintext changes, the odds of every bit of resulting cipher-text changing should be 50/50. Any signs of non-randomness may be used as clues to a cryptanalyst, hinting at the underlying order of the original plaintext or key.

➤ Types of Cryptography

The three primary types of modern encryption are symmetric, asymmetric, and hashing. Symmetric encryption uses one key. The same key encrypts and decrypts. Asymmetric cryptography uses two keys: if you encrypt with one key, and may decrypt with the another. Hashing is a one-way cryptographic transformation without any key but using an algorithm.

➤ Cryptographic Strength

The *strength* of an encryption method depends on the algorithm, the secrecy of the key, the length of the key, the initialization vectors, and how they work together within the cryptosystem. When strength is discussed in encryption, it refers to how hard it is to discover the algorithm or key, whichever is not made public. Attempts to break a cryptosystem usually involve processing an amazing number of possible values in the hopes of finding the one value (key) that can be used to decrypt a specific message. The strength of an encryption method correlates to the amount of necessary processing power, resources, and time required to break the cryptosystem or to discover the value of the key. Breaking a cryptosystem can be accomplished by a brute force attack, which means trying every possible key value until the resulting plaintext is meaningful. Depending on the algorithm and length of the key, this can be an easy task or one that is close to impossible. If a key can be broken with a Pentium Core i5 processor in three hours, the cipher is not strong at all. If the key can only be broken with the use of a thousand multiprocessing systems over 1.2 million years, then it is pretty darn strong. The introduction of dual-core processors has really increased the threat of brute force attacks. The goal when designing an encryption method is to make compromising it too expensive or too time-consuming.

Another name for cryptography strength is *work factor,* which is an estimate of the effort and resources it would take an attacker to penetrate a cryptosystem. How strong a protection mechanism is required depends on the sensitivity of the data being protected. The type of encryption mechanism to be used has its place and purpose. Even if the algorithm is very complex and thorough, other issues within encryption can weaken encryption methods. Because the key is usually the secret value needed to actually encrypt and decrypt messages, improper protection of the key can weaken the encryption. Even if a user employs an algorithm that has all the requirements for strong encryption, if the key is shared with others, the strength of the algorithm becomes irrelevant. Important elements of encryption are to use an algorithm without flaws, use a large key size, use all possible values within the key space, and protect the actual key. If one element is weak, it could be the link that destruct the whole process.

➢ Methods of Encryption

The two main components of the encryption process are the algorithms and the keys. Algorithms used in computer systems are complex mathematical formulas that dictate the rules of how the plaintext will be turned into ciphertext. A key is a string of random bits that will be used by the algorithm to add to the randomness of the encryption process. For two entities to be able to communicate via encryption, they must use the same algorithm and, mostly the same key. In some encryption technologies, the receiver and the sender use the same key, and in other encryption technologies, they must use different keys for encryption and decryption.

7.3   SYMMETRIC ENCRYPTION

In symmetric cryptography, the sender and receiver use two instances of the same key for encryption and decryption, as shown in Figure 7.1. The key has double functionalities as it carry out both encryption and decryption processes. But if an intruder or a hacker gets this key, he could decrypt any intercepted message encrypted with it. Each pair of users who want to exchange data using symmetric key encryption must have two instances of the same key. This means that if Hari and Krishnan want to communicate, both need to obtain a copy of the same key. If Hari also wants to communicate using symmetric encryption with Unni and Gokul, he needs to have three separate keys, one for each friend. This might not sound like a big deal until Hari realizes that he may communicate with hundreds of people over a period of several months, and keeping track and using the correct key that corresponds to each specific receiver can become a daunting task. The equation used to calculate the number of symmetric keys needed is

$$N(N-1)/2 = \text{number of keys}$$

When using symmetric algorithms, the sender and receiver use the same key for encryption and decryption functions. The security of the symmetric encryption method is completely rely on how well the users protect the key. If a key is compromised, then all messages encrypted with that key can be decrypted and read by an intruder. This is complicated further by how symmetric keys are actually shared and updated when necessary. If Hari wants to communicate with Krishnan for the first time, Hari has to issue the right key to Krishnan in a very secure manner. This is a very difficult task, and each technique is very clumsy and can be insecure. Because both users employ the same key to encrypt and decrypt messages, symmetric cryptosystems can provide confidentiality, but they cannot provide authentication or non-repudiation. If two people are using the same key, there is no way to prove through cryptography who actually sent the message.

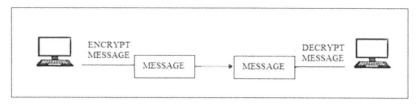

Figure 7.1 Symmetric Cryptography

Compared with asymmetric systems, symmetric algorithms are very fast. They can encrypt and decrypt relatively large volume of data in lesser time when comparing to amount of time to encrypt and decrypt with an asymmetric algorithm. The strengths and weakness of symmetric key systems are summarized in the Table 7.1 below.

Table 7.1 Strength and Weakness of Symmetric Encryption

Strengths	Weaknesses
Much quicker than asymmetric systems.	The key must be securely shared before two parties may communicate securely. Requires a secure mechanism to deliver keys properly.
Cryptographic strength per bit of key.	Each pair of users needs a unique key, so as the number of individuals increases, so does the number of keys, possibly making key management overwhelming.
Hard to break if using a large key size.	Provides confidentiality but not authenticity or non-repudiation.

➤ Stream and Block Ciphers

Symmetric encryption have stream and block modes. Stream mode means each bit is independently encrypted in a *stream*. Block mode ciphers encrypt blocks of data each round: 56 bits for the Data Encryption Standard (DES), and 128, 192, or 256 bits for AES. Some block ciphers can emulate stream ciphers by setting the block size to 1 bit. Stream ciphers require a lot of randomness and encrypt individual bits at a time. This requires more processing power than block ciphers require, which is why stream ciphers are better suited to be implemented at the hardware level. Because block ciphers do not require as much processing power, they can be easily implemented at the software level. Overall, stream ciphers are considered less secure than block ciphers and are used less frequently. One of the difficulties in proper stream cipher implementation is generating an accurately random and unbiased key stream. Stream ciphers has an advantage when compared to block ciphers is that it is more suitable when streaming communication data as it needs to be encrypted speedily. Stream ciphers can encrypt and decrypt more quickly. Hence in real-time applications, it is common that stream ciphers are preferred.

➤ Initialization Vectors (IV) and Chaining

An Initialization Vector is used in some symmetric ciphers to ensure that the first encrypted block of data is random and patterns are not created during the encryption process. IV is used by the algorithm to provide more randomness to the encryption process. If IVs are not used, then two identical plaintext values that are encrypted with the same key will create the same ciphertext. These types of patterns can make the attackers job easier in breaking the encryption method and uncovering the key. Bruce Schneier pointed out that two messages that begin with the same will encrypt the same way up to the first difference.

Chaining seeds the previous encrypted block into the next block to be encrypted. This destroys patterns in the resulting cipher-text. DES Electronic Code Book mode which is described below does not use an initialization vector or chaining. Hence patterns can be clearly visible in the resulting ciphertext.

➤ Padding

Padding is a way to take data that may or may not be a multiple of the block size for a cipher and extend it out so that it is. This is required for many block cipher modes as they require the data to be encrypted to be an exact multiple of the block size. A block cipher works on units of a fixed size, but messages come in a variety of lengths. So some modes especially Electronic Code Book (ECB) and Cipher Block Chaining (CBC), require that the final block be padded before encryption. Several padding schemes exist. The simplest is to add null bytes to the plaintext to bring its length up to a multiple of the block size, but care must be given that the original length of the plaintext can be recovered without error.

➤ Types of Symmetric Systems

The various types of systems are Data Encryption Standard (DES), 3DES (Triple DES), Blowfish, Twofish, International Data Encryption Algorithm (IDEA), RC4, RC5, RC6, Advanced Encryption Standard (AES), Secure and Fast Encryption Routine (SAFER), and Serpent.

➤ Data Encryption Standard (DES)

DES is the Data Encryption Standard, which describes the Data Encryption Algorithm (DEA). DES is the standard and DEA is the algorithm, but generally it is referred as DES. It is a combination of substitution and transposition encryption. DES was designed and developed by IBM to protect financial transactions, based on their older Lucifer symmetric cipher which uses an 128-bit algorithm. Later it has been modified to use a key size of 64 bits with 8 bits used for parity, resulting in an effective key length of 56 bits, instead of the original 128 bits, and named it as *Data Encryption Algorithm (DEA)*.

DES has been implemented in a majority of commercial products using cryptography functionality and in the applications of almost all government agencies. It was tested and approved as one of the strongest and most efficient cryptographic algorithms available.

➤ DES Modes

Block ciphers have several modes of operation. Each mode specifies how a block cipher will operate. One mode may work better in one type of environment for specific functionality, whereas another mode may work better in another environment with totally different requirements. It is important that vendors who employ DES (or any block cipher) understand the different modes and which one to use for which purpose. DES and other symmetric block ciphers have several distinct modes of operation that are used in different situations for different results. The commonly used are,

- Electronic Code Book (ECB),
- Cipher Block Chaining (CBC),
- Cipher Feedback (CFB),
- Output Feedback (OFB), and
- Counter Mode (CTR).

1. Electronic Code Book (ECB)

Electronic Code Book (ECB) is the simplest and weakest form of DES. It uses no initialization vector or chaining. Identical plaintexts with identical keys encrypt to identical cipher-texts. Two plaintexts with partial identical portions such as the header of a letter, encrypted with the same key will have partial identical cipher text portions. ECB may also leave plaintext patterns evident in the resulting cipher text.

2. Cipher Block Chaining (CBC)

In CBC mode, the current plaintext block is added to the previous ciphertext block, and then the result is encrypted with the key. Decryption is thus the reverse process, which involves decrypting the current cipher text and then adding the previous ciphertext block to the result. It is most common legacy encryption mode. It is simple to understand and trivial to implement around an existing ECB mode cipher implementation. It is often mistakenly attributed with providing authenticity for the reason *that a change in the ciphertext will make a nontrivial change in the plaintext.* It is true that changing a single bit of ciphertext will alter two blocks of plaintext in a nontrivial fashion. It is *not* true that this provides authenticity.

Advantage of CBC over ECB is that changing IV results in different ciphertext for identical message. On the drawback side, the error in transmission gets propagated to few further block during decryption due to chaining effect. It is worth mentioning that CBC mode forms the basis for a well-known data origin authentication mechanism. Thus, it has an advantage for those applications that require both symmetric encryption and data origin authentication.

3. Cipher Feedback (CFB)

Cipher Feedback (CFB) mode is very similar to CBC. The main difference is CFB is a stream mode. It uses feedback (chaining when used in stream modes) to destroy patterns. Like CBC, CFB uses an initialization vector and destroys patterns, and errors propagate.

4. Output Feedback (OFB)

Output Feedback (OFB) mode also differs from CFB in the way feedback (chaining) is accomplished. CFB uses the previous cipher text for feedback. The previous ciphertext is the subkey XORed to the plaintext. OFB uses the subkey before it is XORed to the plaintext. Since the subkey is not affected by encryption errors, errors will not propagate.

5. Counter Mode (CTR)

Counter (CTR) mode is like OFB; the difference again is the feedback. CTR mode uses a counter. This mode shares the same advantages as OFB where patterns are destroyed and errors do not propagate. Since the feedback can be as simple as an ascending number, CTR mode encryption can be done in parallel. A simple example would be the first block is XORed to the number 1, the second to the number2, etc. Any number of rounds can be combined in parallel this way.

> ## Triple-DES (3DES)

The Double-DES developed has a key length of 112 bits, but there is a specific attack against Double-DES that reduces its work factor to about the same as DES. Thus, it is no more secure than DES. This prompted to move on to 3DES. Many successful attacks against DES and the realization prompted for a better solution which ended up on AES, but a quick fix was needed in the meantime to provide more protection for sensitive data. This paved the way to 3DES. It is also an encryption cipher and was derived from the original Data Encryption Standard (DES) became prominent in the late nineties. 3DES uses 48 rounds in its computation, which makes it highly resistant to differential cryptanalysis. However, because of the extra work 3DES performs, there is a heavy performance hit. It can take up to three times longer than DES to perform encryption and decryption. 3DES can work in different modes, and the mode chosen dictates the number of keys used and what functions are carried out. There are 4 modes that Triple-DES and they are DES-EEE3, DES-EDE3, DES-EEE2 and DES-EDE2.

- DES-EEE3 Uses three different keys for encryption, and the data are thrice.

- DES-EDE3 Uses three different keys for encryption, and the data are encrypted, decrypted, encrypted.

- DES-EEE2 The same as DES-EEE3, but uses only two keys, and the first and third encryption processes use the same key.

- DES-EDE2 The same as DES-EDE3, but uses only two keys, and the first and third encryption processes use the same key.

The decrypting portion here is decrypted with a different key. When data are encrypted with one symmetric key and decrypted with a different symmetric key.

➤ Blowfish and Twofish

Blowfish is currently one of the faster block ciphers. Security expert Bruce Schneier developed Blowfish as a possible replacement to the aging DES. It can use key sizes of 32 bits to 448 bits. The data blocks go through 16 rounds of cryptographic functions and is a strong encryption protocol. Becrypt is an adaptive hash function based on the Blofish symmetric block cipher cryptographic algorithm. Linux systems use bcrypt to encrypt passwords, and becrypt is based on Blowfish. Becrypt adds 128 additional bits as a salt to protect against rainbow table attacks. While many of the other algorithms have been proprietary and thus encumbered by patents or kept as government secrets, this wasn't the case with Blowfish. *Blowfish* is unpatented, and will remain so in all countries. The algorithm is hereby placed in the public domain, and can be freely used by anyone. Twofish encrypting 128-bit blocks using 128 through 256 bit keys. Both are open algorithms, unpatented and freely available. Both are open algorithms, unpatented and freely available.

➤ International Data Encryption Algorithm (IDEA)

International Data Encryption Algorithm (IDEA) is a symmetric block cipher designed as an international replacement to DES with a key of 128 bits operating on 64- bit blocks of data. The 64-bit data block is divided into 16 smaller blocks, and each has eight rounds of mathematical functions performed on it. IDEA is faster than DES when implemented in software. The IDEA algorithm is patented in many countries. It uses a 128-bit key and 64-bit block size. The IDEA algorithm offers different modes similar to the modes described in the DES section, but it is considered harder to break than DES because it has a longer key size. IDEA is used in the Pretty Good Privacy (PGP) and other encryption software implementations. Although there have been numerous attempts, there have been no successful practical attacks against this algorithm.

➤ RC4

RC4 is one of the most commonly implemented stream ciphers. It has a variable key size, is used in the SSL protocol, and was implemented in the 802.11 WEP protocol standard. RC4 was developed in 1987 by Ron Rivest and was considered a trade secret of RSA Data Security, Inc., until someone posted the source code on a mailing list. Since the source code was released viciously. The stolen algorithm is sometimes implemented and referred to as ArcFour or ARC4 because the title RC4 is trademarked. The algorithm is very simple, fast, and efficient, which is why it became so popular. But because it has a low diffusion rate, it is subject to modification attacks. This is one reason that the new wireless security standard (IEEE 802.11i) moved from the RC4 algorithm to the AES algorithm.

➤ RC5

RC5 is a fast block cipher developed based on RC4. RC5 uses key encryption and decryption as well as key expansion. It is a block cipher that has a variety of parameters which t can be used for block size, key size, and the number of rounds used. It was created by Ron Rivest and analyzed by RSA Data Security, Inc. The block sizes used in this algorithm are 32, 64, or 128 bits, and the key size goes up to 2,048 bits. The number of rounds used for encryption and decryption is also variable. The number of rounds can go up to 255. RC5 finds application in IoT devices used in smart transportation systems.

➤ RC6

RC6 is a derivative of RC5, so it has all the same attributes as RC5. It is a block cipher designed and developed was developed mainly to be submitted as AES, but Rijndael was chosen instead. RC6 uses four working block size registers in its algorithmic computations, whereas RC5 uses only two. Thus, RC6 is faster. RC6 was designed as part of the Advanced Encryption Standard (AES) competition, where it was a finalist. It is a propriety algorithm patented by RSA Security.

➤ Advanced Encryption Standard (AES)

The Advanced Encryption Standard also known as Rijndael is one of the most popular global encryption standards. DES was used as an encryption standard for over 20 years till it was cracked in a relatively short time. This raised a requirement of another encryption algorithm and the Advanced Encryption Standard (AES) is one of the solutions which became most accepted symmetric encryption algorithms. Since 2001, developers have steadily been implementing AES into many other algorithms and protocols. AES encryption has three different block ciphers viz. AES-128 (128 bit), AES-192 (192 bit) and AES-256 (256 bit). These block ciphers are named after the key length they use for encryption and decryption. All these ciphers encrypt and decrypt the data in 128-bit blocks but they use different sizes of cryptographic keys. The Microsoft Encrypting File System (EFS) uses AES for file and folder encryption. The US government has approved AES to protect classified data to top secret. Larger key sizes add additional security, making it more difficult for unauthorized personnel to decrypt the data.

> **Serpent**

It is an open source algorithm developed in 1998 by Ross Anderson, Lars Kundson and Bilham. It is purely Symmetric key cryptography has three main drawbacks, which affect the following.

- *Security services:* Purely symmetric key cryptography provides confidentiality only, not authentication or nonrepudiation.

- *Scalability:* As the number of people who need to communicate increases, so does the number of symmetric keys required, meaning more keys must be managed.

- *Secure key distribution:* The symmetric key must be delivered to its destination through a secure courier.

Despite these drawbacks, symmetric key cryptography was all that the computing society had available for encryption for quite some time. Symmetric and asymmetric cryptography did not arrive on the same day or even in the same decade. The issues surrounding symmetric cryptography exists for quite some time, waiting for someone smarter to come along and save us from some of this grief.

7.4 ASYMMETRIC OR PUBLIC KEY INFRASTRUCTURE (PKI)

Asymmetric encryption or Public Key Encryption was a mathematical breakthrough which finally solved the age-old challenge of preshared keys. It was in 1976, Whitfield Diffie and Martin Hellman, proposed an amazing concept where different keys could be used for encryption, which are not easily derivable from each other. Asymmetric encryption uses two keys. If encrypted with one key, it is decrypted with the other. One key may be made public called the public key. Anyone who wants to communicate with you may simply download your publicly-posted public key and use it to encrypt their plaintext. Once encrypted, the public key cannot decrypt the plaintext but only the private key can do it. As the name implies, the private key must be kept private and secure. Additionally, any message encrypted with the private key may be decrypted with the public key. This is typically used for digital signatures.

The major strength of public key encryption is its ability to facilitate communication between parties previously unknown to each other enabling a wide range of dispersed people to communicate in a secure and predictable fashion. In public key encryption, the key with the sender and the receiver are related but they are different. The information encrypted by the key K can only be decrypted by K' and vice versa. This is made possible by the Public Key Infrastructure (PKI) hierarchy of trust relationships. It is a hybrid system of symmetric and asymmetric key algorithms and methods, along with hashing and digital certificates.

In fact, the Diffie-Hellman key exchange algorithm which lead to the domain of Public Key Encryption. Later the RSA (named after the inventers *Rivest, Shamir and Adleman*) algorithm was invented and is widely used in the field of digital signatures. PKI is made up of many different components such as certificate authorities, registration authorities, certificates, keys, and users to provide a global secure communication.

➤ Certificate Authorities (CA)

The Certificate Authorities are the glue that binds the PKI together. The CA is responsible for creating and handing out certificates, maintaining them, and revoking them if necessary. Each person who wants to participate in a PKI requires a digital certificate, which is a credential that contains the public key for that individual along with other identifying information. The certificate is created and signed (digital signature) by a trusted third party, which is a *Certificate Authority (CA)*. These neutral organizations offer notarization services for digital certificates. To obtain a digital certificate from a reputable CA, one must prove their identify to the satisfaction of the CA. The major CAs are listed below.

- Symantec,
- Thawte,
- GeoTrust,
- GlobalSign,
- Comodo Limited,
- Starfield Technologies,
- GoDaddy,
- DigiCert,
- Network Solutions, LLC, and
- Entrust.

There is an important item to consider when receiving a digital certificate from a third party. If the name of the CA cannot be recognized and trusted, then certificate issued by the CA become totally untrusted and invalid. PKI relies on a hierarchy of trust relationships. If somebody configures their browser to trust a CA, it will automatically trust all of the digital certificates issued by that CA. Browser developers pre-configure browsers to trust the major CAs to avoid placing this burden on users.

➢ Certificates

One of the most important components of a PKI is the digital certificate. A *certificate* is the mechanism used to associate a public key with a collection of components in a manner that is sufficient to uniquely identify the claimed owner. The standard for how the CA creates the certificate is X.509. Most commonly used version is 3 of this standard, which is often denoted as X.509v3. Many cryptographic protocols use this type of certificate. Typical example is SSL. Serial number, version number, identity information, algorithm information, lifetime dates, and the signature of the issuing authority are included in the certificate.

➢ Registration Authority

Registration Authorities (RAs) assist CAs by verifying users' identities prior to issuing digital certificates. The RA establishes and confirms the identity of an individual, initiates the certification process with a CA on behalf of an end user, and performs certificate life-cycle management functions. They do not directly issue certificates themselves, but they play an important role in the certification process, allowing CAs to remotely validate user identities. When users need new certificates, they make requests to the RA, and the RA verifies all necessary identification information before allowing a request to go to the CA.

➢ Certificate Generation and Destruction

The technical concepts behind the public key infrastructure are relatively simple. In the following sections, describe the processes used by certificate authorities to create, validate, and revoke client certificates.

The first step is the enrolment. This is the process where the person who wants to obtain the digital signature has to prove the identity to the CA in some manner. This sometimes requires involves physically appearing before an agent of the certification authority with the appropriate identification documents. Certain certificate authorities provide other means of verification, including the use of credit report data and identity verification by trusted community leaders or authorized Government officials.

Once the CA satisfied with the identity of the applicant, the CA collets the public key of the applicant. The CA next creates an X.509 digital certificate containing the applicant's identifying information and a copy of applicant's public key. The CA then digitally signs the certificate using the CA's private key and provides the applicant with a copy of the signed digital certificate. Once it is received, this certificate can be safely distributed to anyone with whom the applicant wants to communicate securely.

➢ Verification

When you receive a digital certificate from someone with whom you want to communicate, you verify the certificate by checking the CA's digital signature using the CA's public key. Next, you must check and ensure that the certificate was not published on a certificate revocation list (CRL). At this point, you may assume that the public key listed in the certificate is authentic, provided that it satisfies the following requirements:

- The digital signature of the CA is authentic. You trust the CA,

- The certificate is not listed on a CRL, and

- The certificate actually contains the data you are trusting.

Digital certificate verification algorithms are built in to a number of popular web browsing and email clients, so you won't often need to get involved in the particulars of the process. However, it's important to have a solid understanding of the technical details taking place behind the scenes to make appropriate security judgments for your organization. It's also the reason that, when purchasing a certificate, you choose a CA that is widely trusted. If a CA is not included in, or is later pulled from, the list of CAs trusted by a major browser, it will greatly limit the usefulness of your certificate.

➤ Revocation

A certificate may be revoked because the key holder's private key was compromised or because the CA discovered the certificate was issued to the wrong person. It can be due to change in details of certificate or change in security association. Revocation is handled by the CA, and the revoked certificate information is stored on a Certificate Revocation List (CRL). The revocation request grace period is the maximum response time within which a CA will perform any requested revocation. This is defined in the *Certificate Practice Statement* (CPS). The CPS states the practices a CA employs when issuing or managing certificates.

➤ Certificate Revocation Lists (CRLs)

Certificate Revocation Lists (CRLs) are maintained by the various Certificate Authorities and contain the serial numbers of certificates that have been issued by a CA. It has been revoked along with the date and time the revocation went into effect. The major disadvantage to certificate revocation lists is that they must be downloaded and cross-referenced periodically, introducing a period of latency between the time a certificate is revoked and the time end users are notified of the revocation. CRLs are the most common method of checking certificate status.

➤ Online Certificate Status Protocol (OCSP)

This protocol eliminates the latency inherent in the use of certificate revocation lists by providing a means for real-time certificate verification. When a client receives a certificate, it sends an OCSP request to the CA's OCSP server. The server then responds with a status of valid, invalid, or unknown.

➤ Circuit Encryption

Security experts prefer two types of encryption techniques to protect data communication over networks each with different types of protection and consequences. The two general modes of encryption are Link encryption and End-to-end encryption.

Link Encryption

Link encryption protects entire communications by creating a secure tunnel between two points using either hardware or software that encrypts all traffic entering the tunnel and decrypts all traffic when leaving. It encrypts not only the user information, but also encrypts the header, trailers, addresses, and routing data that are part of the packets. The only traffic not encrypted in this technology is the data link control messaging information, which includes instructions and parameters that the different link devices use to synchronize communication methods. Link encryption provides protection against packet sniffers and eaves droppers. Link encryption is usually provided by service providers and is incorporated into network protocols. All of the information is encrypted, and the packets or the header portion of the packet must be decrypted at each hop re-encrypted before it can be sent along its way, which results in retarding the routing. Since due to this decryption and re-encryption, the router, or other intermediate device, knows where to send the packet next. The router must decrypt the header portion of the packet, read the routing and address information within the header, and then re-encrypt it and send it on its way.

Link encryption occurs at the data link and physical layers. Hardware encryption devices interface with the physical layer and encrypt all data that passes through them. Because no part of the data is available to an attacker, the attacker cannot learn basic information about how data flows through the environment.

End-to-End Encryption

End-to-end encryption protects communications between two parties such as a client or a server and is performed independently of link encryption. Here, the headers, addresses, routing, and trailer information are not encrypted, enabling attackers to learn more about a captured packet and where it is headed. Typical example of end-to-end encryption is the use of TLS to protect communications between a user and a web server. This protects against an intruder who might be monitoring traffic on the secure side of an encrypted link or traffic sent over an unencrypted link. With end-to-end encryption, the packets do not need to be decrypted and then encrypted again at each hop because the headers and trailers are not encrypted. The devices in between the origin and destination just read the necessary routing information and pass the packets on their way. End-to-end encryption is usually initiated by the user of the originating computer. It provides more flexibility for the user to be able to determine whether or not certain messages will get encrypted. It is called *end-to-end encryption* because the message stays encrypted from one end of its journey to the other. Link encryption has to decrypt the packets at every device between the two ends.

End-to-end encryption does not encrypt the header, trailer, address, and routing data, so it moves faster from point to point but is more susceptible to sniffers and eaves droppers. When encryption happens at the higher OSI layers, it is usually end-to-end encryption, and if encryption is done at the lower layers of the OSI model, it is usually link encryption. Secure Shell (SSH) is a good example of an end-to-end encryption technique. This suite of programs provides encrypted alternatives to common Internet applications such as FTP, Telnet, and rlogin. There are actually two versions of SSH. SSH1 which is now considered insecure supports the DES, 3DES, IDEA, and Blowfish algorithms. SSH2 drops support for DES and IDEA but adds support for several other algorithms. The main disadvantages of end-to-end encryption is that the headers, addresses, and routing information are not encrypted, and therefore not protected.

7.5 HASHING ALGORITHMS AND USES

A hash value is a numeric value of a fixed length that uniquely identifies data. They are useful for verifying the integrity of data sent through insecure channels the numeric value is commonly referred to as the *message digest*. Message digests can be generated by the sender of a message and transmitted to the recipient along with the full message for two reasons.

First, the recipient can use the same hash function to recompute the message digest from the full message. They can then compare the computed message digest to the transmitted one to ensure that the message sent by the originator is the same one received by the recipient. If the message digests do not match, that means the message was someway modified while in transit. Second, the message digest can be used to implement a digital signature algorithm and is used in Digital Signatures.

The key in PKI is based on a hash value. This is a value that is computed from a base input number using a hashing algorithm. Essentially, the hash value is a summary of the original value. The important thing about a hash value is that it is nearly impossible to derive the original input number without knowing the data used to create the hash value. A hash value is a numeric value of a fixed length that uniquely identifies data. Hash values are useful for verifying the integrity of data sent through insecure channels.

➢ Message Integrity

Message integrity verifies the validity of a transmitted message. It means that a message has not been tampered with or altered. The most common approach is to use a hash function that combines all the bytes in the message with a secret key and produces a message digest that is difficult to reverse. Integrity checking is one component of an information security program.

➢ One-Way Processing

Also called a "one-way hash function," the one- way means that it is extremely difficult to turn the digest back into the original message. It is also exceedingly rare that two different message inputs can result in the same digest output.

➢ Hash-based Message Authentication Code (HMAC)

Hash-based Message Authentication Code (HMAC) is a message authentication code that uses a cryptographic key in conjunction with a hash function. Hash-based message authentication code (HMAC) provides the server and the client each with a private key that is known only to that specific server and that specific client. The client creates a unique HMAC, or hash, per request to the server by hashing the request data with the private keys and sending it as part of a request. What makes HMAC more secure than Message Authentication Code (MAC) is that the key and the message are hashed in separate steps. HMACs are used by IPSec.

➢ CBC-MAC

In cryptography, a Cipher Block Chaining Message Authentication Code, abbreviated CBC-MAC, is a technique for constructing a message authentication code from a block cipher. The message is encrypted with some block cipher algorithm in CBC mode to create a chain of blocks such that each block depends on the proper encryption of the previous block. This interdependence ensures that a change to any of the plaintext bits will cause the final encrypted block to change in a way that cannot be predicted or counteracted without knowing the key to the block cipher.

➢ Various Hashing Algorithms

There are many different types of hash algorithms but the most common type of hashing used for file integrity checks are MD5 and SHA-2. An MD5 hash function encodes a string of information and encodes it into a 128-bit fingerprint.

➢ MD2

MD2 is an earlier, 8-bit version of MD5, an algorithm used to verify data integrity was developed by Professor Ronald L. Rivets of MIT in 1989 to provide a secure hash function for 8-bit processors. MD2 pads the message so that its length is a multiple of 16 bytes. It then computes a 16-byte checksum and appends it to the end of the message. A 128-bit message digest is then generated by using the entire original message along with the appended checksum.

Cryptanalytic attacks exist against the MD2 algorithm, especially, if the checksum is not appended to the message before digest computation, collisions may occur. It has been later proved that MD2 is not a one-way function.

➢ MD4

In 1990, Rivets enhanced his message digest algorithm to support 32-bit processors and increase the level of security. This enhanced algorithm which is known as MD4 is a one-way hash function produces a 128-bit message digest value. It is used for high-speed computation in software implementations and is optimized for microprocessors. It first pads the message to ensure that the message length is 64 bits smaller than a multiple of 512 bits. For example, a 16-bit message would be padded with 432 additional bits of data to make it 448 bits, which is 64 bits smaller than a 512-bit message. The MD4 algorithm then processes 512-bit blocks of the message in three rounds of computation. The final output is a 128-bit message digest.

➢ MD5

In 1991, Rivest released the improved version of his message digest algorithm, which is named as MD5 is also an one way cryptographic hashing algorithm. It also processes 512-bit blocks of the message, but it uses four distinct rounds of computation to produce a digest of the same length as the MD2 and MD4, but offers much more guarantee of data security. Unfortunately, recent cryptanalytic attacks exposed that the MD5 protocol is subject to collisions, preventing its use for ensuring message integrity. Hence no longer in use.

➢ Secure Hash Algorithm (SHA)

The Secure Hash Algorithm (SHA) and its successors, SHA-1 and SHA-2, are standard hash functions designed and developed by NSA to be used with the Digital Signature Standard (DSS). SHA is similar to MD4. It has some extra mathematical functions and produces a 160-bit hash instead of a 128-bit hash, which makes it more resistant to brute force attacks, including birthday attacks. SHA was improved upon and renamed SHA-1.It takes an input of virtually any length and produces a 160-bit message digest. The SHA-1 algorithm processes a message in 512-bit blocks. Therefore, if the message length is not a multiple of 512, the SHA algorithm pads the message with additional data until the length reaches the next highest multiple of 512. Recent cryptanalytic attacks demonstrated that there are weaknesses in the SHA-1 algorithm. This led to the creation of SHA-2, which has four variants viz.

- SHA-256 produces a 256-bit message digest using a 512-bit block size.

- SHA-224 uses a truncated version of the SHA-256 hash to produce a 224-bit message digest using a 512-bit block size.

- SHA-512 produces a 512-bit message digest using a 1,024-bit block size.

- SHA-384 uses a truncated version of the SHA-512 hash to produce a 384-bit digest using a 1,024-bit block size.

➢ HAVAL

HVAL is a modified of MD5 and is a variable-length, one-way hash function and is a modification of MD5. HAVAL uses 1,024-bit blocks and produces hash values of 128, 160, 192, 224, and 256 bits.

➢ Tiger

A hashing algorithm named Tiger has been designed and developed by Ross Anderson and Eli Biham to carry out hashing functionalities on 64-bit systems which is faster than MD5 and SHA-1 The resulting hash value is 192 bits. Design-wise, most hash algorithms (MD5, RIPEMD, SHA-0, and SHA-1) are derivatives or have been built upon the MD4architecture. Tiger was built upon a different type of architecture with the goal of not being vulnerable to the same type of attacks that could be successful on the other hashing algorithms. A summary of hash algorithms are given below in Table 7.2.

Table 7.2 Summary of Available Hash Algorithms

Summary

Beginning with explaining cryptography components and their relationships, definition and need for cryptography, this chapter then move on to explain symmetric cryptography and types of symmetric systems. Various encryption methods such as Data Encryption Standard (DES), 3DES (Triple DES), Blowfish, Twofish, International Data Encryption Algorithm (IDEA), RC4, RC5, RC6, Advanced Encryption Standard (AES), Secure and Fast Encryption Routine (SAFER) and Serpent are then briefly explained for gaining an introductory knowledge of cryptography for automation engineers. A brief explain of Asymmetric or Public Key Infrastructure (PKI), Certificate Authorities, Certificates, Registration Authority, Certificate Generation and Destruction and Key Management are then provided as it is most important in the industrial automation world today. This chapter concludes with hashing algorithms and uses.

CHAPTER EIGHT
CYBER SECURITY: FOREMOST CHALLENGE

8.1 INTRODUCTION

In recent years, with the integration of Information and Communication Technology (ICT), dependency of the electrical power grid on cyberspace grew, cyber-threats have materialized as new vulnerabilities, and the resilience and security of the power grids have become a major concern. The power system automation and integration of Smart Grid technologies transforms the power generation and flow on the Nations electricity grid, with remote controlling mechanisms by means of various ICT technologies. Further new intelligent technologies and Intelligent Electronics Devices (IEDs) utilizing bi-directional communications and other digital advantages are being introduced and optimized with internet connectivity. Modernization of many Industrial Control Systems (ICS) particularly, the Supervisory Control and Data Acquisition (SCADA) system also has resulted in tremendous dependency on the internet and public networks. In fact these dependencies made the cyber-security of the automated power grid, one of the prime focus areas which need serious efforts to protect its integrity.

The advancement in unguided communication media and the Distributed Control System (DCS) technology made the remote access secure and reliable especially in the Smart Grid or SCADA DMS area. Hence engineers working in the power system automation must consider and address the attributes such as interoperability, extent of openness, scalability, simplicity and security, while considering the geographical, operational, and logistical constraints of Smart Grid and Power System SCADA. To achieve these requirements a valid and secure remote access policy is essential. But the implications of communications crossing the physical confines of their immediate network is the major challenge while accomplishing these benefits, and need additional meticulous security requirements. The increasing frequency of cyber intrusions on Industrial Control Systems (ICS) of critical infrastructure certify these requirements. Further the recent reports of intrusions into ICS clearly indicate that the attackers are with sound technical capability, having the capability of taking down the control systems that operate on the power grids, and other critical infrastructure. Today this is a nerve-wracking and challenging issue for power system SCADA and Smart Grid engineers. In fact communication is an essential component of the Smart Grid but security is a crucial concern with highest priority and not at all an add on.

If the system collapses under a cyber-attack it creates hazard and inconvenience to consumers and utilities alike. Hence while implementing the Smart Grid or power system SCADA, the important areas which need considerable special attention are, Secured Remote Access and End Point Security, Control Center Architecture and Security, AMI and secured communication, Firewall deployment and HIPS, and Threats, Vulnerabilities and Solutions. This chapter discusses the difference between IT security and SCADA security, various security concerns, solutions and standards such as remote access techniques, authentication techniques, NERC CIP standards etc. pertaining to power system automation.

8.2   IT SECURITY AND OT SECURITY

The cyber-space which is the present warfront is described as the interdependent network of information technology infrastructures, which includes the internet, communications networks, computer systems, and embedded processors and controllers of critical industries. Today this interdependent cyber-space is a crucial component of National Critical Infrastructure which needs distinct protective measures. Cyber-space is used to exchange information, buy and sell products and services, and enable many online transactions across a wide range of sectors, both nationally and internationally. As a result, a secure cyber-space becomes most critical to the economy and security of any Nation.

Without developing an appropriate cyber-security policy, cloud based process automation can be disastrous. Hence to protect the Nation's critical information infrastructures, from risks such as online fraud, identity theft, and misuse of information online, a well defined cyber-security and mitigation policy in accordance with the utility's safety and security has to be devised with utmost care.

Today the rapid growth of ICTs and social inter-dependency has changed the perception of Critical Information Infrastructure threats and, as a consequence, cyber-security has become international agenda. It is crucial to understand the risks that accompany new technologies in order to maximize the benefits. Growing threats to security, at the level of the individual, the firms, government and critical infrastructures, make security as responsibility of public. It is important to understand and keep conversant contours of fast changing challenges. Present ICS mainly based on the SCADA technology. The security requirement of the SCADA is quite different from IT security as it involves mission critical processes. The basic difference of the IT security and SCADA security are briefly described below.

Generally in SCADA systems, or Industrial Control Systems, the fact that any logic execution within the system has a direct impact in the physical world warranting safety to be paramount. The field devices being on the first frontier to directly face human lives and ecological environment, the field devices in SCADA systems are deemed with no less importance than central hosts. Further certain operating systems and applications running on SCADA systems, which are unconventional and proprietary to IT personnel, may not work correctly with commercial off-the-shelf IT cyber security solutions. Also, factors like the continuous availability demand, time-criticality, constrained computation resources on edge devices, large physical base, wide interface between digital and analog signals, social acceptance including cost effectiveness, user reluctance to change, legacy issues, etc. make SCADA system an extraordinary security engineering task.

ICSs are hard real-time systems as the completion of an operation after its deadline is considered useless and potentially can cause cascading effect in the physical world. The operational deadlines from event to system response impose stringent constraints as a missing deadline can cause a complete failure of the system.

Latency is very important and can be destructive to ICS performance. If the system does not react within a certain time frame can cause great loss in safety, such as damaging the surroundings including fatal accidents. It's not the length of time frame but whether a particular operation meeting its deadline is vital in ICS. Soft real-time systems, may tolerate certain latency and respond with decreased service quality (graceful degradation) which can be tolerated.

Non-major violation of time constraints in soft real-time systems leads to degraded quality rather than system failure. Furthermore due to the physical nature, tasks performed by ICS. A system and the processes within each task are often needed to be interrupted and restarted. The timing aspect and task interrupts can prevent the use of conventional encryption block algorithms. Vulnerability of SCADA rises from the fact that memory allocation is more critical in a Real-Time Operating System (RTOS), than in other operating systems. Many field level devices in ICS system are embedded systems such as RTUs, IEDs, etc. which run years without rebooting but accumulating fragmentation. Thus, buffer overflow is more problematic in ICS than in traditional IT.

8.3   REMOTE ACCESS AND OPEN COMMUNICATION SYSTEMS

For any DCS such as Smart Grid implementation, communication among various automation components is critical. Power measurement devices must talk to real-time control components across the entire power generation, transmission and distribution systems. All automation components must be connected to the SCADA system and these SCADA system must be linked to one another. All of these connections and linkages require open communication systems, often based on Ethernet and the internet. Open systems are preferred today as they reduce communication system costs in the following way as listed below.

1. *Hardware and software are relatively inexpensive:* Open systems cut purchase costs because communications hardware

and software based on Ethernet and the internet are much less expensive than their alternatives.

2. *Installation relies on familiar tools and techniques:* Installation is eased because of a widespread familiarity with these types of systems among implementation agencies.

3. *Existing communications system can be used:* Present communications infrastructure can be used in many cases, dramatically reducing installation and other related costs.

4. *Open protocols cut integration costs:* Integration expenses for connecting different Smart Grid components are reduced because Ethernet is used as a common communications hardware protocol.

5. *Skilled manpower is extensively available:* On-going maintenance and operation costs are reduced because many in the industry are familiar with Ethernet and the internet.

Open communication systems keep costs down, but these systems increases vulnerabilities to cyber-attack than their proprietary because of the following reasons.

1. Large number of interconnections creates multiple vulnerabilities,

2. Armies of professional hackers are familiar with open system protocols,

3. Browser-based internet servers and clients create entry points,

4. Windows-based systems invite attack,

5. Vulnerable TCP/IP software stacks are used across multiple platforms, and

6. Older closed protocols lack security when ported to open protocols like TCP/IP.

Proprietary systems not only have fewer connections to other systems, they are also less familiar to professional hackers, creating a possible *security through obscurity* defense. On the other hand communication systems based on Ethernet, TCP/IP protocols, internet and popular operating systems such as Windows, invite attacks from millions of hackers worldwide.

8.4   VPN AND MPLS IN DCS AUTOMATION

With the advancement in information and communication technology, DCS has taken a new dimension, spanning across geographical boundaries. For the effective implementation of DCS, a secure communication media and technology is most essential. Many utilities do not have their own full-fledged communication network such as optical, copper, or PLCC connectivity to link all remote sites within the automation network. In *such* cases MPLS/VPN is an ideal solution if implemented properly. A Virtual Private Network (VPN) is a secure, private connection through an untrusted network such as the internet normally established between a client device and a server device. It is considered as a private connection in a public network or in an untrusted network because the encryption and tunneling protocols are used to ensure the confidentiality and integrity of the data in transit. It is important to remember that VPN technology requires a tunnel to work and it assumes encryption.

This is very much useful for establishing secured remote access/connectivity in DCS. Here normally, a VPN client might be a Remote Terminal Unit (RTU) and the VPN server might be a server in the critical control network. Typically the client is the one that initiates the connection, and the server accepts and authenticates incoming connection requests from one or more clients. Once a VPN connection is established between a client and a server, the networks upstream of the client and the server are connected together such that network traffic may pass between them.

In the case of the RTU client as aforementioned, the RTU would appear as if it was actually plugged into the network upstream of the VPN server. As such, it would receive a new virtual IP address suitable for local network and could access other devices just as if it was directly connected to the network. When using VPNs, it's critical to remember that the VPN only secures the tunnel and not the client or server. To ensure network security, it's critical that the VPN is seamlessly integrated into a suitable firewall.

During exigent situations, remote VPN access provides secured way of maintaining the operational continuity and support. Remote VPN access permits bulk power organizations to keep personnel away from sites during dangerous weather conditions. This reduction of travel risks during such conditions permits the power utilities to protect some of their skilled manpower, the most critical assets. Remote VPN access allows bulk power organizations to limit the number of personnel at their facilities during periods of heightened physical security threats. During increased security risks, bulk power utilities should limit the number of personnel entering their facilities with greater scrutiny screening. This helps in reduction of operational staffs at risk to a physical attack on the facility.

VPN Architecture

For many years the de facto standard VPN software was Point-To-Point Tunneling Protocol (PPTP), which was made most popular when Microsoft included it in its Windows products. Since most internet-based communication first started over telecommunication links, the industry needed a way to secure PPP connections. The original goal of PPTP was to provide a way to tunnel PPP connections through an IP network, but most implementations included security features also since protection was becoming an important requirement for network transmissions at that time.

The two methods of VPN architecture today used are site-to-site VPN and remote user access VPN. Both these architecture helps the organization to replace long distance dial-up or leased line with local dial-ups or leased line to Internet Service Provider (ISP).

Security Issues of VPN

The advantage of using secure remote access sometimes makes the network susceptible to security breaches. The possibility of accessing enterprises network with laptops having unsecured External Access Points (EAP) cannot be ruled out. If the laptop device or a device connected to the EAP has a virus or some other malicious software, it can spread it to the enterprises network.

Though a properly installed VPN can prevent some of the performance issues associated with supporting multiple protocols and data transmission mediums, VPNs are only as fast as the slowest internet connection between the two endpoints. In addition, most IP applications were designed for low-latency and high reliability network environments. This means that network performance issues will become more pronounced with the increasing use of real-time and interactive applications. While some applications can be reprogrammed or reconfigured to work with increased latency, getting this workaround to work with some applications can be challenging, if not impossible.

Remote Access VPN

A remote access VPN allows individual users to establish secure connections with a remote computer network. Those users can access the secure resources on that network as if they were directly plugged into the network's servers.

An example of a company that needs a remote-access VPN is a large firm with hundreds of salespeople in the field. Another name for this type of VPN is virtual private dial-up network (VPDN), acknowledging that in its earliest form, a remote-access VPN required dialing into a server using an analog telephone system.

There are two components required in a remote access VPN. The first is a Network Access Server (NAS) also called a media gateway or a Remote Access Server (RAS). A NAS might be a dedicated server, or it might be one of multiple software applications running on a shared server. It's a NAS that a user connects to from the internet in order to use a VPN. The NAS requires that user to provide valid credentials to sign into the VPN. To authenticate the user's credentials, the NAS uses either its own authentication process or a separate authentication server running on the network.

VPN Termination in Remote Access

VPN terminating node in remote access is the node where the VPN protocols actually ends. Here the payload is exposed and unwrapped.

Data is no longer cypher rather the plain text. Extra care must be given to decide on VPN termination node else it can be a point of vulnerability. It is a common mistake in substation automation, terminating VPN at routers having multiple access point with connected devices have security holes.

As technology advances, there is an exponential growth of mobile, wireless and widely distributed networks which presents a vastly greater potential for unauthorized remote access. Hence it is better to secure all remote access over VPN with proper End Node Security (ENS) using point to-point IPSec or clientless Secured Socket Layer (SSL) technology.

Site-To-Site VPN

Site-to-site VPN is a type of VPN connection that is created between two separate locations. It provides the ability to connect geographically separate locations or networks, usually over the public internet connection or a WAN connection. Site-to-site VPN typically creates a direct, unshared and secure connection between two end points. Site-to-site VPN can be intranet based or extranet based. Intranet based site-to-site VPN is created between an organization's propriety networks, while extranet-based site to- site VPN is used for connecting with external partner networks or an intranet. The connection in a site-to-site VPN is generally enabled through a VPN gateway device.

Traditional VPN rely on internet Protocol Security (IPSec) to tunnel between the two endpoints. IPSec works on the Network Layer of the OSI Model, securing all data that travels between the two endpoints without an association to any specific application. When connected on an IPSec VPN the client computer is *virtually* a full member of the corporate network which is able to see and potentially access the entire network.

The majority of IPSec VPN solutions require third party hardware or software. In order to access an IPSec VPN, the workstation or device in use must have an IPSec client software application installed. This has both an advantage and disadvantage. The advantage is that it provides an extra layer of security, if the client machine is running the right VPN client software to connect to the IPSec VPN with proper configuration. These are additional hurdles that a hacker would have to get over before gaining access to the customers network.

The disadvantage is that it can be a financial burden for the utilities to maintain the licenses for the client software and for the technical support to install and configure the client software on all remote machines. It is this disadvantage is well projected as one of the negatives by the rival Secure Sockets Layer (SSL) VPN solutions. SSL is a common protocol and most web browsers have SSL capabilities built in. Therefore almost every computer in the world is already equipped with the necessary *client software* to connect to an SSL VPN. Another advantage of SSL VPN is that they allow more precise access control. Primarily, they provide tunnels to specific applications rather than to the entire corporate LAN. So, users on SSL VPN connections can only access the applications that they are configured to access rather than the whole network. Secondly, it is easier to provide different access rights to different users and have more granular control over user access.

A disadvantage of SSL VPN is that the customers are accessing the applications through a web browser which means that they exclusively work for web based applications. It is possible to web enable other applications so that they also can be accessed through SSL VPN, but doing so adds more complexity to the solution and eliminates some of the advantages.

Having direct access only to the web enabled SSL applications also means that the users don't have access to network resources such as printers or centralized storages and are unable to use the VPN for file sharing or file backups.

SSL VPN have been gaining in prevalence and popularity, however they are not the right solution for every instance. Likewise, IPSec VPN is not suited for every instance either. Vendors are continuing to develop ways to expand the functionality of the SSL VPN and it is a technology that a costumer should watch closely if the customer is in the market for a secure remote networking solution. Presently, it is important to consider carefully the needs of the customer's remote uses and consider the pros and cons of each solution to determine what works best for them.

Point-to-Point Tunneling Protocol (PPTP) is a network protocol used in the implementation of Virtual Private Network (VPN). Newer VPN technologies like OpenVPN, L2TP, and IPSec may offer better network security support, but PPTP remains a popular network protocol especially on Windows computers. PPTP uses a client-server design that operates at Layer 2 of the OSI model. PPTP VPN clients are included by default in Microsoft Windows and also available for both Linux and Mac OS X. PPTP is most commonly used for VPN remote access over the internet. In this usage, VPN tunnels are created through the following two step process.

1. The user launches a PPTP client that connects to their internet provider, and

2. PPTP creates a TCP control connection between the VPN client and VPN server.

The protocol uses TCP port 1723 for these connections and General Routing Encapsulation (GRE) to finally establish the tunnel. PPTP also supports VPN connectivity across a local network. Once the VPN tunnel is established, PPTP supports two types of information flow which is mentioned below.

*   *Control messages* for managing and eventually tearing down the VPN connection. It passes directly between VPN client and server, and

*   *Data packets* that pass through the tunnel, to or from the VPN client. Layer 2 Tunneling Protocol (L2TP) is another tunneling protocol used to support VPN or as part of the delivery of services by ISP. It does not provide any encryption or confidentiality by itself. Rather, it relies on an encryption protocol that it passes within the tunnel to provide privacy.

L2TP combines the features of PPTP and Cisco's Layer 2 Forwarding (L2F) protocol. L2TP tunnels Point-to-Point Protocol (PPP) traffic over various network types such as IP, ATM and X.25. In fact it is not restricted to IP networks as PPTP. PPTP and L2TP have very similar focuses, which is to get PPP traffic to an end point that is connected to some type of network that does not understand PPP. Like PPTP, L2TP does not actually provide much protection for the PPP traffic, but it integrates with protocols that do provide security features. L2TP inherits PPP authentication and integrates with IPSec to provide confidentiality, integrity, and potentially another layer of authentication.

Difference between IPSec VPN and SSL VPN

- Generally, to start the IPSec VPN secure connection, the user has to start the application by installing IPSec 3rd party client application or hardware in client PC. This incur financial burden to utilities, as they have to buy licenses for VPN clients. But for SSL VPN, it is not necessary to install separate applications. Almost all the modern standard web browsers can use SSL connections.

- In IPSec communication, once the client is authenticated to the VPN, then the client has the full access of the private network, which may not be necessary, but in SSL VPNs, it provides more precise access control. At the beginning of the SSL authentication, it creates tunnels to specific applications using sockets rather than to the whole network. Also, this enables to provide role based access having different access rights for different users.

- One of the disadvantages of SSL VPN is that, it is only used for web based applications. For other applications, though it is possible to use by web-enabling it adds some complexity for the applications.

- Since it provides access only for Web Enabled Applications (WEA), SSL VPN is difficult to use with applications like file sharing and printing, but IPSec VPNs provide highly reliable printing and file sharing facilities.

- SSL VPNs are becoming more popular due to ease of use and reliability but, as mentioned above, it is not reliable with all the applications. Therefore, selection of the VPN (SSL or IPSec) totally depends on the application and requirements.

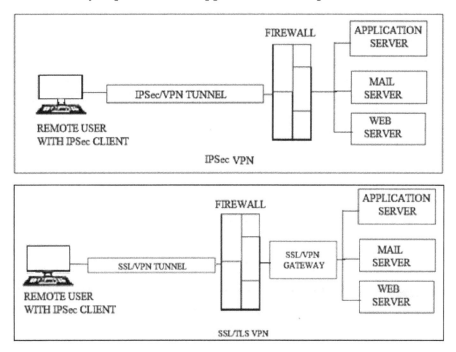

Figure 8.1 IPSec and SSL VPN

An appropriate summary of Tunnelling Protocols are briefly described below.

- PPTP operates in client/server architecture capable of extending and protecting PPP connections. It is a data link layer protocol works and transmits over IP networks only.

- L2TP is a hybrid of Layer 2 Forwarding (L2F) and PPTP. It extends and protects PPP connections. It also operates at the data link layer. It works and transmits over multiple types of networks, joint with IPSec for security.

- IPSec is capable of handling multiple VPN connections at the same time, provides secure authentication and encryption, operates only on IP networks. It mainly focuses on LAN-to-LAN communication rather than user-to-user and operates on the network layer, and provides security on top of IP.

- SSL operates on the transport layer and protects mainly web-based traffic. Most of the web browsers already embedded SSL as it is for deployment. However it can only protect a small number of protocol types, thus is not an infrastructure-level VPN solution. It has granular access control, configuration and better security features as SSL VPNs are closer to the application layer. However, there are a smaller number of traffic types that can be protected through this VPN type.

One VPN solution is not necessarily better than the other, they just have their own focused purposes and are described below.

- PPTP is used when a PPP connection needs to be extended through an IP based network.

- L2TP is used when a PPP connection needs to be extended through a non IP based network.

- IPSec is used to protect IP based traffic and is commonly used in gateway-to-gateway connections.

- SSL VPN is used when a specific application layer traffic type needs protection.

The predecessor to SSL is Transport Layer Security (TLS), which is an actual standard. SSL is a de facto standard and is more popular than TLS because of its large deployment base. Attackers commonly encrypt their attack traffic so that countermeasures which are put into place to analyze traffic for suspicious activity are not effective. Attackers can use SSL, TLS, or PPTP to encrypt malicious traffic as it transverses the network. When an attacker compromises and opens up a back door on a system, the attacker will commonly encrypt the traffic and that will then get exchanged between his system and the compromised system. It is important to configure security network devices to only allow approved encrypted channels.

Deploying VPN

To deploy an efficient and operational VPN, several different elements are needed at various steps along the path, starting from the client, through the cloud, to the network boundary and into enterprise networks. Within the enterprise network, VPN can terminate at Communication Front End (CFE) or at the server, by properly ensuring the secure data transfer. The basic VPN necessities and components are briefly described below.

- Client VPN software to make a secure remote connection,

- VPN aware routers and firewalls which permit authentic unobstructed VPN traffic, and

- VPN appliances, concentrators or servers to handle and manage incoming VPN traffic and to establish and manage VPN sessions and their access to network resources.

➢ **Multi Protocol Label Switching (MPLS)**

Multi Protocol Label Switching (MPLS) was originally presented as a way of improving the forwarding speed of routers based on short path labels rather than longer network addresses but is now emerging as a crucial standard technology that offers new capabilities for large scale IP networks. Directing the data from one network node to the next based on short path labels rather than long network addresses, avoids complex lookups in a routing table. This technique saves significant time over traditional IP-based routing processes. In fact, MPLS is a protocol for speeding up and shaping network traffic flows. Furthermore, MPLS is designed to handle a wide range of protocols through encapsulation. Thus, the network is not limited to TCP/IP and compatible protocols. This enables the use of many other networking technologies, including T1/E1, ATM, Frame Relay, SONET, and DSL. MPLS got its name because it works with the internet Protocol (IP), Asynchronous Transfer Mode

(ATM) and Frame Relay network protocols. Any of these protocols can be used to create a Label Switched Paths (LSPs). It was created initially to save router's idling time by avoiding stop and look up routing tables. A common misconception is that MPLS is only used on private networks, but the protocol is used for all service provider networks including internet backbones. Today, Generalized Multi Protocol Label Switching (GMPLS) extends MPLS to manage Time Division Multiplexing (TDM), Lambda Switching and other classes of switching technologies beyond packet switching.

MPLS allows most packets to be forwarded at Layer 2 (the switching level) rather than having to be passed up to Layer 3 (the routing level). Each packet gets labelled on entry into the service provider's network by the ingress router. The label determines the pre-determined path LSP which the packet has to follow. LSPs, allow service providers to decide the best way for certain types of traffic to flow within a private or public network ahead of time. All the subsequent routing switches perform packet forwarding based only on those labels. These labels never look the IP header until they are badly required. Finally, the egress router removes the labels and forwards the original IP packet towards its final destination.

Service providers can use MPLS to improve Quality of Service (QoS) by defining LSPs that can meet specific Service Level Agreements (SLAs) on traffic latency, jitter, packet loss and downtime. For example, a network might have three service levels and they are,

- level for voice,
- level for time sensitive traffic, and
- level for best effort traffic.

MPLS also supports traffic separation and the creation of virtual private networks (VPNs), Virtual Private LAN Services (VPLS) and Virtual Leased Lines (VLLs).

➢ Choosing MPLS VPN Services

While choosing MPLS VPN service for an utility, one must be clearly aware of the requirements, network design and options of service providers. It is better to keep the following points in mind while selecting the MPLS VPN.

- Carefully evaluate the needs and optimized requirements,

- Gather the service providers offers in the near geographic area,

- Compare between the requirements and options of service providers, which matches the best to the requirements of the utility, and

- Recommendations from an experienced consultant are always better particularly, when the utility is selecting the MPLS services for the first time.

In many cases, selecting the appropriate MPLS/VPN service need to combine multiple services. For example, many enterprises use Layer 3 MPLS VPNs for smaller sites, pseudo wires for point-to-point links between data centers and Virtual Private LAN Service (VPLS) for sites that need high availability to control convergence speed and routing protocol behaviour. If the customer is planning for an MPLS VPN connectivity, it would be better to consider the following points, while finalizing the vendor evaluation.

- *Internet access:* Most vendors allow customer to connect their MPLS VPN directly to the internet through a shared network firewall. However, some of them restrict the outbound traffic, while others allow to establish an IPSec tunnel to the network firewall and then hop into customer's network. Still others allow inbound access through an encapsulated GRE tunnel that dumps off in front of another firewall in control, and

- *The full mesh:* While MPLS technology typically facilitates a full mesh of connectivity among all of the customer sites, this requires a single MPLS network. Some service providers have split their MPLS networks into geographic regions, and customer has to pay more to get connectivity from one region to another. Without this, traffic from one location to another may be forced through a third site acting as a hub. This can unnecessarily complicate the routing and make it inefficient.

Keep the point in mind that MPLS VPNs are not encrypted, rather they logically separate the customer data from other customer's data. The data shares the same physical path with other customers of the service provider, just like Frame Relay or any other WAN. Some vendors may offer additional services that allow the customer to encrypt their traffic. In fact, the customer may want to explore the possibility of using their existing IPSec VPN equipment to create permanent tunnels between sites over a new high-speed MPLS backbone to get the best of both worlds.

8.5 CRITICAL INFRASTRUCTURE PROTECTION

Certain infrastructure which are most essential for the normal function of a Nation such as energy and electric power, banking and finance, transportation, etc. are to be protected at any cost, else no Nation can survive. The following sessions briefly describes the critical infrastructure and its protection.

➢ Critical Infrastructure

Critical Infrastructure is defined as the system that compose the assets, systems, and networks, whether physical or virtual, and/or the computer programs, computer data, content data and/or traffic data so vital to a country that the incapacitation or destruction or interference with such systems and assets would have a debilitating impact on security, national or economic security, national public health and safety, or any combination thereof.

Every day, products and services that support the way of life flow, almost flawlessly in areas of energy and electric power, banking and finance, transportation, Information and Communications Technology (ICT), water systems, Government and private emergency services.

All these are made possible with the proper integration of the systems and networks such as the roads, airports, power plants, and communication facilities. If just one of these systems in the infrastructure is disrupted there could be awful consequences. These infrastructure that are essential for operations of the economy and government are generally termed as Critical Infrastructure of a Nation. Today these critical sectors whose operations greatly depend on ICT and therefore it become inevitable to protect these sectors from cyber-threat.

> **Critical Infrastructure Protection (CIP)**

As explained the operational stability and security of Critical Infrastructure is vital for economic security of a Nation and hence its protection must be given paramount importance. Many Nations consider power sector as Super Critical Infrastructure (SCI) as it is the back bone of almost all industry. One of the purposes of Critical Infrastructure protection is to establish a real-time ability for all sectors of the critical infrastructure community to share information on the current status of infrastructure elements. Ultimately, the goal is to protect the Critical Infrastructure by eliminating the known vulnerabilities and develop a proactive defense mechanism to counter cyber-attacks to Critical Infrastructure. Thus the need of the hour is to chalk out a national policy for Critical Infrastructure Protection (CIP), created through a partnership between the government and private industry.

> **Critical Information Infrastructure Protection**

Within the last two decades, advances in information and communications technologies have revolutionized Government, scientific, educational, and commercial infrastructures. Higher processing power of end devices, miniaturization, reducing memory storage cost, wireless networking technologies capable of supporting high bandwidth and widespread use of internet have transformed stand-alone systems and predominantly closed networks into a virtually seamless fabric of interconnectivity. ICT or information infrastructure enables large scale processes throughout the economy, facilitating complex interactions among systems across global networks. Their interactions propel innovation in industrial design and manufacturing, e-commerce, e-governance, communications, and many other economic sectors. The information infrastructure provides for processing, transmission, and storage of vast amounts of vital information used in every domain of society, and it enables Government agencies to rapidly interact with each other as well as with industry, citizens, state and local governments, and the Governments of other Nations. information infrastructure also encompass interconnected computers, servers, storage devices, routers, switches and other related equipments increasingly support the functioning of such critical national capabilities. Thus ICT has become an integral part of the Critical Information Infrastructure as well and need to be protected from cyber-attack.

8.6 SECURITY CONCERNS IN SUBSTATION AUTOMATION

Substation Automation (SA)is the need of the hour as substations form the base of the most important functions of power utilities. Any major breakthrough in a substation technology is seen as one of the foremost aspects of the Smart Grid revolution. SA not only revolutionized the mode of operation and maintenance, rather it introduced a new culture of managing the utility network. Anticipating the upcoming Smart Grid revolution, many transmission and distribution utilities are explicitly targeting to complete substation automation in a time bound manner. The two main issues are some of the substations are partially automated while the remaining are not. The profusion of the substation and feeder automation equipments from different manufactures, which ranges from SCADA to alarm processing, retrofitting is relatively an easy job today. But an essential knowledge of ICT becomes mandatory without which substation automation can be a bottleneck for implementing Smart Grid.

However many power utilities, mainly due to economic reasons, adopt conventional substation design. Though it caters the present requirements, migration to Smart Grid may become burdensome. Further in the long run O & M costs exceeds relatively high when compared to one-time investment for automated digital substation, as it requires minimal human intervention and has enhanced operation efficiency which saves money.

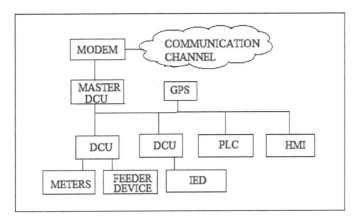

Figure 8.2 Block diagram of an automated substation

A block diagram of a typical automated substation which is shown in Figure 8.2 is generally preferred today as it can accommodate the Smart Grid revolution with relatively lesser investment.

Generally the data concentrator is an integral part of the RTU, which collect the information, and send the data to the control center through a communication channel. Since the substations are remote sites, method like dial-up modem, wireless GSM/CDMA, or dedicated RS232/RS485 serial are to be used. This introduces threat points from hackers as well as insiders. The attack points in a conventional substation with RTU and Human Machine Interface (HMI) are shown in Figure 8.3.

Hence care must be taken to protect the system with proper encryption and authentication between each and every communication nodes. Ensuring the NERC CIP compliance or international equivalent standards is becoming mandatory in power sector today to secure not only the Bulk Electric Supply (BES) but also in all other areas of power generation, transmission and distribution.

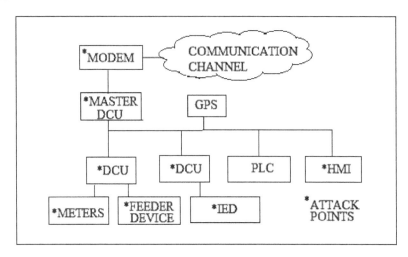

Figure 8.3 Attack points in an automated substation with DCU and HMI

If a local HMI is provided in the substation with connectivity to local data concentrator, it is most critical that the communication between the data concentrator and HMI must be appropriately authenticated and secured by required level of encryption. Today the local HMI or Local Data Monitoring System (LDMS) which are directly linked with the data concentrator or RTU for local monitoring are discouraged due to internal threat, unless the connectivity and communication security is ensured. The other solution is to provide a separate communication channel from the control center to the substation for local monitoring but is expensive and requires recurring cost.

The security threats can be from intruders and from insiders of the corporate network. External intruders can gain access to the system through the SCADA communication link, modem, and any dial up lines to certain systems like IEDs. The lines can be privately owned or leased from a carrier and are vulnerable to eavesdropping and intrusions that can corrupt the data. The intruders could be members of general public or cyber-criminals. Internal intrusion can happen inside the corporate WAN, as many unauthorized users can gain access to the data unless the utility is very strict with the password policy, privileges, and authentication measures. Employees or suppliers of substation equipment may gain access to critical data and can extract crucial information or cause damage unless prevented effectively from doing so.

Encryption is one of the methods that can effectively handle many of the attacks discussed. Inserting IPSec protocol in IP level is a typical example. But this encryption requires RTUs/IEDs with processors of higher computing capability and makes the system very expensive. There is a grave requirement to accelerate the implementation of cyber-security measures in Smart Grid and power system SCADA.

➤ Attack Vector through Substation HMI

Today, within the various SCADA solutions, the Human Machine Interface (HMI), especially the HMI at remote locations for local data monitoring and configuring is the most favourite and most preferred target for attackers. The HMI at the control center acts as a unified hub for managing Critical Infrastructure. If an attacker succeeds in compromising the HMI, nearly anything can be done to the infrastructure itself, causing even physical damage to SCADA equipment. Even if attackers decide not to disrupt operations, they can still exploit the HMI to gather information about a system or disable alarms and notifications meant to alert operators of danger to SCADA equipment.

Many cyber-security professionals found that most HMI vulnerabilities fall into four categories viz. memory corruption, credential management, lack of authentication/authorization and insecure defaults, and code injection. All of which are preventable through secure development practices. It is also observed that the average time needed between disclosure of a Zero Day Initiative (ZDI) of a SCADA vendor and the time for releasing a patch takes up to 150 days. This delay in releasing patches must be minimized by the HMI vendors by giving special attention and respond accordingly. Also the ZDI developers should start with basic fuzzing techniques to find new vulnerabilities in HMIs.

Software developers should also look for new file associations during installation to aid in fuzzing, as many of the file formats are wide open. Developers of HMI and SCADA solutions would be well advised to adopt the secure life cycle practices implemented by OS. By taking simple steps such as auditing for the use of banned APIs, vendors can make their products more resilient to attacks. SCADA developers also should expect that their products may be used in manners that they did not intend to and developers have to indeed assume that their products and solutions will be connected to a public network. Hence developers must have a mindset that assumes the worst-case scenario while developing the applications. It is better that if developers implement more defense-in-depth strategy to enhance protection.

The SCADA HMI malware specifically targeting ICS aggressively aim HMIs. The ZDI program encourages researchers to find and report the bugs associated with HMI and other SCADA systems to the bounty program. By working together, the developers receive compensation for their work while the vendors receive valuable data for improving their products. Present scenario indicates that bugs in SCADA systems will likely be present for many years to come. Again by working together, the security of these systems will continue to improve though a completely secure system will never be created. Implementing strong research and development tactics will be the best chance to keep the lights on as long as needed else HMI may become a Hacker Machine Interface.

➢ Security Concerns of ICS Control Center

The control center architecture must be designed with utmost security and with proper disaster recovery center. Secured ingress and egress must be ensured with the field devices, IEDs, Smart Meters, other control centers, etc. Usually the field devices and Smart Meters communicate with the Communication Front End (CFE) server through VPN preferably SSL/VPN. Obviously the CFE should have the capability of handling very large data, and certain situation act as a Data Management Server with Web server capabilities. Front End Processor (FEP) of CFE server should have very high processing capability and must be hot redundant. Today it is a general practice that the control center architecture is logically segmented to various zones and critical networks are isolated. The data transfer between these zones is generally through firewalls with proper configuration. One of the usual recommended practice is to separate the SCADA network from the corporate network.

The nature of network traffic on these two networks should be different. internet access, FTP, e-mail, and remote access will typically be permitted on the corporate network but should not be on the SCADA network. Rigorous change control procedures for network equipment, configuration, and software changes may not be in place on the corporate network. If SCADA network traffic is carried on the corporate network, it could be intercepted or be subjected to a Denial of Service (DoS) attack. Having separate networks, security and performance problems on the corporate network will not be able to affect the SCADA network. A typical control center architecture of Power System SCADA having Firewall with De Militarised Zone (DMZ) between corporate network and control network are shown in Figure 8.4.

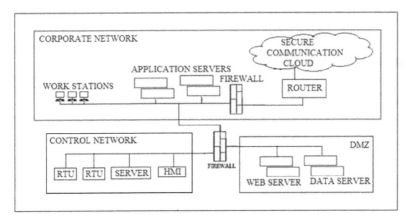

Figure 8.4 Firewall with DMZ between Corporate and Control Networks

Using firewalls with the ability to establish a DMZ between the corporate and control networks are preferred today in MCC architecture. Each DMZ holds one or more critical components, such as the data historian, the wireless access point, or remote and third party access systems. In effect, the use of a DMZ capable firewalls allows the creation of an intermediate network.

Creating a DMZ requires the firewall to offer three or more interfaces, especially when linking public and private interfaces. One of the interfaces is connected to the corporate network, the second to the control network, and the remaining interfaces to the shared or insecure devices such as the data historian server or wireless access points on the DMZ network.

Non-firewall based solutions will not provide suitable isolation between control networks and corporate networks. The two zone solutions especially without DMZ are marginally acceptable but should be only be deployed with extreme care. The most secure, manageable, and scalable control network and corporate network segregation architectures are typically based on a system with at least three zones, incorporating a DMZ.

> **Defense-in-Depth Architecture**

Another SCADA control center architecture which gained much popularity with the incorporation of modern firewall technology is the Defense-in-depth architecture. A single security product, technology or solution cannot adequately protect a SCADA by itself. A multiple layer strategy involving two or more different overlapping security mechanisms is desired so that the impact of a failure in any one mechanism is minimized. A defence-in-depth architecture strategy includes the use of firewalls, the creation of demilitarized zones, intrusion detection capabilities along with effective security policies, training programs and incident response mechanisms. In addition, an effective defense-in-depth strategy requires a thorough understanding of possible attack vectors on a SCADA. These include,

- backdoors and holes in network perimeter,
- vulnerabilities in common protocols,
- attacks on field devices,
- database attacks, and

- communications hijacking and Man-In-The-Middle (MITM) attacks.

Figure 8.5 shows a typical SCADA defense-in-depth architecture strategy that has been developed with improved control systems cyber-security. The control systems cyber-security using *defence-in-depth strategies* for organizations use control system networks which maintain a multi-tier information architecture is elaborated in detail in succeeding chapter.

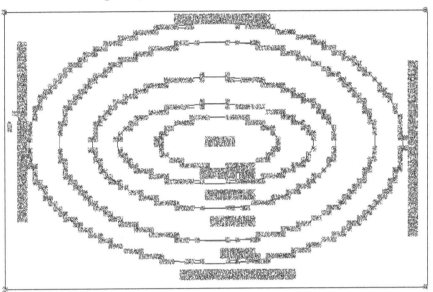

Figure 8.5 Defense-in-Depth Architecture

➢ Firewall deployment and Policies

Once the defence-in-depth architecture is in place, the security engineers have to determine exactly the traffic that should be allowed through the firewalls. Configuring the firewalls to deny all except, for the traffic absolutely required for business needs of every organization. Cyber-security engineers of the utility must be aware of the data flow requirements of business and the security impacts of allowing that traffic through. Typical example is, many organizations considered allowing SQL traffic through the firewall as required for business for many data historian servers. Unfortunately, SQL was also the vector for the Slammer worm. Many important protocols used in the industrial world, such as HTTP, FTP, OPC/DCOM, Ethernet/IP, and MODBUS/TCP, have significant security vulnerabilities.

While deploying the firewalls in SCADA which is the heart of ICS, the following points are most important from the point of security. When installing a single two-port firewall without a DMZ for shared servers particular care needs to be taken with the ruleset design. The best practice is to keep rules which should be stateful with IP address and port specific. The address portion of the rules should restrict incoming traffic to a very small set of shared devices on the control network from a controlled set of addresses on the corporate network. Allowing any IP addresses on the corporate network to access servers inside the control network is not recommended. In addition, the allowed ports should be carefully restricted to relatively secure protocols such as Hypertext Transfer Protocol Secure (HTTPS). Allowing HTTP, FTP, or any unencrypted SCADA protocol to cross the firewall is a security risk due to the potential for traffic sniffing and modification. Rules should be added to deny inbound communication with the control network.

Rules should allow internal devices in the control network to establish connections outside the control network in a most secured manner. On the other hand, if the DMZ architecture is being used, then it is possible to configure the system so that traffic will not pass directly between the corporate network and the control network. With a few special exceptions which are mentioned below, all traffic from either side can terminate at the servers in the DMZ. This allows more flexibility in the protocols allowed through the firewall. A typical example, MODBUS/TCP might be used to communicate from the RTUs/IEDs to the data historian, while HTTP might be used for communication between the historian and enterprise clients. Both protocols are inherently insecure, yet in this case they can be used safely because neither actually crosses between the two networks. An extension to this concept is the idea of using *disjoint* protocols in all control networks to corporate network communications. That is, if a protocol is allowed between the control network and DMZ, then it is explicitly not allowed between the DMZ and corporate network. This design greatly reduces the chance of a worm such as Slammer actually making its way into the control network, since the worm would have to use two different exploits over two different protocols.

One area of considerable variation in practice is the control of outbound traffic from the control network, which could represent a significant risk if unmanaged. Typical example is Trojan horse software that uses HTTP tunnelling to exploit poorly defined outbound rules. Thus, it is important that outbound rules be as stringent as inbound rules. A summary of the preferred outbound and inbound rules for the secure data flow are described below.

- Inbound traffic to the control system should be blocked. Access to devices inside the control system should be through a DMZ.

- Outbound traffic through the control network firewall should be limited to essential communications only.

- All outbound traffic from the control network to the corporate network should be source and destination-restricted by service and port.

In addition to these rules, the firewall should be configured with outbound filtering to stop forged IP packets from leaving the control network or the DMZ. In practice this is achieved by checking the source IP addresses of outgoing packets against the firewall's respective network interface address. The intent is to prevent the control network from being the source of spoofed communications, which are often used in DoS attacks. Thus, the firewalls should be configured to forward IP packets only if those packets have a correct source IP address for the control network or DMZ networks. Finally, internet access by devices on the control network should be strongly discouraged. Usually the firewalls deployed in PSS come with the default configuration as described below. However the installation and security engineers do confirm the ruleset of the firewalls without any compromise, else can be catastrophic.

- The base rule set should be deny all, permit none.

- Ports and services between the control network environment and the corporate network should be enabled and permissions granted on a specific case-by-case basis. There should be a documented business justification with risk analysis and a responsible person for each permitted incoming or outgoing data flow.

- All permit rules should be both IP address and TCP/UDP port specific, and stateful if appropriate.

- All rules should restrict traffic to a specific IP address or range of addresses.

- Traffic should be prevented from transiting directly from the control network to the corporate network. All traffic should terminate in the DMZ.

- Any protocol allowed between the control network and DMZ should explicitly NOT be allowed between the DMZ and corporate networks (and vice-versa).

- All outbound traffic from the control network to the corporate network should be source and destination-restricted by service and port.

- Outbound packets from the control network or DMZ should be allowed only if those packets have a correct source IP address that is assigned to the control network or DMZ devices.

- Control network devices should not be allowed to access the internet.

- Control networks should not be directly connected to the internet, even if protected via a firewall.

- All firewall management traffic should be carried on either a separate, secured management network or over an encrypted network with two-factor authentication.

Traffic should also be restricted by IP address to specific management stations.

These are only guidelines, hence a vigilant assessment of each control environment is required before finalizing and implementing the firewall ruleset.

Summary

This chapter gives a description about how the SCADA security is different from IT security and its importance. The requirement of open communication system and standardization are discussed with emphasis on security. The VPN and MPLS technology and selection criteria are also discussed. The critical infrastructure protection requirements are described in a succinct and palatable manner. Security concerns of the substation automation and control center architecture are discussed with mitigation solutions. Malware threats especially the attack of the lethal malware Stuxnet which is a nightmare for ICS implementing agencies because of the ZDVs of the Windows Operating System is described. These attack vectors and proposed solutions are discussed in this chapter. The chapter concludes with describing threats and vulnerabilities of ICS and power system SCADA with various types of attacks and mitigating techniques.

.

CHAPTER NINE
DEFENSE IN DEPTH ARCHITECTURE

9.1 INTRODUCTION

Presently one of the ICS architecture which gained much popularity with the incorporation of modern firewall technology is the defense-in-depth architecture. A single security product, technology or solution cannot adequately protect a SCADA by itself. A multiple layer strategy involving two or more different overlapping security mechanisms is desired so that the impact of a failure in any one mechanism is minimized.

A defense-in-depth architecture strategy includes the use of firewalls, the creation of demilitarized zones, intrusion detection capabilities along with effective security policies, training programs and incident response mechanisms. In addition, an effective defence-in-depth strategy requires a thorough understanding of possible attack vectors on a ICS. These include,

1. backdoors and holes in network perimeter,

2. vulnerabilities in common protocols,

3. attacks on field devices,

4. database attacks, and

5. communications hijacking and *Man-In-The-Middle (MITM)* attacks.

The control systems cyber-security using *defense-in-depth strategies* for organizations use control system networks which maintain a multi-tier information architecture which requires,

- maintenance of various field devices, telemetry collection, and/or industrial level process systems,

- access to facilities via remote data link or modem, and

- public facing services for customer or corporate operations. This strategy includes firewalls, the use of demilitarized zones and intrusion detection capabilities throughout the ICS architecture.

This chapter presents the *defence-in-depth strategies starting from the Purdue Reference Architecture, and explain the five level security needed to secure the ICS viz.* Physical Security, Network Security, Computer Security, Application Security and Device Security.

9.2 COMMON SCADA NETWORK SECURITY ATTACKS

1. DOS and DDOS attack

There are many cases where a website's server gets overloaded with traffic and simply crashes. But more commonly, this is what happens to a website during a DoS or DDoS attack. When a website has too much traffic, it's unable to serve its content to visitors.

A DoS attack is performed by one machine and its internet connection, by flooding a website with packets and making it impossible for genuine users to access the content of flooded website.

A distributed denial-of-service attack, is similar to DoS, but is more forceful. It's harder to overcome a DDoS attack. It's launched from several computers, and the number of computers involved can range from just a couple of them to thousands or even more. Since it's likely that not all of those machines belong to the attacker, they are compromised and added to the attacker's network by malware. These computers can be distributed around the entire globe, and that network of compromised computers is called botnet. Since the attack comes from so many different IP addresses simultaneously, a DDoS attack is much more difficult for the victim to locate and defend against.

2. Phishing

Phishing is a method of gathering personal information using misleading e-mails and websites. A method of a social engineering with the goal of obtaining sensitive data such as passwords, usernames, credit card numbers mainly using deceptive e-mails. The recipient of the email is tricked into opening a malicious link, which leads to the installation of malware on the recipient's computer. It can also obtain personal information by sending an email that appears to be sent from a bank, asking to verify the identity and stealing away the private information.

3. Rootkit

Rootkit is a collection of software tools that enables remote control and administration level access over a computer or computer networks. Once remote access is obtained, the rootkit can perform a number of malicious actions as it come equipped with key loggers, password stealers and antivirus disablers. Rootkits are installed by hiding in legitimate software when the user give permission to that software to make changes to the OS, the rootkit installs itself in the computer and waits for the hacker to activate it. Other ways of rootkit distribution include phishing emails, malicious links, files, and downloading software from suspicious websites.

4. SQL Injection Attack

Many servers store data for websites using SQL. SQL Injection Attack is a common attack vector that uses malicious SQL code for backend database manipulation to access information that was not intended to be displayed. This information may include any number of items, including sensitive company data, user lists or private customer details. With the advancement of technology, network security threats become sophisticated, making threat of SQL injection common and dangerous to privacy issues and data confidentiality.

5. Man-In-the-Middle Attacks

Man-in-the-middle attacks are cyber security attacks that allow the attacker to eavesdrop on communication between two targets. It can listen to a communication which should, in normal settings, be private. As a typical example, a man-in-the-middle attack happens when the attacker wants to intercept a communication between person A and person B. Person A sends their public key to person B, but the attacker intercepts it and sends a forged message to person B, representing themselves as A, but instead it has the attackers public key. B believes that the message comes from person A and encrypts the message with the attackers public key, sends it back to A, but attacker again intercepts this message, opens the message with private key, possibly alters it, and re-encrypts it using the public key that was firstly provided by person A. Again, when the message is transferred back to person A, they believe it comes from person B, and this way, it has an attacker in the middle that eavesdrops the communication between two targets. Some of the various types of MITM attacks are mentioned below.

- DNS spoofing
- HTTPS spoofing
- IP spoofing
- ARP spoofing
- SSL hijacking
- Wi-Fi hacking

6. Computer Virus

A computer virus is a type of computer program that, when executed, replicates itself by modifying other computer programs and inserting its own code. When this replication succeeds, the affected areas are then said to be *infected* with a computer virus for everyday Internet users, computer viruses are one of the most common threats to cyber security. Statistics show that approximately 33% of household computers are affected with some type of malware, more than half of which are viruses.

Computer viruses are pieces of software that are designed to be spread from one computer to another. They're often sent as email attachments or downloaded from specific websites with the intent to infect the computer and other computers on contact list by using systems on the user network. Viruses are known to send spam, disable the security settings, corrupt and steal data from the computer including personal information such as passwords, even going as far as to delete everything on the hard drive.

7. Rogue security software

Rogue security software poses a growing threat to computer security. It is malicious software that mislead users to believe there is a computer virus installed on their computer or that their security measures are not up to date. Then they offer to install or update users' security settings. They'll either ask the user to download their program to remove the alleged viruses, or to pay for a tool. Both cases lead to actual malware being installed on the computer.

8. Trojan horse

Trojan horse or Trojan refers to tricking someone by inviting into a securely protected area to deceive. In computing, it holds a very similar meaning. It is a malicious bit of attacking code or software that tricks users into running it willingly, by hiding behind a legitimate program. The spread of Trojan horse is often by phishing email. When user click on the email and its included attachment, malware got downloaded immediately to the computer. Trojans also spread when click on a false advertisement. Once inside the computer, a Trojan horse can record the user passwords by logging keystrokes, hijacking the webcam, and stealing any sensitive data from the computer.

9. Adware and spyware

Adware is deceptive software that earns its creators money through fraudulent user clicks. Fortunately, it's one of the most detectable types of malware. Adware may slow down your computer and affect browsing experience. It could also add vulnerabilities to the computer that could be exploited, and at times, it can collect and send the browsing history to third parties without the user consent. It can also trick you into installing a real malware using its ad network.

Spyware works similarly to adware, but is installed on the computer without the user's knowledge. It can contain key loggers that record personal information including email addresses, passwords, even credit card numbers, making it dangerous because of the high risk of identity theft.

10. Computer worm

Computer worms are pieces of malware programs that replicate quickly and spread from one computer to another. A worm spreads from an infected computer by sending itself to all of the computer's contacts, then immediately to the contacts of the other computers.

A worm spreads from an infected computer by sending itself to all of the computer's contacts, then immediately to the contacts of the other computers. Interestingly, they are not always designed to cause harm; there are worms that are made just to spread. Transmission of worms is also often done by exploiting software vulnerabilities.

9.3 PURDUE REFERENCE ARCHITECTURE FOR ICS

Purdue model is an Enterprise Reference Architecture developed by Theodore J.Willaims and colleagues of Purdue University for ICS and was adopted model by ISA-99 as a concept model for ICS network segmentation. This reference model is a resource for segmenting the modern ICS architecture and also help to understand the Industrial Cyber Security Landscape.

The Purdue model divides the ICS architecture into three zones and they are, Enterprise zone, Industrial Demilitarized zone and Industrial or process zone. Process zone is further divided into four levels and they are,

- Level 3: Site operations- managing production work flow to produce the desired products. Batch management such as manufacturing execution/operations management systems, (MES/MOMS) such as laboratory, maintenance and plant performance management systems, data historians and related middleware, Time frame such as shifts, hours, minutes, and seconds, etc.

- Level 2: Area supervisory control- supervising, monitoring and controlling the physical processes. Real-time controls and software; DCS, human-machine interface (HMI), supervisory and data acquisition (SCADA) software.

- Level 1: Basic control- sensing and manipulating the physical processes. Process sensors, analyzers, actuators and related instrumentation.

- Level 0: The process- defines the actual physical processes.

The enterprise zone has been divided into two levels viz. enterprise network and site business and logistics. These levels manage the business-related activities of the manufacturing operation. ERP is the primary system; establishes the basic plant production schedule, material use, shipping and inventory levels. Time frame: months, weeks, days, shifts. In fact Purdue model Increases resiliency by segmenting the OT network.

The enterprise zone

The enterprise zone is the part of the ICS where business systems such as ERP and SAP typically live. Here, tasks such as scheduling and supply chain management are performed.

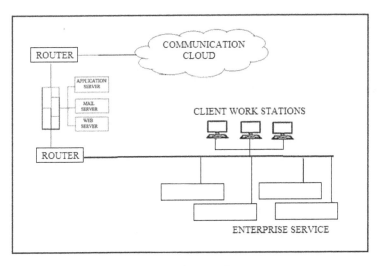

Figure 9.1 Enterprise zone

The can be subdivided into two levels viz.

- Level 5: Enterprise network
- Level 4: Site business and logistics

Level 5 - Enterprise network

The systems on the enterprise network normally sit at a corporate level and span multiple facilities or plants. They take data from subordinate systems out in the individual plants and use the accumulated data to report on the overall production status, inventory, and demand. Technically not part of the ICS, the enterprise zone relies on connectivity with the ICS networks to feed the data that drives the business decisions.

Level 4 - Site business planning and logistics

Level 4 is home to all the **Information Technology (IT)** systems that support the production process in a plant of a facility. These systems report production statistics such as uptime and units produced for corporate systems and take orders and business data from the corporate systems to be distributed among the Operation Technology (OT) or ICS systems. Systems typically found in level 4 include database servers, application servers (web, report, MES), file servers, email clients, supervisor desktops, and so on.

Industrial Demilitarized Zone (IDMZ)

Usually the Industrial Demilitarized Zone (IDMZ) lies between the enterprise zone and the Industrial zone as shown in Figure 9.3. Like the traditional (IT) DMZ, the OT-IDMZ allows to securely connect networks with different security requirements. Here different make firewalls at the two different levels are recommended for improves security.

DMZs are in essence a network between networks, and in the industrial security context, an added network layer between the OT, ICS, or SCADA, network and the less-trusted IT or enterprise network. Deploying the DMZ between two firewalls means that all inbound network packets are screened using a firewall or other security appliance before they arrive at the servers the organization hosts in the DMZ. There are many organizations and standard bodies that recommend segmenting the enterprise zone from the industrial zone by utilizing an industrial demilitarized zone (IDMZ). It acts as a zone and conduit system protecting physical processes, separating networks according to their different purposes, requirements and risks.

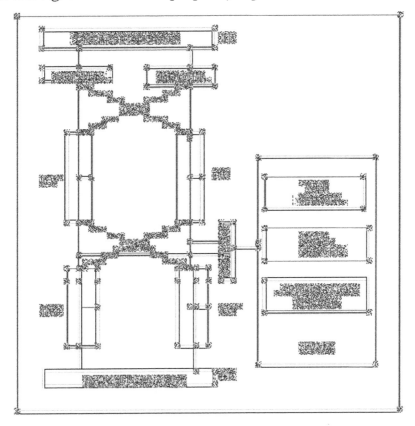

Figure 9.2 Industrial Demilitarized Zone (IDMZ)

In the Purdue model, the Industrial DMZ is information sharing layer between the business or IT systems in levels 4 and 5 and the production or OT systems in levels 3 and lower created as per security standards such as the NIST cyber security Framework and NERC CIP. Direct communication between IT and OT systems is prevented and having a proxy service in the IDMZ relay adds an extra layer of separation and scrutiny. Systems in the lower layers are not directly exposed to attacks or compromise. If something were to compromise a system at some point in the IDMZ, the IDMZ is configured such a manner that it will automatically shut down without compromising and the production will be continued. Systems typically kept in the

Industrial Demilitarized Zone are WEB servers, Microsoft domain controllers, Mail servers, etc.

The manufacturing zone

The manufacturing zone is where the action is; it is the zone where the process lives, by all means, this is the core of the. The manufacturing zone is subdivided into four levels viz. Level 3: Site operations, Level 2: Area supervisory control, Level 1: Basic control and Level 0: The process.

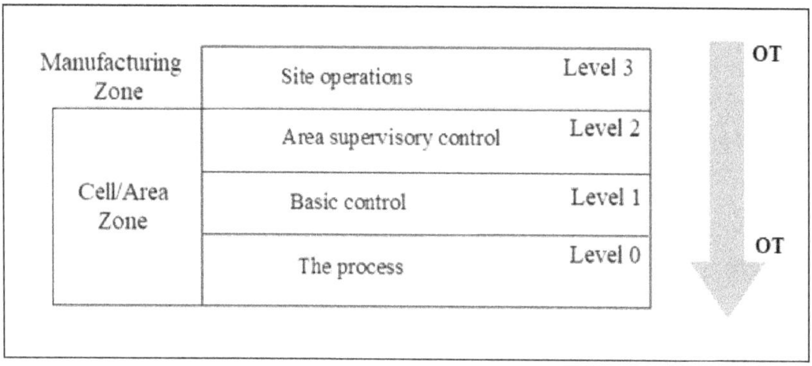

Figure 9.3 Manufacturing Zone

Level 3 - Site operations

Level 3 is where systems that support plant wide control and monitoring functions reside. At this level, the operator is interacting with the overall production systems. Think of centralized control rooms with HMIs and operator terminals that provide an overview of all the systems that run the processes in a plant or facility. The operator uses these HMI systems to perform tasks such as quality control checks, managing uptime, and monitoring alarms, events, and trends.

Level 3, site operations, is also where the OT systems that report back up to IT systems in level 4 live. Systems in lower levels send production data to data collection and aggregation servers in this level, which can then send the data to higher levels or can be queried by systems in higher levels (push versus pull operations).

Systems typically found in level 3 include database servers, application servers (web and report), file servers, Microsoft domain controllers, HMI servers engineering workstations, and so on.

Level 2 - Area supervisory control

Many of the functions and systems in level 2 are the same as for level 3 but targeted more toward a smaller part or area of the overall system. In this level, specific parts of the system are monitored and managed with HMI systems. Think along the lines of a single machine or skid with a touch screen HMI to start or stop the machine or skid and see some basic running values and manipulate machine or skid-specific thresholds and set points.

Systems typically found in level 2 include HMIs (standalone or system clients), supervisory control systems such as a line control PLC, engineering workstations, and so on.

Level 1 - Basic control

Level 1 is where all the controlling equipment lives. The main purpose of the devices in this level is to open valves, move actuators, start motors, and so on. Typically found in level 1 are PLCs, Variable Frequency Drives (VFDs), dedicated proportional-integral-derivative (PID) controllers, and so on. Although one could find a PLC in level 2, its function there is of supervisory nature instead of controlling.

Level 0 - Process

Level 0 is where the actual process equipment that we are controlling and monitoring from the higher levels lives. Also known as Equipment under Control (EUC), level 1 is where we can find devices such as motors, pumps, valves, and sensors that measure speed, temperature, or pressure. As level 0 is where the actual process is performed and where the product is made, it is imperative that things run smoothly and uninterrupted. The slightest disruption in a single device can cause mayhem for all operations.

9.4 PHYSICAL SECURITY

Physical security is the first line of defense against environmental risks and fickle human behavior. It is the protection of physical property, encompasses both technical and nontechnical components. Most of the information security experts often-overlooked physical security as they do about information and computer security and the associated hackers, ports, viruses, and technology-oriented security countermeasures. But information security without proper physical security could be very dangerous. The physical threats that an organization faces fall into the following categories viz.

- Natural disaster like floods, earthquakes, fires etc.,

- Strikes, riots, terrorist attacks etc.,

- Location and layout of building infrastructure,

- Power supply failure, communications interruptions, water supply interruption etc.,

- Unauthorized access and damage by disgruntled employees, employee errors and accidents, fraud, theft etc.,

- Unsecure network devices used.

In all situations, the primary consideration, above all else, is that nothing should obstruct life safety goals as it has given the highest priority. A wise planning can balance life safety and other security measures.

9.4 PHYSICAL SECURITY

Physical security is the first line of defense against environmental risks and fickle human behavior. It is the protection of physical property, encompasses both technical and nontechnical components. Most of the information security experts often-overlooked physical security as they do about information and computer security and the associated hackers, ports, viruses, and technology-oriented security countermeasures. But information security without proper physical security could be very dangerous. The physical threats that an organization faces fall into the following categories viz.

- Natural disaster like floods, earthquakes, fires etc.,
- Strikes, riots, terrorist attacks etc.,
- Location and layout of building infrastructure,
- Power supply failure, communication interruptions, water supply interruption etc.,
- Unauthorized access and damage by disgruntled employees, employee errors and accidents, fraud, theft etc.,
- Unsecure network devices used.

In all situations, the primary consideration, above all else, is that nothing should obstruct life safety goals as it has given the highest priority. A wise planning can balance life safety and other security measures.

The physical security of computers and their resources in the decades back was not as challenging as it is today because computers were mostly mainframes that were locked away in server rooms, and only a few people knew what to do with them. Presently, a computer is available with almost every desk in every utility, and access to devices and resources is spread throughout the environment. Organizations have server rooms, and remote access, resources out of the facility. Properly protecting these computer systems, networks, facilities, and employees has become an overwhelming task to many companies.

Theft, fraud, sabotage, and accidents are raising costs for many companies because environments are becoming more complex and dynamic. Security and complexity are at the opposite ends of the spectrum. As environments and technology become more complex, more vulnerabilities are introduced that allow for compromises to take place. Most companies have had memory or processors stolen from workstations, while some have had computers and laptops taken. Even worse, many companies have been victims of more dangerous crimes, such as robbery at gunpoint, a shooting rampage by a disgruntled employee, anthrax, bombs, and terrorist activities.

Many companies may have implemented security guards, closed-circuit TV (CCTV) surveillance, intrusion detection systems (IDSs), and requirements for employees to maintain a higher level of awareness of security risks. These are only some of the items that fall within the physical security boundaries. If any of these does not provide the necessary protection level, it could be the weak link that causes potentially dangerous security breaches.

From a holistic view of physical security, there are so many components and variables such as secure facility construction, risk assessment and analysis, secure data center implementation, fire protection, IDS and CCTV implementation, personnel emergency response and training, legal and regulatory aspects of physical security, etc. Each has its own focus and skill set, but for an organization to have a solid physical security program, all of these areas must be understood and addressed.

Many thefts and deaths could be prevented if all organizations were to implement physical security in an organized, mature, and holistic manner. When security professionals look at *information* security, they think about how someone can enter an environment in an unauthorized manner through a port, wireless access point, or software exploitation. When security professionals look at *physical* security, they are concerned with how people can physically enter an environment and cause an array of damages.

Physical security must be implemented based on a *layered defense model,* which means that physical controls should work together in a tiered architecture. The concept is that if one layer fails, other layers will protect the valuable asset. Layers would be implemented moving from the perimeter toward the asset.

➤ Mitigation Strategies

Presently the physical security is implemented based on a layered defense model and it generally falls in to the following categories.

- Building Location And Layout
- Building Infrastructure.

- Utilities Such as Power, Water, Fire Suppression, etc and
- Network Devices Used.

Layered security includes

- Fencing
- Reinforced Barricades
- Walls
- Gates/Entry Points
- Vehicle Barriers
- On-Site Security Guards
- CCTV Cameras
- Motion Detectors
- Intrusion Detection Systems
- Vibration Detectors
- Secured Cabling

Control room should be highly secured, such as the control room access may be depend on time, employment status, work assignment, level of training etc. The authentication for the access to the control room should be reliable such as biometric devices, cipher locks or access cards. The devices in the control room must be fixed permanently. Adequate lighting should be provided. Regular auditing of access logs must be done. Natural disasters must not affect the proper functioning of the firm. Field devices must be protected from the intruders using proper alarms, cipher locks with proper authentication.

9.5 NETWORK SECURITY

The ICT network security is the most important as it connects the field devices, corporate networks, SCADA networks, DR network, etc. A proper zone base segmentation and security based on functionalities using firewalls, gateways, data diodes, etc are the present techniques employed for ensuring network security.

From a mitigation perspective, simply deploying IT security technologies into an ICS may not be a viable solution. Although modern control systems use the same underlying protocols that are used in IT and business networks, the very nature of control system functionality may make even proven security technologies inappropriate. Some sectors, such as energy, transportation, and chemical, have time sensitive requirements, so the latency and 'throughput' issues associated with security strategies may introduce unacceptable delays and degrade or prevent acceptable system performance. Due to these facts, currently the main mitigation strategy is a security conscious segmentation. A network segment is also known as a network security zone which is a logical grouping of information and automation systems in an ICS network. Usually an Industrial Control Network has been segmented into four security zones with different trust levels as described below.

- Enterprise Zone-   Low Trust Level
- Industrial Demilitarised Zone-   Medium Trust Level
- Industrial Zone-   High Trust Level
- Cell Area Zone-   High Trust Level

Understanding attack vectors is essential to building effective security mitigation strategies. The degree of understanding of the control system by the security engineers regarding these vectors are most essential to mitigate these vulnerabilities effectively and efficiently. Effective security depends on how well the security engineers and vendors understand the ways that architectures can be compromised. Critical cyber security issues that need to be addressed include those related to,

- Backdoors and holes in network perimeter
- Vulnerabilities in common protocols
- Attacks on Field Devices

- Database Attacks

- Communications hijacking and *Man-in-the-middle* attacks

Demilitarized Zone (Level 3.5). This first line of defence in isolating the OT network from IT network. This is a critical segmentation because IT network are generally targeted before OT network. Manufacturing Zone (Level 3). This segmentation protects each ICS system / remote sites / factories. The purpose of this segmentation is to keep this site operational even if other ICS systems / sites come under attack. Cell Zone (Level 2). To further increase resiliency of each ICS environment, each functional cell or production line within the ICS network is further segmented. This will ensure that if a functional cell is attacked, other adjacent functional cell are still functioning. A SCADA network security engineer must perform the following tasks without any compromise.

- Ensure the firewalls and Intrusion Prevention Systems (IPS) are properly placed in the network with proper configuration as per the organisation's security policy and standards adopted such as NERC CIP,IEC62443 etc.

- Security engineer must be aware of the port scan by the external attackers and their capability of exploiting vulnerabilities.

- Must be aware of internet connections, remote access capabilities, layered defenses and placements of hosts on networks.

- Aware of the interaction of the security devices installed in the network such as firewalls, IPSec, antivirus etc. and their routable protocols if supports.

- Must be aware of the vulnerable protocols such as SSL.

- Unprotected ports which are commonly attacked.

- Network monitoring and maintenance.

For nearly three decades, digital network DMZs or *demilitarized zones* have been used as a data protection strategy in IT networks to broker access to information by external untrusted networks. This IT DMZ model and approach is well established, but is not necessarily an effective security measure when applied to OT networks.

In ICS network, DMZs is a network between networks, an added network layer between the OT, ICS, or SCADA, network and the less-trusted IT or enterprise network. If correctly implemented, no TCP or any other connection exchanging messages should ever traverse between IT and OT; through DMZ, it is a place where information originates from, or terminates completely.

For industrial purposes, what should be placed inside the DMZ is all of the applications and servers that have TCP connections out to the IT network. In practice, this can be a whole range of things; so when designing IT/OT network integration architectures, one must generally see customers deploy an intermediate system to aggregate OT data which needs to be shared with the enterprise. The most common aggregator is one of the many process historians, or one of the many variants of OPC server.

The modern industrial DMZ acts as a zone and conduit system protecting physical processes, separating networks according to their different purposes, requirements and risks. The best practice for implementing an IT/OT DMZ is to put two firewalls around the DMZ, one between the OT network and DMZ network, the other between the DMZ and the IT network. This practice supports the assumption that two firewalls reduce the likelihood that single firewall software vulnerability will open an attack pathway straight in to control system networks. In addition, all three networks must be on separate domains with their own authentication systems and no sharing of domain credentials.

Network segmentation has traditionally been accomplished by using multiple routers. Firewalls should be used to create DMZs to protect the control network. Multiple DMZs could also be created for separate functionalities and access privileges, such as peer connections, the data historian, the Inter Control Center Communications Protocol (ICCP) server in SCADA systems, the security servers, replicated servers, and development servers. All connections to the Control

System LAN should be routed through the firewall, with no connections circumventing it. Network administrators need to keep an accurate network diagram of their control system LAN and its connections to other protected subnets, IDMZs, the corporate network, and the outside.

Generally it is observed that, most sites deploy only a single firewall with three ports -one connected to IT, one connected to OT and one to the DMZ network - meaning single vulnerabilities are again a concern. More fundamentally, modern attacks don't exploit software vulnerabilities, modern attacks exploit permissions. From an attack perspective, exploiting vulnerabilities involves a lot of work and code writing unless of course someone else has already done the work and released an attack tool to the public. Exploiting permissions, on the other hand, can be as easy as stealing the firewall password or stealing a password on the IT network that the OT network then trusts or allows an attacker to go into a historian or other system in the DMZ right through the firewall.

9.6 COMPUTER/SERVER SECURITY

When consider the computer/server security, one of the important task is the patch management. Keeping regular IT systems and applications with the latest firmware, software, and patch management is a daunting task especially in the industrial zone of the ICS network.

Uptime requirements for the critical ICS computer systems do not allow them to reboot after updates. For those critical systems that are allowed to be altered, a different strategy to protect them is better and generally employed. For systems that can be updated and patch especially in the field operation zone, a readily available, update and convenient patching solution should be provided. Typical examples are windows server updates services and system center configuration manger of Microsoft.

End node protection is another important task in the computer system. This defensive control in the form of end node protection software and can be installed locally with remote administrative capability. Some of the generally available end node protection software are

- Host Based Firewalls,
- Anti Malware software, and
- Application Whitelisting software.

9.7 APPLICATION SECURITY

Application security is the process of making applications more secure by finding, fixing, and enhancing the security of apps. Much of this happens during the development phase, but it includes tools and methods to protect apps once they are deployed. This is becoming more important as hackers increasingly target applications with their attacks. SCADA systems need to have a strategy that supports not only management of knowledge and training but security knowledge that include policy, standards, design and attack patterns, threat models, code samples, reference architecture and security framework. Application security can help organizations protect all kinds of applications used by internal and external stakeholders including customers, business partners and employees. Vulnerabilities in SCADA applications include the following key components.

- Input Validation Vulnerabilities
- Software Tampering
- Authorisation and Authorisation Vulnerabilities
- Configuration Vulnerabilities
- Session Management Vulnerabilities
- Parameter management Vulnerabilities

SCADA software security must be viewed holistically. It is achieved through the combination of effective people, process and technology with none of these three on their own capable of fully replacing the other two entities. This also means that just like software quality in general, software security requires that we focus on security throughout the application's life cycle.

➢ Input Validation Vulnerabilities

An input validation attack is any malicious action against a computer system that involves manually entering strange information into a normal user input field. Input validation attacks take place when an attacker purposefully enters information into a system or application with the intentions to break the system's functionality. The best form of defense against these attacks is to test for input validation prior to deploying an application. A few common types of input validation attacks include:

- Buffer Overflow: This is a type of attack that sends too much information for a system to process, causing a computer or network to stop responding. A buffer overflow might also cause excess information to take up memory that was not intended for it, sometimes even overwriting memory.

- Canonicalization attacks: A canonicalization attack takes place when someone changes a file directory path that has digital permissions to access parts of a computer in order to allow access to malicious parties that use this unauthorized entry to steal sensitive information or make unapproved changes.

- XSS attacks (cross site scripting): These attacks involve placing a malicious link in an innocuous place, like a forum, which contains most of a valid URL with a dangerous script embedded. An unsuspecting visitor might trust the site they are on and not worry that a comment or entry on the site contains a virus.

- SQL injection attacks: SQL injection attacks involve taking a public URL and adding SQL code to the end to try to gain access to sensitive information. An attacker might enter code into a field commanding a computer to do something like copy all of the contents of a database to the hacker, authenticate malicious information, reveal hidden entries in a database or delete information without consent.

➢ Software Tampering

Modifying the application code before or while running the application is known as software tampering. Software tampering can lead to override or bypass the security or protective controls. Modifying the unauthorised application's runtime behaviour to perform unauthorised actions, exploitation via binary patching, code substitution,, software licence cracking, trojenisation of applications, etc are the common attacks associated with software tampering vulnerabilities.

➢ Authorization & Authentication

Authorization and Authentication deal with appropriate mechanisms to enforce access control on protected resources in the system. Authentication vulnerabilities include failure to properly check the authentication of the user or bypassing the authentication system altogether. Login bypassing, Fixed parameter manipulation, Brute force and dictionary attacks, Coockie replay and Pass-the-hash attacks are generally identified as authentication vulnerabilities.

Authorization is the concept that follows access to resources only to those who are permitted to use them. It comes after the successful authentication. Authorization flaws could result in either horizontal or vertical privilege escalation. The usage of strong protocols to validate the identity of a user or components. Further, issues such as the possibility or potential for authentication attacks such as brute-force or dictionary based guessing attacks. Elevation of privileges, disclosure of confidential data, data tampering are some of the authorization vulnerabilities.

➢ Configuration Vulnerabilities

This will consider all issues surrounding the security of configuration information and deployment. It is very crucial in the security of an application. Usually the systems and applications will run with a default configuration as it has been described in the manual. This helps attackers to guess the passwords, bypass login pages and finding setup vulnerabilities. Hence configuration especially the configuration of Firewalls must be done as per the requirement of the security policy of the organization.

➢ **User and Session Management Vulnerabilities**

This concerns how a user's account and session is managed within the application. The quality of session identifiers and the mechanism for maintaining sessions are some of the considerations here. Similarly, user management issues such as user provisioning and de-provisioning, password management and policies are also covered as part of this category. By mismanaging a session handling, an attacker can guess or reuse a session key and take over the session and the identity of a legitimate user. Session management and session replay are the common session management vulnerabilities associated with session management.

➢ **Parameter Management Vulnerabilities**

The manipulation of parameters exchanged between a client and the server inorder to modify application data, such as user credentials and permissions, price and quantity of products, etc. Cookie manipulation, form field manipulation and query string manipulation are common parameter manipulation vulnerabilities.

➢ **Security requirements in the Software Development Cycle**

Developing security architecture and engineered approach to the problem are generally recommended because current technology is not enough to prevent cyber attacks. Developing requirements for control systems with security features and use of simulation

- models based on a framework could improve the definition of requirements and reveal problems early in the software development cycle.

➢ **Auditing and Logging**

This concerns with how information is logged for debugging and auditing purposes. The security of the logging mechanism itself, the need and presence of an audit trail and information disclosure through log files are all important aspects.

> **Compliance to standards for software development**

Software development for control systems can be improved by following documents such as NIST published guidelines SCADA Security, Configuration, Guidelines, general assessment methods and tools for SCADA vulnerabilities and Holzman's rules

> **Data Protection in Storage & Transit**

This includes handling of sensitive information such as social security numbers, user credentials or credit card information. It is also covers the quality of cryptographic primitives being used, required/ minimum key lengths, entropy and usage of industry standards and best practices.

9.8   DEVICE SECURITY

Devices such as routers, firewalls and even network hosts including servers and workstations must be assessed as part of the security testing process. certain high level security vulnerabilities usually found on many network devices can also create many problems, hence one must ensure that HTTP and Telnet interfaces to the routers, switches and firewalls are properly configured and not with a blank, default or easy to guess passwords. If a malicious insider or other attacker gains access to the network devices, he can own the network and can lockout administrative access, setup backdoor user accounts, reconfigure ports, and even bring down the entire network.

When HTTP, FTP and TELNET are enabled in network devices with the help of free tools and a few minutes of time one can sniff the network and capture login credentials as they are sending clear texts. In case of wireless devices one must watch out for unauthorised Access Points (APs) and wireless clients that are attached to the network, else chances for social engineering and there are chances of connecting in to the malicious network and systems.

Mobile computing is convenient for personal, business and hacking. If secured mobile devices are not properly connected to the enterprise networks which represents thousands of unprotected islands as the phones, tablets and laptops which running numerous operating system platforms with a number of applications and infinite number of risks are associated with mobile computers.

> **Physical attack**

- Manipulation of the mechanical and electrical part of an ICS device is always feasible if the attacker gets physical access to the device which is not a matter of IT security. However being able to manipulate the programmed functionality of an ICS device, such an attack can be simultaneously applied to a large number of devices by a single attacker. A manipulated device can also be used by an attacker as a platform to compromise other parts of the system. A device that is compromised by a physical attack might have privileged access to other components and its segments, and there for act as a backend to attack farther devices.

- As a counter measure against physical security problems, ensure that APs,. Antennas and other wireless and network infrastructure equipment are located away in secure closets, ceilings or places which are difficult to access physically. Terminate the APs outside any firewall or any network perimeter security devices wherever possible. placing unsecured wireless equipment inside the secured network, it can negate any benefits which can be obtained from the perimeter security devices such as the firewall.

> **Device hardening**

- One of the areas of the device hardening is disabling unnecessary and unused options and features on ICS devices if the ICS devices do not provide the ability to disable unnecessary and unused options place these behind an industrial firewall and blocking the corresponding service port. Industrial firewalls are available with CISCO, TOFFINO, ROCKWELL, etc.

- Another method for ICS device hardening is restricting physical access to the device. It can be done by both administratively disabling the unused communication ports and physically block those ports from being connected to with block out devices. Keep the ICS devices in an enclosure that can be safely locked is another option. As the availability is more important than integrity and confidentiality, the device hardening of ICS presently have to confirm redundant power supplies, redundant communication port/paths, redundant I/O and redundant computing and controls.

> **Device patching**

- Make sure that the ICS devices are installed with latest firmware and software releases on a consistent basis and within a reasonable time and updates with new releases ensure that the software, firmware, patches and manuals are from reputable reliable sources or from OEMs also check that the ICS vendors offers cryptographically signed firmware versions for their devices this feature prevents installing and using tampered firmware.

- New firmware images, OS and patches to ICS should be tested in a testing and or developing environment to make sure that the new revisions works with the existing setup approximately before deploying to the production network this indeed save lots of headache and down time.

9.9 MODERN APPROACH TO IT/OT INTEGRATION

In other than airgapped or stand alone ICSs, the most crucial area of concern is the IT/OT integration especially in critical infrastructure. Modern approach describes and recommends that one side of the IT/OT DMZ be protected with unidirectional gateways to replicate OT systems to the IT network. The defining feature of a unidirectional gateway is that it is hardware-enforced. A combination of hardware and software that physically moves information in one direction only which means no messages whatsoever (including attacks) can enter the protected OT network from external sources, thus fulfilling the mission and purpose of implementing an IT/OT DMZ. The software element of unidirectional gateways replicates industrial servers and applications in two common scenarios with a Modern IT/OT DMZ.

Today many countries are strictly enforcing this approach while integrating the IT networks with OT networks especially in critical infrastructure domain like power system, oil & gas, water supply, etc.

- either replicating a historian or OPC server insider the OT network with a unidirectional gateway to the DMZ network whereby the IT network accesses the replicated server inside the DMZ through a firewall as shown in Figure 9.4,

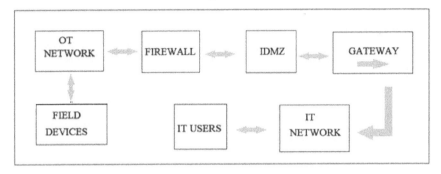

Figure 9.4 Modern IT/OT DMZ Scenario No.1

- or, replicating the historian or OPC server which sits inside the DMZ with a unidirectional gateway to a replica server sitting on the IT network for corporate use as shown in Figure 9.5. In both scenarios, the IT replica of the DMZ OPC or historian server is still the focus for IT/OT data exchange. It is now thoroughly protected in its original operational state.

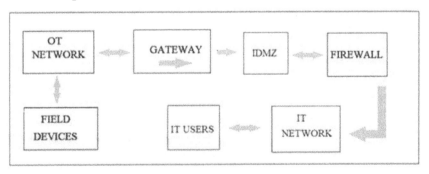

Figure 9.5 Modern IT/OT DMZ Scenario No.2

Enterprise Zone

This is in fact the ERP and administrative zone which deals with the complete information regarding the functionality of enterprise, its planning, operations, etc. All IT data protection strategies are expected to be implemented at this zone. A network security engineer in an ICS has to be aware and ensure that

- the devices, such as firewalls and IPS are properly placed on the network and configured.

- should be aware how the attackers perform part scans and exploit vulnerabilities.

- while designing the IDMZ, the security engineers must be aware of the internet connections, remote access capabilities, layered defenses and placement of ho the network.

- should be aware of ports which are unprotected.

If any attacker, compromises any one of the systems in the network, exploiting vulnerabilities due to the lack of proper security implementation, then

- the attacker can launch a Denial of Service (DoS) whichever can take down the internet connection, or entire network.

- with the use of a network analyser can steal confidential information of emails and files send over the network.

- a hacker can set up a backdoor access to the network.

Hence while integrating IT and OT; a prompt testing must be carried out between IDMZ and internal network of the enterprise. Obtain permissions from the predetermined and remotely connected other network for vulnerabilities on other systems that can affect the enterprise network mainly due to open ports, lack of firewalls and improper configured routers.

9.10 INCREASING RESILIENCY BY SEGMENTING THE OT NETWORK

Industrial Control Systems (ICS) and Supervisory Control and Data Acquisition (SCADA) systems are being increasingly targeted by attackers involved in terrorism and cyber warfare. Besides factories, these systems run critical infrastructure like power plants, water treatment systems, and traffic control systems. At stake is not just financial loss and brand reputation, but these attacks can result in national security threats and even death.

Based on our experience when evaluating ICS and SCADA systems, we almost always find security weaknesses that can be easily taken advantage of. These weaknesses allow the ICS components to be manipulated and controlled beyond its intended parameter. The root of the problem can be trace to,

- Patching: Unable to install the latest patch because it is not approved by Original Equipment Manufacturer (OEM)

- No or weak authentication: Any device that can get connected to the system can change value and configuration of PLCs easily or bypass its authentication.

- Backdoors: Use of undocumented and unrestricted access to critical functions

- Buffer overflow: Poorly written software that allows restrictions to be bypassed or functions to be manipulated

- No encryption: Data and information can be deciphered easily for manipulation.

The previous best-practice for ICS systems was to keep them segregated (air-gapped) from IT networks to prevent outside interference. However, we are seeing ICS networks increasingly being connected to the IT network. This convergence event is exposing ICS systems to threats and vulnerabilities that were previously protected through isolation.

Summary

It can seem as a difficult task to keep track of all the ICS security threats those are out there, and the new ones that just keep emerging. Whether the media is creating a culture of fear out of being online and placing trust in leaving the information out for all to see and manipulate, or whether the threats that wait in the dark corners of the internet are truly serious and can happen to anyone. The best thing one can all do is to be prepared to mitigate with preventive and counter measures. There is no way to be completely sure that a system is impenetrable by cyber threats. The responsibility of the computer professionals and automation engineers is to ensure that the ICS systems are secure as much as possible. This chapter gives the modern aspects of ICS security based on the *Defense-in-Depth architecture* describing all the five levels of security *viz.* Physical Security, Network Security, Computer Security, Application Security and Device Security.

CHAPTER TEN
RISK ASSESSMENT

10.1 INTRODUCTION

This chapter describes some risk assessment methods, which the ICS systems are commonly followed especially in critical infrastructure sectors. Many review reports of cyber attacks reveals that the following vectors are the most prevalent presently for cyber attacks on ICS.

- Weak authentication,
- Network scanning/probing,
- Removable media,
- Brute force intrusion,
- Abuse of access authority,
- Spear phishing, and
- Structured query language (SQL) injection.

10.2 RISK CALCULATION

With threats to sensitive data and ICS growing in both number and sophistication every day, organizations cannot afford a chaotic approach to security. Instead, they need to focus their limited cyber security budgets and resources on the specific vulnerabilities in their unique security posture. To do this, organizations need to identify, analyze and prioritize the risks to the confidentiality, integrity or availability of their data or information systems, based on both the likelihood of the event and the level of impact which would have on the business.

The definition of Risk and Risk assessment in industry are defined as follows.

Risk: A probability or threat of damage, injury, liability, loss, or any other negative occurrence that is caused by external or internal vulnerabilities, and that may be avoided through pre-emptive action.

Risk Assessment: Identification, evaluation, estimation and prioritisation of degree of risks involved in a situation, their comparison against the standards, and determination of an acceptable level of risk.

The risk calculation is based on the severity, criticality, likelihood and the impact. In fact risk is a function of these variables and many formulae has been developed depending upon the significance of the ICS. A general accepted risk calculation formula is

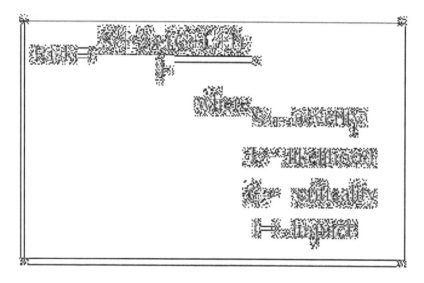

Severity: It is a number ranging from zero to ten, given to the vulnerability by a service like National vulnerability Database Scoring System by applying an algorithm like the common Vulnerability Scoring System.

Criticality: It is a number between 1 and 5 that reflects the importance of the system under control to the overall ICS functionality.

Likelihood: It is a number between 1 and 5 reflecting the chance of the vulnerability becoming a successful threat event.

Impact: It is a number between 1 and 5 that reflects the financial impact on the company, the associated damage to the image of the company, the potential impact on the environment, and the associated risk to employees.

10.3 RISK ASSESSMENT STEPS

Asset identification, system characterization, mapping the network, vulnerability identification, threat modelling and mitigation strategies are the major steps in risk assessment. They are briefly described below.

➤ Asset Identification

Asset identification is particularly intended to decide the potential targets of the attackers in an ICS and identify the weaknesses and the attack vectors to that target which allow the attackers to launch the successful attack.

➤ System Characterization

Many methods are used to gather information about a system such as physical surveillance, public domain information aggregation, scanning, etc. Physical characterization methods can range from simply observing the facility to entering the facility and carrying out a tour secretly posing as a vendor or maintenance person. This helps a security professional to gather amazing information about the ICS. Tours can provide huge information, including how well an organization has physically protected, information about the control systems at a site and how well the organization protects them, etc. Electronic asset discovery methods can range from simply collecting and aggregating using freely available tools to fingerprint systems. It is very important to gather information regarding the spear-phishing targets and possibilities when a plant or office is unattended. The device-specific intelligence, and air gaped systems in the organization must be specially identified. Threat actors can easily obtain IP address ranges through domain registry searches. Crafting an Internet query designed to return an error message can also yield information about the system. Free tools, such as nMap (Network Mapper), can be used to gather about devices, ports, protocols, and services which are open;

whether a firewall is in place, what type of firewall is in use and its location in the network.

➢ Mapping The Network

Thoroughly verify the industrial network and prepare an up-to-date network diagram with all IP addresses, active services, firewall rules, etc with thorough verification. This helps the security professional to understand the present data flow and the configurations in detail. Make sure that the network diagram is updated with the changes made.

➢ Vulnerability Identification

Improper configuration management is one of the most common ways that an attacker can find an opening into the control system domain. Hence proper configuration and monitoring should be done with utmost importance. General purpose Operating Systems (OS) platforms provide numerous processor and network services that automatically run by default. The result is unmonitored, open ports that are vulnerable to network exploits and actively executing code that may be subject to attacks such as buffer overflows. Unused ports and servers should not be kept active as it permits intruders to access the industrial network easily.

Because of the requirement of high or constant availability and critical response time of ICS, any change to the system necessitates exhaustive testing for software and security updates. Schedule all patching or update activities far in advance and permit them on a very infrequent basis. In addition, ICS components may not tolerate security software because of critical timing requirements. Control system components are often so processor-constrained that running security software itself creates unacceptably high delays in response, threatening system stability. The result is outdated OS revision levels and outdated or no malware protection software. Even if antivirus software is up to date and configured for proper execution, ICSs built on standard platforms are vulnerable to newly discovered malware threats that, once again, cannot be patched in a timely fashion.

Technology-related vulnerabilities within TCP/IP-based control system environments leave critical networks and systems open to compromise. Examples of vulnerabilities in IT system technologies that could migrate to control system domains include the susceptibility to malicious software such as viruses, worms, etc., escalation of privileges through code manipulation, network reconnaissance and data gathering, covert traffic analysis, and unauthorized intrusions into networks, either through or around perimeter defenses. System vulnerabilities also include hostile mobile code such as malicious active content involving JavaScript, applets, Visual Basic (VB) Script, and Active-X. With a successful intrusion into ICS networks come new issues such as reverse engineering of control system protocols, exploits leveraging vulnerabilities on operator consoles, and unauthorized access into trusted peer networks and remote facilities.

Outdated, inherently insecure protocols, such as FTP and Telnet, are generally used for ICS operations. Personnel often send passwords in the clear. One standard protocol for data communication between control devices, Object Linking and Embedding (OLE) for Process Control (OPC), must run without authentication. SCADA and ICS communication protocols for control devices, such as Modbus/TCP, Ethernet/IP and DNP3, do not typically require authentication to remotely execute commands on a control device, and no encryption options are available.

Most devices lack even the most basic access control, separating system software mode and application program mode. Server and terminal authentication is often nonexistent or completely ineffective. Differentiation of access privileges between administrators and end users is also generally unavailable or not implemented.

➢ Threat Modelling

Threat modelling starts with combining information of threat sources and threat vectors to create possible threat events to exploit vulnerabilities existing in the ICS.

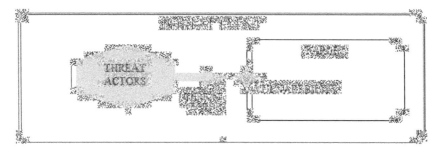

Figure 10.1 Threat Event

A threat source can be an internal threat sources such as employees or contractors or implementation agencies. It can be also former employees, hackers, enemy nations, terrorists, and malwares. Preparing a list of threat sources is one of the basic functions of the threat modelling. The next stage is identifying the threat vectors used by the threat sources which mostly include the following components.

- SCADA network,
- Business LAN,
- Internet,
- Spear fishing,
- DCS and ICS systems and devices,
- Workstations and applications,
- Environment and physical security,
- Mobile systems and devices, and
- Remote access.

10.4 PENETRATION TESTING

Network is the nerve system of an organization by storage its information and driving its communication. Network penetration test is to identify exploitable vulnerabilities in network, systems, hosts, and network devices such as routers, switches, etc. before hackers are able to discover and exploit them. Penetration testing will reveal the actual opportunities for hackers to be able to compromise systems and networks in such a way that allows for unauthorized access to sensitive data or even-over systems for malicious purposes. The main objectives of the penetration test is to

- identify seemingly flaws present in the environment,
- understand the level of risk for the organization (risk assessment),
- mitigate and fix the identified network security flaws,
- identify the misconfigured setting,
- identify the vulnerabilities associated with discovered OS and applications, and
- identify the active and vulnerable ports on hosts.

Penetration testing is commonly known as PenTest (PT) or ethical hacking. A proper PenTest can make recommendations for fixing problems within the network that were discovered during the PenTest. The main purpose of the PenTest is to improve network security and provide protection for the entire network and connected devices against future attacks.

Generally there is a misconception among the risk assessment and the penetration testing. They are often used interchangeably in reality. Vulnerability assessment refers to the process of evaluating the network systems and the services that provides for potential security problems while PenTest involves methods used to perform legal exploits to prove that a security issue actually exists. PenTest usually designed to go beyond a vulnerability assessment by performing a simulation of the same scenario a hacker would use to penetrate a network. Vulnerability assessment usually covered within the PenTest. The purpose of the simulation is to identify security issues before hackers can locate them and perform an exploit.

As PenTests simulate the methods which hackers would use to attack a network, network security professionals should obtain the appropriate authorization from utility management before proceeding to carry out the PenTest on the network. An improperly conducted PenTest can be detrimental to routine process and business operations.

There are various methodologies used in penetration testing and they are mainly black box testing, white box testing and grey box testing. Other network monitoring testing such as intrusion detection, packet sniffing, etc. are also use to determine the status of the network security.

Black box PenTest is conducted without the knowledge of any information related the technical aspect of a network. This mainly used to conduct a comprehensive network exploration in an effort to determine the best way to organize a simulated attack. White box attack usually carried out after gathering all data and information associated with a network and the architecture and its configuration. Grey box approach of penetration testing is performed according to internal information for a network including technical documents, user privilege credentials, etc. Based on the internal information collected, a highly sophisticated network attack can be launched to determine what can happen when hackers gain access to critical information and infrastructure.

While carrying out the penetration testing, security issues/flaws can be identified and confirmed. It also determines how the issues/flaws should be fixed. It provides a list of all network vulnerabilities that were discovered during the test. Usually PenTest reports contains priority wise security risk levels, suggestions for tightening the network security as a whole and recommendations to fix the issues as well. In addition, it may explain how the risks can affect business or process continuity and potential financial losses that can be incurred in case of security breach occurs.

Depending upon the security objectives and management goals of the organisation the type of the PenTest has been decided. Some organisations perform periodic penetration tests using different types of tools. PenTest is used to evaluate web servers, Domain Name System (DNS) servers, router configurations, work stations vulnerabilities, remote access, open ports, and available services. In fact the properties that a real attacker might use to compromise the utilities overall security can be identified. Some test can be extrusive and disruptive.

Hence before starting the PenTest careful evaluation and agreement upon the impact on the productivity.

Summary

Risk and vulnerability assessment are very important issues in ICS and SCADA systems. Unless security flaws are not properly identified, they cannot be fixed. For this computer professionals and automation engineers have to have an in-depth knowledge of industrial networking to guide and implement right solutions to fix the security holes. This chapter begins with describing Risk Calculation, Risk Assessment Steps such as Asset Identification, System Characterization, Threat Modelling and Mitigation Strategies. Chapter concludes with a short description about PenTest.

CHAPTER ELEVEN
ICS SECURITY STANDARDS

11.1 INTRODUCTION

Currently, there are quite a few OT cyber-security standards in existence, but each of these cyber security standards have a specific focus or objective and they are described below.

- ISA 99/IEC 62443: ISA 99 standards are intended for industrial automation devices. IEC 62443 is a superset of ISA99, incorporating all the specification of ISA 99, but in addition there are ongoing works for new specifications and updates under it.

- NERC (North American Electric Reliability Corporation): This is primarily intended to electrical T&D (Transmission & Distribution) equipment. The Standards are called North American Electric Reliability Corporation-Critical Infrastructure Protection (NERC CIP). ISA 99/IEC 62443 and NERC CIP have many common requirements, but not complementary each other.

- NIST (National Institute of Standard Technology) standards: NIST is US federal government body and though they have their own set of requirements for control system security, it endorses mainly the ISA99 standards.

- ISO 27001: This is intended for security practice to be implemented at organization level, mainly by IT department.

Whichever standard is selected, it is a fact that no foolproof cyber security protection does exist. But by making a device comply with available standards, its immune system gets strengthened and probabilities of withstanding attacks can be elevated considerability. The best way to keep the entire industrial control system secure is keeping it isolated from the external network but has many practical difficulties. This chapter briefly explain these security standards and its compliance requirements.

11.2 SELECTION OF STANDARDS

For embedded device, especially embedded device that goes into manufacturing, industrial machines, controllers used in industrial automation, ISA99/IEC62443 is most relevant standard to comply with. The following areas such as

- embedded devices used in mining trucks to control the movements,

- controller used in process automation to control a refinery plant,

- embedded device to control the air conditioning of building, and

- embedded device that control elevator/escalator movement, etc.

follow the IEC 62443 security standards.

Further it is accepted that anywhere where an embedded device is not a standalone device and whose operation or mal-operation could risk or cause injury to human lives, ISA99 is applicable. Other than the power system devices and automation devices used in transmission and distribution which need to comply with NERC CIP or its equivalent, for all other embedded devices that need to be cyber secure may follow the ISA99 /IEC62443 standards. Following proper security standards and strictly complying the selected standards, the immunity of the device gets strengthened. This improves the capability of withstanding the physical-cyber attacks. The best way to secure an ICS is keeping the entire system *AirGapped* and keeps the system totally isolated from external network.

Today complying the NERC CIP is becoming a mandatory security standard for power system automation especially when implementing automation in power Transmission and Distribution (T&D) sector.

Though it is a complex process to ensure NERC CIP requirements, it offers reasonably flawless physical-cyber security for automated power system. Further many nations realizing the need and necessity of complying and implementing NERC CIP standards in power system automation from the lessons learned from the BlackEnergy attack on Ukraine power grid, strictly enforcing NERC CIP compliance.

11.3 ISA 99/IEC 62443 STANDARD

ISA/IEC-62443 is a series of standards, technical reports, and related information that define procedures for implementing electronically secure Industrial Automation and Control Systems (IACS). This guidance applies to end-users (i.e. asset owner), system integrators, security practitioners, and control systems manufacturers responsible for manufacturing, designing, implementing, or managing industrial automation and control systems. All ISA work products are now numbered using the convention ISA-62443-x-y and previous ISA99 nomenclature is maintained for continuity purposes only. Corresponding IEC documents are referenced as IEC 62443-x-y. The approved IEC and ISA versions are generally identical for all functional purposes.

➢ Compliance Procedure

The procedure to get an embedded device compliant is very much similar to getting a device safety certified. The very first step is to have a certified system/product development process. Though it is not a must to have a mature process, it is an advantage in obtaining the IEC 62443 certification. Compliance to CMMI (Capability Maturity Model Integration), level 3 certification and above quality standards is good benchmark of a mature process.

The device needs to be designed considering the requirements as specified in ISA99 /IEC62443. The processes and design of device have to be approved by an Assessor. The Assessor is usually from an external organization that has track record of certifying compliance to ISA99. Testing the device based on set of test procedures usually carry out in an accredited lab such as Achilles Test Platform.

➤ Organization certifying embedded devices

There are two well recognized organizations certifying embedded devices on cyber security viz. Wurldtech and ISASecure. The choice between the two certification bodies would be purely based on specific project teams or cost or comfort level or previous project experiences.

1. Wurldtech, a GE company, offers the Achilles certification for devices. There are 2 levels of certification viz. level 1 and level 2. Level 2 requires more number of tests to be passed. Wurldtech does not publicly state the requirements that need to pass to obtain the certification rather they recommend the use of Achilles Test Platform during the development stage to test the embedded device.

2. ISASecure, an association of Industrial control system users and manufacturers. ISASecure's EDSA (Embedded Device Security Assurance) certification is intended for embedded devices. ISA Secure EDSA certification comprises of,

   • certifying the processes,

   • the design of embedded device and

   • passing the conformance testing.

The ISA Secure have come out with their own specifications on all 3 above mentioned steps and publicly available on their website. It is largely based on IEC 62443 standards and also some specifications from NERC and NIST. There are 3 levels of EDSA certification with level 3 being the stringent.

One thing to be noted is both the organizations offer their own named certification- Achilles certification or ISA Secure EDA certification and do not explicitly certify complying to ISA 99/IEC 62443. The choice between the 2 certification bodies would be purely based on specific project teams or cost or comfort level or previous project experiences.

11.4 NERC CIP STANDARD FOR BES

The digital innovation of power system automation is booming and shows no signs of slowing down. Advances in Information and Communication Technology (ICT) bring new vulnerabilities which threaten the reliable functioning of the power grid that is critical to any Nation's energy future. With critical infrastructure attacks on the rise, compliance mandates seem more timely than ever. North American Electric Reliability Corporation (NERC)- Critical Infrastructure Protection (CIP) standards are made up of nearly 40 rules and almost 100 sub-requirements are today most preferred security standard in power system automation. These provisions are critical for ensuring that electric systems are prepared for mitigating the cyber threats. Understanding certain definitions such as *Critical Assets and Responsible Entities* are better to conceive the concepts well.

Critical Assets: These assets include but are not limited to: Control systems, data acquisition systems and networking equipment, as well as hardware platforms running virtual machines or virtual storage.

Responsible Entities: They are defined as reliability coordinators, balancing authorities, interchange authorities, transmission service providers, transmission owners, transmission operators, generator owners, generator operators; load servicing entities and NERC/regional entities. All responsible entities are required to adhere to standards as defined by NERC.

The set of standards the NERC CIP standards covers mainly the Electronic Security Perimeter (ESP) and the protection of critical cyber-assets, personnel and employee training, security management and disaster recovery planning which are briefly described below.

CIP-002-5.1a-Cyber-Security Cyber Security- BES Cyber System Categorization

This standard requires the security engineer of the utility to identify and categorize BES cyber systems and their associated BES cyber assets for the application of cyber security requirements commensurate with the adverse impact that loss, compromise, or misuse of those BES cyber systems could have on the reliable operation of the BES. Identification and categorization of BES cyber systems support appropriate protection against compromises that could lead to mal-operation or instability in the BES. During this time the security engineer will identify each critical asset, categorize the asset, prioritize how the asset coincides with compromise or loss and, ultimately, highlight the overall relationship or operating dependency the asset has to the facility. This is helpful when submitting to the NERC Compliance Registry (NCR), and it also aids in creating compliance monitoring objectives.

CIP-003-6-Cyber Security-Security Management Controls

This standard requires to specify consistent and sustainable security management controls that establish responsibility and accountability to protect Bulk Electric Supply (BES) cyber systems against compromise that could lead to mal-operation or instability. This necessitates consistent and sustainable security management controls be enacted by an organization to protect all identified critical cyber assets from compromise, mal-operation or instability. Cyber security policy, leadership, exceptions, information protection, access control, change control and configuration management are all included in CIP-003-6, while adherence to sub-requirements may vary by organization, criticality of assets and impact rating.

CIP-004-6-Cyber Security-Personnel & Training

This standard requires minimizing of risk against compromise that could lead to mal-operation or instability in the BES from individuals accessing BES cyber systems by requiring an appropriate level of personnel risk assessment, training, and security awareness in support of protecting BES Cyber Systems. This necessitates that all personnel with authorized access to critical cyber assets have an adequate degree of personnel screenings and risk assessments, employee training and security awareness programs. Power utility also needs to maintain a list of credentialed access lists, including service providers and contractors. Moreover, CIP-004-6 also requires the organization to document, review and update such training and programs on an annual basis.

CIP-005-5-Cyber Security-Electronic Security Perimeter(s)

This standard requires to manage electronic access to BES cyber systems by specifying a controlled Electronic Security Perimeter in support of protecting BES cyber systems against compromise that could lead to mal-operation or instability in the BES. This standard primarily focuses on the perimeter and efforts to address vulnerabilities encountered during remote access. The perimeter that houses all critical cyber assets should be protected and any and all access points be secured. Key components to this include, but are not limited to, the following: remote session encryption, multi-factor authentication, anti-malware updates, patch updates and using extensible authentication protocol (EAP) to limit access based upon roles.

CIP-006-6-Cyber Security-Physical Security of BES Cyber Systems

This standard requires managing physical access to BES cyber systems by specifying a physical security plan in support of protecting BES cyber systems against compromise that could lead to mal-operation or instability in the BES.

This standard emphasizes the physical security perimeter and tasks the responsible entity with implementing a physical security program. The goal is to address the physical security zone and create preventative controls aimed at protecting and controlling access to cyber assets based upon risk-based security zones. A physical security plan, protection of physical access control systems, protection of electronic access control systems, physical access controls, physical access monitoring, physical access logging, log retention access, and maintenance and testing are all requirements of the security program for CIP-006-6.

CIP-007-6-Cyber Security-System Security Management

This standard requires managing system security by specifying select technical, operational, and procedural requirements in support of protecting BES cyber systems against compromise that could lead to mal-operation or instability in the BES. This requires that create, implement and maintain processes and procedures for securing systems for both critical and non-critical cyber assets. This also means documenting security measures, including records of test procedures, ports and services, security patch management and malicious software prevention.

CIP-008-5-Cyber Security-Incident Reporting and Response Planning

This standard requires mitigation of the risk to the reliable operation of the BES as the result of a cyber security incident by specifying incident response requirements. Security incidents related to any critical cyber assets must be identified, classified, responded to and reported in a manner deemed appropriate by NERC. Utility has to create an incident response plan that should include the actions, roles and responsibilities of those involved, as well as details of how incidents should be handled and reported to governing bodies. This plan will need to be updated annually and tested for applicability.

CIP-009-6-Cyber Security-Recovery Plans for BES Cyber Systems

This standard requires that recover reliability functions performed by BES cyber systems by specifying recovery plan requirements in support of the continued stability, operability, and reliability of the BES. Utility critical cyber assets must have recovery plans that align with their energy utilizes organization and adhere to disaster recovery best practices. A recovery plan, change control, backup and restoration processes and testing or backup media are all requirements of CIP-009-6.

CIP-010-2-Cyber Security-Configuration Change Management and Vulnerability Assessment

This standard requires preventing and detecting unauthorized changes to BES cyber systems by specifying configuration change management and vulnerability assessment requirements in support of protecting BES Cyber Systems from compromise that could lead to mal-operation or instability in the BES.

CIP-011-2-Cyber Security-Information Protection

This standard requires to prevent unauthorized access to BES cyber system Information by specifying information protection requirements in support of protecting BES cyber systems against compromise that could lead to mal-operation or instability in the BES.

CIP-014-2-Cyber Security-Physical Security

This standard requires to identify and protect transmission stations and transmission substations, and their associated primary control centers, that if rendered inoperable or damaged as a result of a physical attack, could result in instability, uncontrolled separation, or cascading within an interconnection.

➢ ACHIEVING NERC CIP COMPLIANCE

As NERC CIP is becoming mandatory in power system automation as presently no other equivalent standards are available or developed. Achieving NERC CIP compliance is a complex process, needs in-depth knowledge of ICT. To be NERC CIP compliant, bulk power supply operators must ensure that they've enacted the measures contained in all of the enforceable CIP standards. The steps below outline what an operator would need to do to ensure they're compliant with NERC's program.

Step 1: Categorization

The very first step in achieving NERC CIP compliance is categorizing an organization's assets. CIP-002 outlines the system used to determine which assets are critical. This allows bulk power suppliers to determine what risks pose the most immediate threats to their systems and so rationalize their security operations.

Step 2: Management and Training

The next steps outlined by the CIP are the management of security (CIP-003) and the training of personnel (CIP-004). CIP-003 requires the creation and maintenance of a security plan, which should outline the measures and processes for the other security measures contained in the other standards. For example, CIP-003 requires operators to create procedures for training personnel according to CIP-004, and to maintain documents pertaining to those procedures. CIP-003 recommends review of the security processes once every 15 months. CIP-004 includes requirements about keeping staff up to code, such as going through quarterly reviews of security practices.

Step 3: Creating and Managing Perimeters

In order to achieve NERC CIP compliance, operators must also implement the requirements of CIP-005 and 006.CIP-005's recommendations focus on creating electronic security perimeters, including creating access limitations for both inbound and outbound network traffic, and the use of measures such as password protection, encryption, and firewalls. CIP-006 moves security into the real world, setting out requirements for ensuring physical security, such as limiting unescorted access to the assets. Measures might include requiring someone to sign in and sign out when accessing the facility. CIP-007 provides information on managing system security. Items covered include keeping lists of listening ports, configuring firewalls, and documenting ports, as well as patch installation and management.

Step 4: Reporting and Recovering from Incidents

CIP-008 and 009 deal with what happens after an incident occurs: how to report it and implement recovery plans. CIP-008 emphasizes the need to adhere to a reporting procedure for incidents, and requires operators to have clear response procedures in place. The plans must be tested once every 15 months. CIP-009 outlines the requirements for recovery plans, which must set forth criteria for triggering a response and the roles and responsibilities of responders, among other things.

Step 5: Changing Environments

CIP-010 addresses change management and vulnerabilities. Operators are required to develop baseline configurations for system assets and use those to monitor and implement changes to the system. They must also document software and patches that are installed on the system. Vulnerability assessments are required once every 15 months.

Step 6: Protecting Data and Physical Assets

Keeping operators' assets, both digital and physical, safe is the goal of the CIP. CIP-011 lays out standards for protecting information and the new CIP-014 addresses the need for physical security. CIP-011 includes requirements for ensuring the staffs to know how to recognize and handle sensitive system information, and for protecting such information. CIP-014 discusses the need to perform vulnerability and risk assessments for the physical operating environment.

The current set of NERC's standards which almost cover all cyber issues of a Bulk Electric System (BES) is flexible and acceptable. Presently it is observed that the power utilities move towards an active consideration of NERC CIP versions 5 & 6 system security, needs rather than just compliance but an effective implementation especially after the cyber-attack on Ukraine power sector. It is largely due to the concerns that some owner/operators are not designating their bulk electric power facilities as *cyber-assets*, leaving potential holes in power system cyber-security.

11.5 ISO/IEC 27001 STANDARD

The ISO released the ISO/IEC 27000 family of standards in 2005 and has been making periodic updates to the various policies. Ownership of ISO 27001 is shared between the ISO and the International Electrotechnical Commission (IEC). It is part of a set of standards developed to handle information security. It is the leading international standard focused on information security, published. Both ISO and IEC are leading international organizations that develop international standards. ISO 27001 is developed to help organizations, of any size or any industry, to protect their information in a systematic and cost-effective way, through the adoption of an Information Security Management System (ISMS). It not only provide companies with the necessary know-how for protecting their most valuable information, but a company can also get certified against ISO 27001 and, in this way, prove to its customers and partners that it safeguards their data.

The certification helps the customers, governments, and regulatory bodies to believe that the organization is secure and trustworthy. This will enhance the company reputation and help to avoid financial damages or penalties through data breaches or security incidents. If the organization once qualified to receive a certification, it could be at risk of failing a future audit and losing the compliance designation. Receiving an ISO 27001 certification is typically a multi-year process that requires significant involvement from both internal and external stakeholders. It is not as simple as filling out a checklist and submitting it for approval. Before even considering applying for certification, one must ensure the ISMS is fully mature and covers all potential areas of technology risk.

The ISO 27001 certification process is typically broken up into three phases:

- The organization hires a certification body who then conducts a basic review of the ISMS to look for the main forms of documentation.

- The certification body performs a more in-depth audit where individual components of ISO 27001 are checked against the organization's ISMS. Evidence must be shown that policies and procedures are being followed appropriately. The lead auditor is responsible for determining whether the certification is earned or not.

- Follow-up audits are scheduled between the certification body and the organization to ensure compliance is kept in check.

The two most important mandatory certification requirements when implementing ISO 27001 are scoping the ISMS in which define what information needs to be protected and conducting a risk assessment and defining a risk treatment methodology in which identify the threats to the information. ISO 27001 is broken into 12 separate sections which are explained below.

- *Introduction* which describes what information security is and why an organization should manage risks.

- *Scope which* covers high-level requirements for an ISMS to apply to all types or organizations.

- *Normative References* which explains the relationship between ISO 27000 and 27001 standards.

- *Terms and Definitions which* covers the complex terminology that is used within the standard.

- *Context of the Organization* which explains what stakeholders should be involved in the creation and maintenance of the ISMS.

- *Leadership* which describes how leaders within the organization should commit to ISMS policies and procedures.

- *Planning which* covers an outline of how risk management should be planned across the organization.

- *Support* which describes how to raise awareness about information security and assign responsibilities.

- *Operation* which covers how risks should be managed and how documentation should be performed to meet audit standards.

- **P**erformance *Evaluation* which provides guidelines on how to monitor and measure the performance of the ISMS.

- *Improvement which* explains how the ISMS should be continually updated and improved, especially following audits.

- *Reference Control Objectives and Controls* which provides an annex detailing the individual elements of an audit.

➢ **Audit Controls for the ISO 27001**

- The documentation for ISO 27001 breaks down the best practices into 14 separate controls. Certification audits will cover controls from each one during compliance checks. Here is a brief summary of each part of the standard has been given below.

- *Information Security Policies* which covers how policies should be written in the ISMS and reviewed for compliance.

- *Organisation of Information Security* which describes what parts of an organization should be responsible for what tasks and actions.

- *Human Resource Security* which covers how employees should be informed about cyber security when starting, leaving, or changing positions.

- *Asset Management* which describes the processes involved in managing data assets and how they should be protected and secured.

- *Access Control* which provides guidance on how employee access should be limited to different types of data.

- *Cryptography* which covers best practices in encryption.

- *Physical and Environmental Security* which describes the processes for securing buildings and internal equipment.

- *Operations Security* which provides guidance on how to collect and store data securely.

- *Communications Security* which covers security of all transmissions within an organization's network.

- *System Acquisition, Development and Maintenance* which details the processes for managing systems in a secure environment.

- *Supplier Relationships* which covers how an organization should interact with third parties while ensuring security.

- *Information Security Incident Management* which describes the best practices for how to respond to security issues.

- *Information Security Aspects of Business Continuity Management* which covers how business disruptions and major changes should be handled.

- *Compliance* which identifies what government or industry regulations are relevant to the organization.

Organisations are also required to complete the following mandatory clauses.

- Information security policy and objectives
- Information risk treatment process
- Risk Treatment plan
- Risk assessment report
- Records of training, skills, experience and qualifications
- Monitoring and measurement results
- Internal Audit Program
- Results of internal audits
- Results of the management review
- Results of corrective actions

➢ **Maintaining ISO 27001 Compliance**

Obtaining an initial ISO 27001 certification is only the first step to being fully compliant. Maintaining the high standards and best practices is often a challenge for organizations, as employees tend to lose their diligence after an audit has been completed. It is leadership's responsibility to maintain ISO 27001 compliance. Given how often new employees join a company, the organization should hold quarterly training sessions so that all members understand the ISMS and how it is used and required to pass a yearly test that reinforces the fundamental goals of ISO 27001. In order to remain compliant, organizations must conduct their own ISO 27001 internal audits once every three years. Cyber security experts recommend doing it annually so as to reinforce risk management practices and look for any gaps or shortcomings.

An ISO 27001 task force should be formed with stakeholders from across the organization. This group should meet on a monthly basis to review any open issues and consider updates to the ISMS documentation. One outcome from this task force should be a compliance checklist such as mentioned below.

- Obtain management support for all ISO 27001 activities.

- Treat ISO 27001 compliance as an ongoing project.

- Define the scope of how ISO 27001 will apply to different parts of the organization.

- Write and update the ISMS policy, which outlines the cyber security strategy at a high level.

- Define the Risk Assessment methodology to capture how issues will be identified and handled.

- Perform risk assessment and treatment on a regular basis once issues have been uncovered.

- Write a Statement of Applicability to determine which ISO 27001 controls are applicable.

- Write a risk treatment plan so that all stakeholders know how threats are being mitigated. Using threat modelling can help to achieve this task.

- Define the measurement of controls to understand how ISO 27001 best practices are performing.

- Implement all controls and mandatory procedures as outlined in the ISO 27001 standard.

- Implement training and awareness programs for all individuals within the organization who have access to physical or digital assets.

- Operate the ISMS as part of the organization's everyday routine.

- Monitor the ISMS to understand whether it is being used effectively.

- Run internal audits to gauge the ongoing compliance.

- Review audit outcomes with management.

- Set corrective or preventive actions when needed.

11.6 NIST SP 800-53

NIST sets the security standards for agencies and implementers. It's structured as a set of security guidelines, designed to prevent major security issues that are making the headlines nearly every day. It is a non-regulatory agency of the U.S. Commerce Department, tasked with researching and establishing standards across all federal agencies. NIST SP 800-53 defines the standards and guidelines for federal agencies to architect and manage their information security systems. It was established to provide guidance for the protection of agency's and citizen's private data. In many cases, complying with NIST guidelines and recommendations will help federal agencies ensure compliance with other regulations, such as the Health Insurance Portability and Accountability Act (HIPAA), Federal Information Security Management Act (FISMA), or Sarbanes-Oxley Act (SOX). NIST guidelines are often developed to help agencies meet specific regulatory compliance requirements. NIST has outlined the following nine steps toward FISMA compliance.

- Categorize the data and information you need to protect

- Develop a baseline for the minimum controls required to protect that information

- Conduct risk assessments to refine your baseline controls

- Document your baseline controls in a written security plan

- Roll out security controls to your information systems

- Once implemented, monitor performance to measure the efficacy of security controls

- Determine agency-level risk based on your assessment of security controls

- Authorize the information system for processing

- Continuously monitor your security controls

Summary

This chapter briefly explains the various security standards presently existing in the industrial sector and their selection requirements. IEC 62443, NIST 800, NERC CIP and ISO 27001 standards are briefly explained. The compliance procedure for IEC 62443 and NERC CIP are also described as they are most pertinent today.

CHAPTER TWELVE
DOCUMENTED ICS CYBER ATTACKS

12.1 INTRODUCTION

Cyber security is becoming an increasingly challenging in process automation. Continuous innovation with modern technologies has taken manufacturing processes from initial industrial age into the information age. Hence there is a greater scope of cyber threats from various sources. Internet helped in boosting productivity and efficiency to unimaginable levels. Industrial automation thundered into today's data-driven, Internet-associated world, it sped past computerized security without taking its foot off the accelerator. For many years, malicious cyber-actors have been targeting the industrial control systems (ICSs) that manage our critical infrastructures. Most of these events are not reported to the public, and the threats and incidents to ICSs are not as well-known as enterprise cyber-threats and incidents. This chapter briefly explain certain publically reported cyber threats to critical infrastructure, which sheds light on the growing cyber threats to ICS devices.

12.2 DOCUMENTED POWER SYSTEM CYBER INCIDENTS

➤ *Crashed Ohio Nuke Plant Network by Slammer Worm (2003)*

In January 2003, a Slammer worm penetrated a private computer network at Ohio's Davis-Besse nuclear power plant and disabled a safety monitoring system for more than 5 hours, despite a belief by plant personnel that the network was protected by a firewall. The Slammer worm spread from the enterprise network to the ICS network by exploiting the vulnerabilities of the MS-SQL. It was reported that process computers had crashed for hours, aggravating the system operators.

➤ Taum Sauk Hydroelectric Power Station Failure (2005)

The Taum Sauk incident on December 14, 2005, was not an attack but instead a failure of a hydroelectric power station. Various explanations, including design or construction flaws, instrumentation malfunction, and human error, have been attributed to the catastrophic failure of an upper reservoir. Investigation revealed that the sensors failed to indicate that the reservoir was full and the pumps were not shut down until the water overflew for about 5 to 6 min. This overflow damaged the parapet wall, resulting in the collapse of the reservoir. Apparently this incident was (apparently) not an attack, but the idea behind it could be exploited to perform undetectable attacks in safety-critical infrastructures. This can be a means for a stealthy attack on a SCADA by sending compromised sensor measurements to the control center.

➤ Cyber Incident on Georgia Nuclear Power Plant (2008)

In July 2008, a nuclear power plant in Georgia was forced into an emergency shutdown for 48 hours because a computer used to monitor chemical and diagnostic data from the corporate network rebooted after a software update. When the updated computer restarted, it reset the data on the control system. The safety systems interpreted the lack of data as lowering of the levels in the water reservoirs that cool the plant's radioactive nuclear fuel rods, and triggering a system shutdown.

➤ PSS Giant Telvent Compromised in Canada (2013)

A breach on the internal firewall and security systems of Telvent, Canada, one of the most reliable company which supplies remote monitoring and control tools to the energy sector, was discovered on September 10, 2012. After penetrating the network, the intruders stole project files related to the OASyS SCADA product, a highly sophisticated remote administration tool allowing companies to combine older IT equipment with modern Smart Grid technology. It is very likely that the adversaries gathered information about this new product to find its vulnerabilities and to prepare for future stealthy attacks against PSS.

➢ *Ukraine Power Grid Cyber-attack December (2015)*

The Ukraine power grid Cyber-attack took place on 23 December 2015 and is considered to be the first known successful cyber-attack on a power grid. Hackers were able to successfully compromise information systems of three energy distribution companies in Ukraine and temporarily disrupt electricity supply to the end consumers. The cyber-attack was complex and comprised of the following steps,

- prior compromise of corporate networks using spear fishing emails with BlackEnergy malware, seized the ICS under control, and switched off substations remotely,

- disabled IT infrastructure components such as uninterruptable power supplies, modems, RTUs, commutators,

- destroyed files stored on servers and workstations with the KillDisk malware, and

- denial-of-service attack on call-center to deny consumers up-to-date information on the blackout.

A brief account on the Ukraine attack has been already described in chapter one.

➢ Stuxnet attack on Iran's Natanz nuclear facility (2012 & 2017)

In 2012 Iranian nuclear facilities were attacked and infiltrated by the first *cyber-weapon* or the *digital missile* of the world known as the Stuxnet. It is believed that this Natanz nuclear facility attack was initiated by a random worker's USB drive. By current estimations this attack results in 30% decrease in enrichment efficiency. It is reported that in 2017, once again Iranian critical infrastructures and networks have been vehemently attacked by a new variant of the lethal Stuxnet which is many fold sophisticated than its former variant leaving extreme concerns to the security of the industrial automation world. A brief account on the Iranian nuclear facility attack has been described in chapter one.

➤ ICS CYBER ATTACKS ON US

It has been reported by IBM X-Force that the the number of events targeting the ICS assets in 2019 increased over 2000 percent since 2018. In fact, the number of events targeting OT assets in 2019 was greater than the activity volume observed in the past three years combined. As the US is the most cyber targeted nation they have stepped up security measures by strictly implementing the mandatory standards in ICSs. In 2019 June US grid regulator NERC issued a warning that major hacking group with suspected Russian ties was conducting reconnaissance into the networks of electrical utilities. Some of the significant successful aatacks are described below.

- *Penetration of Electricity Grid of US by Spies (2009)*

On August 14, 2003, the Northeast and Midwest regions of the United States and some provinces in Canada suffered a serious blackout because of a software bug. These incidents have raised concerns about the security of electric power grids, because disrupting national power systems might cause catastrophic damage. *The Wall Street Journal* reported that on April 8, 2009, Cyber-attackers have penetrated the US electric power grid and left behind a software program that can be used to disrupt the system.

- **Water Tower Decoy in US (2012)**

In December 2012, a malicious computer virus concealed in an MS Word document sent from Chinese hacking group, APT1, successfully took over a water tower control system in the US. Fortunately for anyone nearby, the tower was actually a trap set up to attract such would-be industrial attacks. So, while nothing was hurt or destroyed in this incident, it did demonstrate the frightening reality of these attacks.

- **US Wind farm attack (2019)**

The largest renewable energy developer in US located at Utah was hit by a cyber attack that briefly break contact of a number of wind and solar farms. Later it has been reported that it was a DoS attack that left grid operators temporary blinded generation sites totalling a loss of 500MW. The cyber attack took advantage of a known weakness in Cisco firewalls to trigger a series of a five minute communication outage over a span of about 12 hours.

➢ CYBER THREATS TO INDIAN ICS

The US was the most cyber targeted nation in the world in 2019 for power sector cyber attacks. However India surpassed US and topped in the list for three months and remained within the top 5 cyber targeted countries in 2019 leaving extreme concerns to India's power sector automation and Smart Grid projects which are struggling to comply the relevant physical-cyber security standards. If any cyber security flaws are introduced by chance to the Indian power grid by the implementation agencies, likelihood of exploiting these vulnerabilities by our enemy nations are very high. Government of India (GoI) and Central Electricity Authority (CEA) are giving directions to implement the proper cyber security measures without any lapse to the various power Transmission and Distribution utilities while moving to digital energy. Realising the possibility supply chain attacks, the GoI recently cautioned the power utilities to test all the Chinese products especially the industrial networking products used in power sector automation.

• Indian North-Eastern Grid Blackout (2012)

In 2012 one of the world's worst blackout has occurred in India. The exact cause for this blackout is yet to be confirmed as many speculations/reports of a cyber attack from enemy nations are live though official explanation denies it. But the Nation has realised the consequences of a blackout if it happens due to a cyber attack. The security experts point out it may occur at any times as India is facing 30 cyber attacks daily on its power sector mostly from China, Slovania, Mexico, Ukraine and Pakistan unless India identify and fix the flaws of the imported industrial networking and automation products. The 2012 blackout left almost 710 million people without power. The noted other impacts due to this blackout are briefly described below.

More than 700 million people in India have been left without power in the world's worst blackout of recent times, leading to fears that protests and even riots could follow if the country's electricity supply continues to fail to meet growing demand. First to fail was India's northern grid, leaving an estimated 350 million people in the dark for up to 14 hours. It was quickly followed by the eastern grid, which includes Kolkata, then the north-eastern grid. Twenty of India's 28 states were hit by power cuts, along with the capital, New Delhi, when three of the country's five electricity grids failed at lunchtime.

As engineers struggled for hours to fix the problem, hundreds of trains failed, leaving passengers stranded along thousands of miles of track from Kashmir in the north to Nagaland on the eastern border with Burma.Traffic lights went out, causing jams in New Delhi, Kolkata and other cities. Surgical operations were cancelled across the country, with nurses at one hospital just outside Delhi having to operate life-saving equipment manually when back-up generators failed. Electric crematoriums stopped operating; some with bodies left half burnt before wood was brought in to stoke the furnaces. As Delhiites sweated in 89% humidity and drivers honked their horns even more impatiently than usual, in West Bengal the power cut left hundreds of miners trapped underground for hours when their lifts broke down. All the state's government workers were sent home after the chief minister announced it would take 10 to 12 hours for the power to return. There were some agitations, riots and protests in urban areas which were very reliant on electricity. TVs and computers were not worked for a week and one-third of India's households do not even have electricity to power a light bulb. By early evening, 50 of the trapped miners in West Bengal had been rescued and power had been restored to the north-east of the country, as well the most affluent areas of Delhi.

India has five electricity grids viz. northern, eastern, north-eastern, southern and western. All are interconnected. The blackout and its impacts were an eye opener to the Indian energy engineers that the present power grid of India needs to be cyber secured in every respect with appropriate architecture with approved standards as the all the five regional grids are interconnected, operated and controlled by NLDC, New Delhi. It also given a lesson to the grid security to engineers on the need of PMU based power system monitoring and control when national grids integrates and operates as a single grid.

- ***Breach at the Kudankulam Nuclear Power Plant (2019)***

Towards the end of October 2019, reports were spreading in social media regarding a cyber attack at Kudankulam Nuclear Power Plant. On October 29, the Plant authorities, denied such an attack and informed that both the reactors (1000MW and 600MW) were running without any operational or safety concerns. But unexpectedly, Nuclear Power Corporation of India Limited (NPCIL) within 24 hours admitted that there indeed was an incident and Dtrack RAT has been located within the plant. Source code included hard coded credentials to KNPP indicating that it was a targeted attack. It also contains methods to collect browser history, passwords, host IPs, running processes and all files on disk volumes.

The matter was conveyed to Computer Emergency Response Team (CERT-In) as soon as it was noticed. CERT-In said that they had identified a malware attack that breached India's largest nuclear power facility's administrative network on September 4. They further emphasised that the nuclear plant's operational systems were safe they are air gapped and the administrative network was not connected to it. Hence there was nothing to be panic.

This clearly exposed the lack of the technical awareness of the plant authorities regarding the air gap jumpers. Further the malware, DTRACK, was developed by a North Korean hacker group called LAZARUS who specialised in stealing information from a system. It is suspected that a large amount of data was stolen during the breach. This data could be used to plan the next attack more efficiently. As per the cyber security experts and ethical hackers, Domain Controller level access has been gained by the hackers at KNPP.

In the modern environment, most of the ICS networks are air gapped/stand-alone having no connectivity to cyber-space to make it secure. Hence the ICS threat actors usually carried out the attacks to ICS in two stages as explained in previous chapters. Hence it can be observed that the stage I attack has been carried out successfully by the threat actors. The chances of the stage II attack which will be the real objective behind the ICS attack cannot be ruled out. The CERT-In and the NPCIL authorities might have taken all necessary actions without any compromise to prevent such attack else it will be extremely disastrous.

12.3 COMMON ICS SECURITY ISSUES

Security solutions developed for traditional IT networks are not adequate and effective in DCS because of the major differences between them. Their security objectives are different in the sense that security in IT networks aims to enforce the three security principles viz. confidentiality, integrity and availability, while the security in DCS networks aims to provide human safety, equipment and the mission critical operations, etc. Furthermore, the security architecture of IT networks is different from that of the DCS network since security in IT networks is achieved by providing more protection at the center of the network where the data is kept, while the protection in automation networks is done both at the network center and end nodes or edge. Their underlying topology is also different as IT networks use a well-defined set of operating systems and protocols, while DCS networks use multiple propriety operating systems and protocol specific to vendors. Hence Quality of Service (QoS) metrics are different in the sense that it is acceptable in IT networks to reboot devices in case of failure or upgrade, while this is not at all acceptable in DCS networks since services must be available 24x7. These major differences between the IT and DCS network security objectives necessitate the need for new security solutions specific for the ICS network. As explained in the previous chapters, the development of DCS security solutions faces many challenges and mainly they are,

- many ICS components use propriety operating systems to control functionality without security features,

- most of the legacy ICS network was designed without regard to security,

- security should be integrated with existing systems without relegation the latency and efficiency and performance,

- remote access to grid devices must be monitored and controlled, and

- the new protocols selected should have the capability of incorporating future security solution.

12.4 MITIGATION STRATEGIES

Employing zone based architecture is one of the means of managing different parts of the DCS to provide protection. The defense-in-depth zone based architecture has been explained in previous chapter, can be used to categorize as customer operations, business, communication and control systems. Each zone is independently comprised of field devices, systems, communication media, and data centers which serve the specific operational functions of that zone. Implementing a set of security features common to all zones and security features required explicit to that zone can form an effective, modular and segmented security system. The following modular security zones are minimum suggested for DCS.

- Customer operations security zone,

- Corporate security zone, and

- Communication and control systems security zone.

Customer operations security zone: The customer operations security zone contains devices and processes that extend product management to customers. Smart Grid is a typical example of a complex DCS, where security has to be provided, access to home systems and the data gathered by Advanced Metering Infrastructure (AMI) must be limited to authorized people and devices. Customer energy management systems must ensure integrity of command and meter data, authenticate devices, and protect the grid from compromised devices.

Corporate security zone: The corporate security zone includes all the features and functions of the customer operations security zone plus security for IT functions vital to a business, such as email, internet, telephony, messaging, and a wide variety of corporate applications. To meet these requirements, an IDMZ with consistent security policies must be applied across the entire product line of the DCS.

Communication and control systems security zone: The communication and control systems security zone defines the processes used to manage the routing of product from the manufacture area to the end user. It contains data centers involved in the production, testing, marketing and reliable distribution of products. Information collected and processed here supports equipment maintenance, troubleshooting, load capacity, and supply chain re-routing in the event of break down.

To protect the integrity of transmitted data and control, utilities must ensure individual and device authentication, computer health verification, correlation of alarm data with other sensors to prevent false positives, regulatory compliance and enable forensic analysis. Data encryption, intrusion detection and prevention and secure sharing of information between various data centers are critical and must be addressed with utmost care.

As utilities innovate with ICT based modern automation technologies, they need a foundation of converged IP networks, proven security principles, industry-leading networking equipment and software with integrated security capabilities. The maturity, reliability, and success of these products and services can shorten the learning curve for utilities to evolve operations to meet new standards and regulations.

➢ *Follow Standards and Guidelines*

An OT security expert must strictly follow security the standards and guidelines to ensure the ICS security requirements without any compromise. Following a security standard with proper updating will indeed help to make ICS smarter against cyber-attacks. The chief cyber-security officer of the utility must be very keen in enforcing the following steps without compromise while designing and implementing the ICS.

- Develop a security policy,
- Establish physical security,
- Lockdown perimeter security,
- Enable existing security features,
- Secure operational traffic,
- Secure management traffic,
- Properly manage the system configuration,
- Eliminate security shortfalls.
- Continuous security training, and
- Perform security audits.

Moreover to build a secure ICS strictly follow the key reminders without any compromise as shown in Figure 12.1.

- Be always on the defensive,
- Be always vigilant for cyber-attacks,
- Have safety, security and disaster recovery plans,
- Implement physical-cyber-security without any compromise, and
- Proper documentation and reporting of cyber incidents, attempts and attacks.

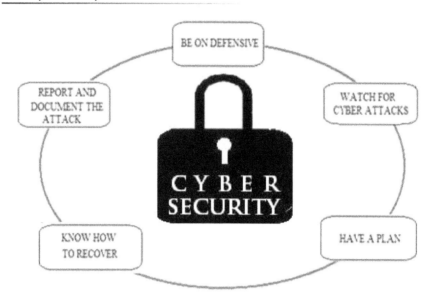

Figure 12.1 ICS Security Key Reminders

Summary

In recent years ICS is one of the main target of cyber-attackers and a number of cyber incidents have occurred to the power systems. Chapter twelve describes some of the cyber-incidents as well as different sources of attacks are described to make the ICS engineers aware of the severity of the attacks. It also briefly describes the different types of threats that ICS may encounter from the perspective of the utility and implementation agencies. It then explains the lethal malware threats like Stuxnet which is a nightmare for Power System SCADA and ICS as it mainly exploits the Zero Day Vulnerabilities of the Windows OS. Various proposals for making the automated power system smarter than cyber-attacks by cyber-security expert groups also have been discussed.

LIST OF ACRONYMS

3GPP	Third Generation Partnership Project
AC	Alternating Current
ADO	Advanced Distribution Operation
ADU	Application Data Unit
AER	All Electronic Range
AES	Advanced Encryption Standard
AH	Authentication Header
AMI	Advanced Metering Infrastructure
AMR	Automatic Meter Reading
ANSI	American National Standard Institute
AP	Access Point
API	Application Programming Interface
APT	Advanced Persistent Threat
ARP	Address Resolution Protocol
ASAI	Average System Availability Index
ASCII	American Standard Code for Information Interchange
ASD	Adjustable Speed Drives
ATM	Asynchronous Transfer Mode
BCMAC	Block Chaining Message Authentication Code
BES	Bulk Electric System
BGP	Border Gateway Protocol
BPLC	Broadband Power Line Communication
BSD	Berkeley Software Distribution
CATV	Coaxial Cable TV
CBC	Cipher Block Chaining
CCF	Common Cause Failure
CDMA	Code Division Multiple Access
CERC	Centre Electricity Regulatory Commission
CFB	Cipher Feedback
CFE	Communication Front End

CIP	Critical Infrastructure Protection
CMF	Common Mode Failure
CMMI	Capability Maturity Model Integration
COSEM	Companion Specification for Energy Metering
CPS	Cyber Physical Systems
CRC	Cyclic Redundancy Check
CRL	Certificate Revocation Lists
CSMA/CD	Carrier Sense Multiple Access/Collision Detection
CTR	Counter Mode
DA	Distribution Automation
DAS	Certificate Authorities (CA)
DCS	Distributed Control Systems
DCU	Data Control Unit
DER	Distributed Energy Resources
DES	Data Encryption Standard (DES)
DLC	Direct Load Control
DLL	Dynamic Link Library
DLMS	Device Language Message Specification
DMS	Distributed Management System
DMZ	De Militarized Zone
DNP	Distribution Network Protocol
DNS	Domain Name Servers
DOS	Denial Of Service
DOS	Data Acquisition System (DAS)
DP	Distributed Power
DPSCI	Documented Power System Cyber Incidents
DRMS	Demand Response Management System
DSL	Denial-of-Service (DoS)
DSM	Demand Side Management
DSM	Dispatch Training Simulator
DST	Decision Support Tools
EAP	External Access Point
EBCDIC	Extended Binary Coded Decimal Interchange Mode

ECB	Electronic Code Block
ECC	Energy Control Center
ECM	Equipment Condition Monitor
EDGE	Enhanced Data Rates For GSM Evaluation
EIA	Electronic Industry Association
EMC	Electro Magnetic Compatibility
EMS	Energy Management System
ENS	End Node Security
EPA	Enhanced Power Architecture
ESP	Encapsulating Security Payload
ESZ	Enterprise Security Zone
ESZ	Enterprise Security Zone
ETDR	Endpoint Threat Detection and Response
EU	European Union
EUC	Equipment Under Control
FCC	Federal Communication Commission
FDDI	Fiber Distributed Data Interface
FDMA	Frequency Division Multiple Access
FEP	Front End Processor
FES	Flywheel Energy Storage
FMS	Fieldbus Message Specification
FOCS	Fibre Optical Current Sensor
FTP	File Transfer Protocol
FTS	Fault Tolerant System
FTTH	Fibre To The Home
FTTP	Fibre Transmission Transfer Protocol
GIF	Graphic Interchange Format
GMPLS	Generalizes Multi-Protocol Label Switching
GOOSE	General Object Oriented Substation Event
GPS	Global Positioning System
GRE	General Routing Encapsulation
GSM	Global System For Mobile Communication
HA	High Availability

HASR	High Availability Seamless Redundancy
HDLC	High Level Data Link Control
HHU	Hand-Held Unit
HMAC	Hash-based Message Authentication Code
HMI	Human Machine Interfaces
HSDPA	Speed Downlink Packet Access
HTTP	Hypertext Transfer Protocol
IANA	Internet Assigned Numbers Authority
IBM	International Business Machine
ICCP	Intercontrol Centre Communication Protocol
ICMP	Internet Control Message Protocol
ICS	Industrial Control System
ICT	Information and Communication
IDEA	International Data Encryption Algorithm
IDS	Intrusion Detection System
IEC	International Electrotechnical Commission
IED	Intelligent Electronic Device
IEEE	Institute Of Electrical and Electronics Engineering
IGMP	Internet Group Management Protocol
IMAP	Internet Message Access Protocol
IP	Internet Protocol
IP FRR	IP Fast Reroute
IPS	Intrusion Prevention System
IPSec	Internet Protocol Security
IPX	Internetwork Packet Exchange
ISA	International Society for Automation
ISDN	Integrated Service Digital Network
ISO	International Organisation for Standards
IT	Information Technologies
IV	Initialization Vectors
JPEG	Joint Photographic Experts Group
L2TP	Layer 2 Tunnelling Protocol
LAN	Local Area Networks

LDMS	Local Data Monitoring System
LDP	Label Distribution Protocol
LLC	Logical Link Control
LPD	Line Printer Daemon
LSA	Load Shed Application
LSE	Lead Serving Entity
LSP	Label Switched Path
LTE	Long Term Evaluation
MAC	Media Access Control
MAU	Multistation Access Unit
MBP	Manchester Bus Powered
MCC	Master Control Centre
MDMS	Meter Data Management
MITM	Man In The Middle attack
MMS	Manufacturing Messaging Specification
MPLS	Multi-Protocol Label Switching
MU	Merging Unit
NAS	Network Access Server
NERC	North American Electric Reliability Corporation
NFS	Network File System
NIC	Network Interface Card
NIST	National Institute For Standard and Technology
NNTP	Network News Transport Protocol
O&M	Operation and Maintenance
OAREC	Optimal and Automatic Residential Energy Consumption
OCSP	Online Certificate Status Protocol
OFB	Output Feedback
OFDMA	Orthogonal frequency division multiple access
OS	Operating System
OSI	Open System Interconnection
OSPF	Open Shortest Path First
OT	Operational Technology

PAC	Programmable Automation Controller
PC	Personal Computer
PCI	Peripheral Component Interconnect
PCMCIA	Personal Computer Memory Card International Association
PDF	Portable Document Format
PDU	Protocol Data Unit
PKI	Public Key Infrastructure
PLC	Programmable Logic Controller
PLCC	Power Line Carrier Communication
POP3	Post Office Protocol version 3
PPA	Profibus Process Automation
PPP	Point-To-Point Protocol
PPTP	Point To Point Tunnelling Protocol
PSS	Power System SCADA
QR	Quick Removing
RAS	Remote Access Server
REA	Rural Electric Association
ROW	Right Of Way
RSVP	Resource Reservation Protocol
RTO	Regional Transmission
RTOS	Real Time Operating System
RTP	Real Time Pricing
RTU	Remote Terminal Unit
SCADA	Supervisory Control And Data Acquisition
SDO	Standard and Specification Development Organization
SE	State Estimation
SERC	State Electricity Regulatory Commission
SG	Smart Grid
SHA	Secure Hash Algorithm
SHEMS	Smart Home Energy Management System
SIL	Safety Integrity Level

SM	Smart Meter
SMTP	Simple Mail Transfer Protocol
SNMP	Simple Network Management Protocol
SONET	Synchronous Optical Networking
SPS	Special Protection System
SQL	Sructured Query Language
SSH	Secured Shell
SSL	Secured Socket Layer
TC	Technical Committee
TCP	Transmission Control Protocol
TDM	Time Division Multiplexing
TDMA	Time Division Multiple Access
TFTP	Trivial File Transfer Protocol
TIFF	Tagged Image File Format
TLD	Top Level Domains
TLS	Transport Layer Security
UDP	User Data Protocol
UN	United Nation
USB	Universal Serial Bus
UTP	Unshielded Twisted Pair
V Ring	Virtual Ring
VFD	Variable Frequency Drives
VPDN	Virtual Private Dial-Up Network
VPN	Virtual Private Network
WAN	Wide Area Network
WG	Working Group
WWW	World Wide Web
ZDA	Zero Dynamic Attack
ZDV	Zero Day Vulnerability

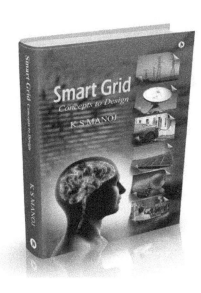

Salient Features of the Book

- Covers power grid networks, including how they are developed and deployed for power delivery and other Smart Grid services.

- Discusses power systems, advanced communications, and required machine learning that define the Smart Grid.

- Clearly differentiates the Smart Grid from the traditional power grid as it has been for the last century.

- Provides the reader with a fundamental understanding of both physical-cyber-security and computer networking.

- Presents the complexity and operational requirements of the evolving Smart Grid to the ICT professional and presents the same for ICT to the power system engineers.

- Provides a detailed description of the cyber vulnerabilities and mitigation techniques of the Smart Grid.

- Provides essential information for technocrats to make progress in the field and to allow power system engineers to optimize communication systems for the Smart Grid.

- Explains how contemporary grid networks are developed and deployed and presents a collection of cutting-edge advances to improve current practice.

Size: 9" × 6", Pages:424

ISBN : 978-1-64650-999-7

MRP: 850/-

www.ingramcontent.com/pod-product-compliance
Lightning Source LLC
Chambersburg PA
CBHW051045050326
40690CB00006B/598